REDLAND:
RUBRA TERRA,
REDLAND COURT AND
REDLAND HIGH SCHOOL

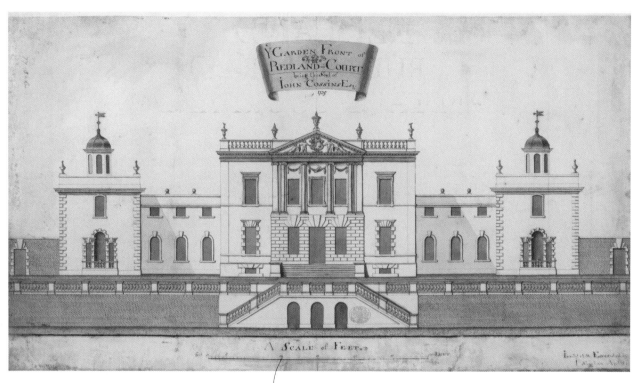

Frontispiece 1735. Architectural drawing of Redland Court by Wilstar, map-maker.
Note the suggestion of two weathervanes on the West and the East cupolas which are not the later additions
added in 1761 featuring Halley's Comet. *Reproduced with permission from the British Library*

REDLAND:
RUBRA TERRA,
REDLAND COURT AND
REDLAND HIGH SCHOOL

Jennifer Allen-Williams

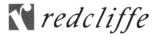 redcliffe

First published in 2012 by Redcliffe Press Ltd.,
81g Pembroke Road, Bristol BS8 3EA

www.redcliffepress.co.uk
info@redcliffepress.co.uk

© Jennifer Allen-Williams

ISBN 978-1-908326-07-2

British Library Cataloguing-in-Publication Data
A catalogue record for this book is available from the British Library

Unless indicated otherwise all images are courtesy of the R.H.S. Archive Collection

Set in Minion 12/14pt

Cover design: Mark Cavanagh
Typesetting: Harper Phototypesetters Ltd
Printed by HSW Print, Tonypandy, Rhondda

CONTENTS

INTRODUCTION

It is my privilege and pleasure to be the Headmistress of Redland High, a school which has a proud tradition of educating generations of Bristol's girls.

Working and learning in Redland Court one is immediately struck by the feeling of history all around. The beautiful Redland Court has contributed hugely to the sense of community at Redland High: girls are imbued with a sense of history, of continuity and of tradition. Former students speak fondly of the buildings and campus and current pupils enjoy the elegance of the eighteenth-century house alongside modern facilities.

Redland High has remained true to its foundation, having opened in 1882 as an all-through Junior and Senior School for girls and continuing so today. By nurturing and encouraging every girl to find her strengths and giving her the confidence to tackle every subject to the best of her ability, students have left the school for distinguished careers and have also fulfilled important roles in family and neighbourhood life.

Governors, headmistresses and staff have always been mindful of current educational thinking and have continued to move with the times, ensuring that we offer educational experiences and preparation for modern, young women to forge successful lives. Breadth and depth of interest, academic excellence, a spirit of community, strong pastoral care and clear moral values have been at the heart of the school for the past 130 years. Successive headmistresses and generations may articulate them differently, but they remain fundamental and we remain true to our founding principles.

I should like to congratulate Jenny Allen-Williams on the many months of research and scholarship which have led to the production of this fascinating book. She has captured the essence of Redland High and brought to life a proud history in presenting its development against a national context.

Mrs Caroline P. Bateson. BA (Hons), MA
Headmistress 2006-

PART ONE

1
THE 'RED' LAND (RUBRA TERRA)

All good stories have a 'beginning', a 'middle', and an 'end'. Hopefully, this story of the development of Redland High School for Girls has a never-ending 'end' and the story starts, or should it be 'commences', with the name 'REDLAND'.

Only trains start (on time) everything else commences.
Miss Sylvia Peters, Headmistress, 1947-1968.

A glance at the colour of the soil, whether in gardens or revealed by excavations deeper down, gives an obvious explanation of the origin of the name for the district. A legacy of Roman occupation was revealed as Roman coins were dug up on Redland Green during the Second World War when public open space was turned over to temporary allotments.

The Romans disregarded any previous land ownership when they constructed their roads and created direct routes passing through hills, not around them. It is speculation that a road was constructed from their military camp at Abona (Sea Mills) through to Bath and the area of Redland, or even that part of Durham Downs, known as Roman Road, might have led to a stopover on Redland Green. By the year 410 AD Britain was left to its own fate. An inscription on a building at the corner of Lower Redland Road and Redland Road indicated that Redland Road originated as a Roman road, 'Via Julia'.

The main west-east axis route was established in ancient times by the Roman road from Sea Mills to Bath, VIA JULIA, which came across the Downs. The line of the Roman road lay under the eastern part of Lower Redland Road and was then carried further east by Redland Road.[1]

The name 'Redland' has been suggested as being a corruption of the name 'Thirdland' being the result of the division of an area into Ridings. Various forms of Thridland and Threadland do not appear until the sixteenth century and the translation into Latin, 'Rubra Terra', revealed in the earliest relevant charter, suggests the distinctive soil of the area was responsible for the name.[2]

The district of Redland appears to have been part of the See of Worcester from the late eighth century when the district of Westbury, including Redland, belonged to Offa, King of Mercia. After Offa's death in 835 the country was invaded by the Danes and stability was only established when Alfred became King and came to power in 872. Church lands in the Westbury district fell into the hands of laymen and under Alfred's jurisdiction power was restored to the Church, namely the Benedictine monks at Westbury-on-Trym. Again there was turmoil in England and it was not until 1093 that the monastery of Westbury became a College of Canons which enabled them for the next four hundred and fifty years to hold the land later known as Redland.

The best cultivated land was leased out to tenants who were on good terms with their ecclesiastical owners.[3]

In 1539 King Henry VIII decided to break away from Papal authority and oversaw the dissolution of the monasteries and the selling of land to new ownership. In some instances the owners treated the tenants badly. The new owners were often profiteers and changed the arable land to sheep grazing, thus reducing the number of tenant farmers. Speculation in land brought changes in ownership of a manor as happened in Redland with pockets of land changing hands as many as five times.[4]

The first definite reference to the Manor of Redland appears in the *Valor Ecclesiasticus* of 1539 under the heading of the Manor of Westbury. A land grant in the year 1229 gave the name in Latin, 'unam hidam terre in Yriddelond', one hide of land in Redland.[5]

The *Valor Ecclesiasticus* refers to manor lands at Redland and 'manor' usually implies a manor house. There is evidence for a permanent house on the site in the early sixteenth century as it was near a roadway and the existence of a fishpond was often associated with monastic buildings. The curious name of 'Gastons' survives on a map of nearby fields and the origin of the name suggests it was an area for the 'gasts' (guests) to be able to graze their horses. There is mention of a 'great stable' used as a guest house and in 1714 lived in as additional family accommodation. The whole 'manor' house may have been a monastic 'guest house'.[6]

At the time of the Dissolution the area known as Redland, along with the rest of the Worcester lands, passed into the hands of Henry VIII and was sold in 1544 to Sir Ralph Sadlier for 1,000 marks. Tenants were found for the Manor of Redland whose work involved maintaining the pastures and the income supported a gentlemanly lifestyle with an array of servants. The district of Redland appears to have been unaffected by the Civil Wars although some historic and ancient aristocratic Somerset farming families found themselves selling off their unproductive properties to wealthy merchants from London. These London merchants sought a more relaxed lifestyle for themselves, a 'home in the country'.[7]

One such entrepreneur was John Foxton who bought lands in the early 1550s. All purchases were subject to the 'foot o' fine' whereby a document was copied in triplicate on one sheet of vellum and cut into three pieces with each wavy cut line, often drawn decoratively with a pen, each shape matching as proof of belonging to the original document. Hence the term 'indenture' came to be applied to any formal agreement.[8]

In 1552 John Foxton purchased the Redland estate and sold it on to a London gentleman, Egion Wilson, formerly from Berwick, and a licensed victualler. Together with his son, Miles Wilson, he commenced the building of a house on the site of the original guest house, the Manor of Thrylande.[9]

NOTES

1 Malpass, P., 2010. *The Development of Redland.* Unpublished manuscript. p.2.
2 Charlton, J. and Milton D.M., 1951. *Redland 791-1800.* Bristol: Arrowsmith. p.2.
3 ibid. pp.4-7.
4 ibid. p.8.
5 ibid. p.14.
6 ibid. pp.20-21.
7 ibid. pp.9-10.
8 ibid. p.13.
9 ibid. p.24.

2
THE MANOR OF THRYLANDE, A TUDOR HOUSE AND A GEORGIAN MANSION

In the years before 1650 the concept of an architect, in the sense of a man who both designed and supervised the erection of a building, did not exist. Building was in the hands of a mason who employed bricklayers, stonemasons, carpenters, plumbers, plasterers and glaziers. The overall design was determined by the client and the planned oblique perspective drawing of the proposed house evolved as a frontal view with side elevations where the immediate shapes are drawn as seen from the front and the sides added on as in a child's drawing of a house. Without a three-dimensional drawing in true perspective interior mistakes occurred. Staircases had to be accommodated in

the available allowed space, particularly if they were curved.

A plan and elevation drawing from a later estate map of 1732 (below) shows the Wilsons's house as an irregular L-shaped house with gables and mullioned windows each with its own hood-mould. Unusual features are two bay-windows, crenellated, and rising through the two storeys, one of which is over a doorway and the other is blocked over. Nothing is known of this house apart from this drawing and a note in Miles Wilson's will.[1] After Egion's death the house passed to his son, Miles. Miles Wilson's will of 1567 refers to *my mansion house of Redlande with the garden and orchard there.*[2] Miles Wilson's

1. Drawing from a later estate map of 1732 showing the Wilsons's Elizabethan house, the Manor of Thrylande, built between 1552 and 1567 and demolished in the 1730s. *Reproduced with permission from the British Library*

13

death on April 14, 1567 is recorded in the Westbury Parish Register, and his body, along with his daughter's, is buried in an impressive monument/tomb in Westbury Church.[3]

The property was left to his widow, Elizabeth, until she remarried or until the marriage of his youngest daughter, Elizabeth. In 1571 the young Elizabeth married Roger Revell and a family dispute over the future of the property passing to their son resulted in the sale of the property to Sir Richard Hill in 1604.

At Westminster on the Morrow of Souls, 2 James between Richard Hill kt.q. and Richard Revell esq. def. of the Manor of Thrydlande alias Rydlande, alias Ridlande with appurts. And 2 messuages etc and common pasture for 240 sheep in Thydlande, alias Rydelande, alias Rudlande… given £240.[4]

Copying of deeds or local documents saw many variations on the spelling of the word representing the modern day name of 'Redland'. The two messauges referred to are presumed to be the house itself and the Great Stable.[5]

Sir Richard Hill appears to have lived at Redland until his death and was related to a Bristol family of goldsmiths. His and his family deaths were also recorded in the Westbury Parish register.[6] After 1627 the estate passed to his brother and then to his nephew who resold the property in 1653 to Dr. Jeremy Martin, a physician. The Tudor house and the Great Stable suited the Martin's family of nine children.[7] Information about the Redland estate is more precise than any recorded earlier and details of the surrounding land of forty two acres showed only five acres were arable.

The messuage appears to be leased as a farm and the house was a separate entity. The income generated from the sheep farming areas was enough to support the widowed Elizabeth Martin and on her death the property reverted to her son, William.[8]

In 1678 William married Mary Geering. William was borrowing money from his wife's family and in order to bring the house into a fashionable update with resale in mind a brick arbour under the present terrace and a Dutch-style garden were constructed in 1711.[9] William Martin was succeeded by his son, Gregory, who was also borrowing money to pay his debts and those of his father. William Martin's expenses had included providing for two unmarried daughters and a dowry for the third. In 1712 Gregory Martin sold the Great Stable and adjoining land to Andrew and Martin Innys. Other parts of the estate were mortgaged but Gregory Martin failed to redeem these. In 1732 the estate, including the mortgages, passed into the hands of John Cossins, husband of Gregory Martin's cousin, Martha Innys.[10]

2. Drawing of Redland Court, built between 1732 and 1735. The frontal view of the house, architect, John Strachan (Strahan). Extra bays added by Thomas Paty in 1747. *Reproduced by permission of Nicholas Kingsley. The Country Houses of Gloucestershire, Vol II, 1660-1830.* p. 203

John Cossins, grocer, was the son of a respected London grocer who was Master of the Grocers' company. John had inherited his father's coat-of-arms which included the golden lion of Cossins, also the silver owls of Saville of Lower Siddington, near Cirencester, through his wife's lineage.[11] In 1714 John Cossins married Martha, daughter of Andrew Innys, a Bristol merchant and daughter of Innys' second wife, Elizabeth Martin. Martha was the youngest of fourteen children.[12]

The Tudor house built for the Wilson family was demolished in 1730. Between 1732 and 1735 the house was replaced by an elegant Georgian building known as Redland Court, designed for John Cossins by John Strachan, a pupil of John Wood who had been responsible for the development of Georgian buildings in Bath.[13] The small, square-shaped, oak panelling from the Tudor house was reused for some rooms in the Georgian mansion and can be seen today.[14]

Redland was a country area a mile from the city of Bristol with a rural village atmosphere although not a village like Westbury or Henbury with their own parish churches. There were two distinct parts, one of which included a small settlement on the eastern side of what is now called Blackboy Hill and labelled Redland on Wilstar's map of Clifton in 1746, and further east the Redland Court estate founded on the historic Redland Manor and the Tudor house.[15]

John Cossins was not reliant on rural farming as his main source of income was his business interest in London and acquisition of properties. The area was free from other buildings and had a commanding view over the city of Bristol. Surrounding land was for sale or for mutual exchange and could be released for personal reasons such as a family chapel. The two-storey white limestone mansion of classical design covered much of the same ground as the demolished Tudor building whilst retaining the arbour and the Dutch garden.

Jon. Cosins Esqr. to Tho: Paty Dr.				
1747				
June 10th	Paid for two Tun of Rock Stone	£01 : 15 :		4
	Do for Tools	00 : 02 :		0
	Do: Mr. Whitehurch for Landing	00 : 02 :		0
	Do: Freight at 5s p. Tunn	00 : 10 :		0
	Mens time Landing & Loading		*unreadable blot*	
	To Halling Do. to Redland	00 : 4 :		0
20th	To 32 feet coping under the Pallisados at 1/6	02 : 8 :		0
	Two Caps on the Pillers at 4s	00 : 8 :		0
	28 Quines on the Sumer House at 12d	01 : 8 :		0
	Door Case	01 : 15 :		6
	two Side Windows at 15s	01 . 10 :		0
	Side Windows at 22	02 ; 4 ;		0
	2 Stretching Quines & 2 Steaders in the Back Front	00 : 3 :		6
	18 Caps on the Batlements at 12d.	00 : 18 :		0
	4 Quine Do at 1s 5d	£00 : 05 :		8
	22 Do between the Batlements at 8d	00 : 14 :		8
	47 : 4 of Facia Course at 9d	01 : 15 :		6
	52 : 2 of Cornice at 1/6	03 : 18 :		3
	13 : 6 of 18 in coping back of the Alcoves at 9d	00 : 10 :		$1\frac{1}{2}$
	13 : 0 of Do 8 In Wide at $3\frac{1}{2}$	00 : 03 :		$9\frac{1}{2}$
	4 Caps on the Wing Battlements	00 : 04 :		0
	2 Quine Do	00 : 02 :		10
	4 Do in the Opes at 8d.	00 : 02 :		8
	17 ft of 6 in Facia Course 6d	00 : 08 :		6
	14 ft 6 of Impost at 6d	00 : 07 :		3
	2 Key Stones at 2s	00 : 04 :		0
	1 day Jon Wilton new Setting the coping	00 : 02 :		2
	$\frac{1}{4}$ day Dce. Ford abt. the Hatch	00 : 00 :		7
	$1\frac{3}{4}$ Do Piecing the Plinth in the Tarras	00 : 03 :		11
	6 Days Do abt. Do	00 : 13 :		0
	8 foot of Frestone at 12d	00 . 08 .		0
	Quarter of Peck of Plaster	00 : 02 :		4
	$\frac{3}{4}$ Day Jon Reeley Sawing the Stones off Bottom of the Doors	00 : 01 :		6
	To a Panswick Chimny piece and Cornice & Setting Do	01 : 10 :		0
	8 Iron Cramps for Do at 2d	00 : 01 :		4
		£25 : 11 :		9

Recd Nov. ye 10th 1747 of Jon Cosins Esq.
the full of the above Note and all Accouts to this Day
Tho: Paty

3. Bill of costs for extensions. Complete transcripts, Bristol City Archives as reported in Appendix II. Ref. Charlton, J., and Milton, D., 1951. *Redland. 791-1800.*

The Palladian-style building, with basement, thirteen-window frontage, no visible roof, set high on a hill, would have been an imposing structure seen by all through an open, elegant, carriage driveway lined with trees and entered through wrought-iron gates bearing the Cossins's Coat of Arms. As a Grade II listed building it is remarkable that very little has been changed from the original design and where changes were made they were reasonably sympathetic.[16]

In the 1890s a second storey was added to the west wing for an apartment for the first Headmistress, Miss Cocks, and although losing the cupola and pillared parapet the addition was given a replacement parapet which is in line with the central part of the house. In the 1920s, Miss Edghill, the school's third Headmistress, under the guidance of Mr Oatley, a sympathetic architect, used money earmarked for the purchase of a sports ground to purchase new facing stone in order to save the crumbling limestone from being rendered over.

The frontal view of the building is of a symmetrical composition of a central seven-window block. The central block has steps up over the basement level to a slightly projected centre, with rusticated ground floor and three nineteenth-century French windows beneath a tent-shaped glassed verandah. Above the verandah is an Ionic portico with four pilasters and three windows with architraves. The triangular pediment is decorated with a

4. c.1920s. Urn on parapet before deterioration. The bird is probably a parrot

cartouche of the family coat of arms surrounded by cherubic figures. Below the pediment and between the pilasters are flamboyant swags of leafy foliage. Atop the frontal roof balustrade are seven urns.[17] The central urn is topped with a stone carving of a pineapple, signifying 'sweetness' and 'goodness'. Swathes and putti (cherubic figures), are carved around the urns. The damaged carvings are less decipherable and may once have been symbolic representations of birds. 1920s photographs of the toppings show human forms of sculptured heads. Acorns were a symbol for 'strength' and 'growth'; as in the growth of surviving ancient oak trees. Two other urns are placed on the far corners of the parapet. The stone urns added to the impression of height and attention was paid to the south side as it faced the carriageway leading to the house, an avenue later to be lined with lime trees.

John Cossins and his wife moved to Redland Court in about 1736. The house was approached by stone steps built over the existing arbour leading onto a terrace framed by balusters. In addition to John and Martha Cossins, who did not have any children, the household included John's widowed sister, Mary, and three of Martha's brothers, one of whom was William Innys. The attic rooms provided accommodation for the servants. Water came from wells dug into a stream under the house and used in the basement kitchen areas.[18] One of the wells was discovered years later when a hole developed in the floor of a room being used by a Redland High School secretary. Later, when extensive buildings revealed an underground spring, it was found necessary to divert the water away from the foundations.

The rear of the house, now used as the main entrance, has a row of steps protected by an overhanging verandah and iron railings. The basement areas can be clearly seen and delineated by large, faceted, stone blocks. Many alterations occurred after 1860 with additional windows and ground-floor entry doors. Seen

5. 1932. Redland Court. Note the the large Cedar of Lebanon flourishing at that time

from the rear there is a curious mixture of styles developed by many owners. The three main rooms on the ground floor in the central part of the building are fully panelled. The former drawing room is now the Headmistress's study after Miss Taylor, Headmistress, changed it from a Sixth-Form classroom into a room for her own use in 1931. The six-panelled mahogany door is surrounded by a Doric structure composed of fluted half-columns raised on block pedestals and supporting an entablature surmounted by a broken pediment with a curved pedestal intended for a bust or a cartouche.[19]

Folding doors allowed for the drawing-room to be extended into the adjoining room to create a large area for entertainment and fine dining. Fluted Ionic pillars and cornices are featured in the room along with the central room's Italian marble fireplace which features a carving of a lion's mask with paws and scrolled drapes. A

deep crack has developed across the front of the fireplace suggesting some movement in the old foundations which is not surprising when new building foundations were drilled into the solid stone hillside on which the mansion was built. The carved marble fireplace in the adjoining room shows a classical woman's head with garlands and drapes. A gazetteer of notable homes in Gloucester, c.1820 reported the house as *A spacious and handsome building.*[20]

The entry hall is flagged and tiled with staircases either side leading to the second floor. These may not be the originals, although eighteenth-century in style, as they cut across the windows.[21] Perhaps Elizabethan stairs, which are broader in tread and may have had fewer stairs to reach the second floor, were saved from the Tudor house. These may have suffered woodworm damage or were not seen as 'elegant' and were replaced by the new owners after

Martha Cossins had left. Repairs and replacements have been made to recent woodworm damage and strengthening has been added to take the volume of traffic now using the stairways.

The immediate surroundings were of eighteenth-century taste which included the fashionable planting of Cedar of Lebanon trees. These grew enormously over a period of two hundred and forty years eventually succumbing to destruction by a fungus and others removed for buildings necessary for future use. There was no artificial lake of the 'Capability Brown garden design' and the grounds were left as wilderness with a semi-circular courtyard cut into the hillside for horse and carriage use. Mr John Innys was visited by Sir Joseph Banks, President of the Royal Horticultural Society, who was examining the gardens of extensive properties on the outskirts of Bristol. Recording the visit in his journal, 'The End of an Excursion', he writes,

After breakfast we set out for Mr Innis's garden at Redland, which I had heard a great Character of, found it very trifling, scarce one good Plant in the whole collection. Mr Innis Values himself chiefly upon officinal Plants, consequently is well stored with nettles, docks and c (clover?) yet we were not able to puzzle out the name of LYSIMACHA NUMMULARIA, at Least so the Gardener told me who askd me the name and desird me to set it down on paper which I did.[22]

(Lysimachia, Creeping Jenny, or Moneywort)

The Dutch garden has remained and some of the land was used for orchards and a kitchen garden. At some stage a caretaker's/gardener's cottage was added in the stable area and later pulled down to accommodate a school hall.

At the west gateway are another set of wrought-iron gates with an overthrow arch containing a cartouche. They were saved from demolition in the Second World War through the intervention of the School Council and are known to have been made by Nathaniel Arthur. The garden wall and balustrade are dated as c.1735 but bear the remains of an earlier brick wall belonging to the sixteenth-century Tudor house.

In 1740 work began on a private chapel for John Cossins and his family on his estate which is now part of Redland Green. It is attributed to the architect, John Strachan, although he died in 1741 before Redland Court was finished. William Halfpenny was left to complete the work and is recorded as providing estimates as well as designs. The walls were of limestone and lead was used for the dome. Overall the chapel can be said to be in the style of English Rococo.[23] A bill presented by Richard Williams gives detail of the work carried out from September 1741 to November 1741. William Halfpenny is mentioned on bills in May 1742 when he agrees to:

Give proper directions as is usuall by Architests and Directors of Buildings, to all his Workmen employ'd At his Chapple at Redland and to See Said Workmen do their Work in a Workmanlike Manner, and See that they Make proper Use of his Materials without Waste and to See the Whole Completed for the Sum of ten pounds, ten shillings Sterling.[24]

The accounts for the building of the chapel have been preserved and have been well documented.

Two Tun (tonne) of rock stone £1.15.4. 2 Key stones, 4 shillings.[25]

The private chapel, now the Redland Parish Church, can be seen through an avenue of lime trees planted by the Bristol City Council in the 1920s leading to the ornamental wrought-iron gates presented by the Cossins family in 1753. The west front has pairs of pilasters with a pediment and a cupola. The pediment has a half-circular window. Rising behind the pediment is a bell tower which begins as a square form, the juncture marked by urns, and transforms into an octagonal structure supporting a cupola with orb and cross. In 1742 Lewis Casteels received two guineas (£2 2s 0d) for gilding the ball and cross.[26] Entry is by way of a flight of five steps of black marble leading to the chapel doors and into an octagonal meeting hall area with stairs to the gallery seats. The nave with carved cherub heads has a towering proscenium arch over the sanctuary. A massive stone screen is in place. The original wooden pews have been replaced at some stage. The chapel's interior is harmonious and compact for its relatively small size.[27]

John Cossins hired the master craftsman, Thomas Paty, to decorate the chapel. The chancel ornamentation was completed in 1743 and substantial restoration work was needed to replace the central carvings which were stolen several years ago but which could be identified through earlier photographs. The walls and the dado are panelled in oak. Paty's use of oak leaves and acorns echo the theme of 'prosperity' and 'growth'; 'from little acorns big trees grow'.

John Cossins was anxious to establish himself as a country gentleman and to leave his association with trade as being not socially acceptable.[28] A 'country gentleman' was in keeping with having one's portrait painted by an artist of some stature. John Cossins commissioned two family portraits, to be painted by John Vanderbank (1694-1739). The portraits of John and Martha Cossins now hang in the entrance hall of the Redland High School.

John Vanderbank was the son of John Vanderbank, Senior, of Dutch origin, who worked in London as a tapestry weaver. John the Younger showed promise as an artist and worked in the London studio of Godfrey Kneller, a former European artist established in England in 1676 as a portrait painter. Assistants were employed by the master to learn skills and to help with finishing areas of the painting. John Vanderbank set up his own studio in St Michael's Lane, London. His commissions included portraits of Sir Isaac Newton, Thomas Gray (Founder of Guy's Hospital) and George I (1725) and Queen Charlotte (1736). Although a number of paintings and etchings exist Vanderbank never achieved great fame because of his early death from tuberculosis at the age of forty-five years.[29]

In Vanderbank's portrait John Cossins is depicted wearing a brown, velvet jacket in the manner of a country squire and bewigged in a long white shoulder-length wig. He appears to be a man of strong character but the sadness in his face shows he is in poor health. Martha is depicted in the fashion of the day, with low-cut gown revealing a little of her pink bosom, suggesting coquettishness and daring. The blue silk sleeve is rendered in the manner of the French artist, Chardin (1699-1779). In Chardin's painting, *The Lesson*, which hangs in the National Gallery, luminosity of the blue silk sleeve is achieved by applying a white undercoat and then painting over with a cobalt and cerulean blue mix. There is also quality in the way Vanderbank has painted the blue silk of Martha's sleeve, brought forward to the front of the picture plane.

Vanderbank had also been commissioned by John Cossins to make a copy of the painting, *Embalment*, by Annibak Carracci (1560-1609), which originally hung in the gallery at Houghton Hall and was later destroyed by fire. Vanderbank's copy can be seen today in Redland Parish Church, formerly the Cossins' family chapel. The family portraits originally housed in the private chapel were later transferred to the Vicarage on Redland Green built for John Cossins in 1751. In the 1900s the paintings were restored at the expense of the Vicar.[30] However, they were insufficiently cleaned at this time and by 1950 were again in a poor state. The portrait of John Cossins was acquired by Redland High School in 1950 on loan from Church authorities. Staff donations were spent on its cleaning and presentation for the School's seventieth Anniversary in 1952. A pupil reported she had seen 'a portrait of a lady, in the same frame' at the Vicarage and this was later acquired, although it was badly damaged by earlier attempts at 'patching' and 'repainting and varnishing'. Despite this damage the two portraits are a welcome addition to the entrance hall. The portraits are not signed and are only identified through written records. They were loaned and catalogued for an exhibition of eighteenth-century paintings held in the Bristol Art Gallery in the 1980s.

John Cossins died in 1759 aged seventy-seven years. In 1761, the year of the sighting of Halley's Comet, Martha Cossins ordered a weathervane featuring the comet, which is now on the west cupola, although an etching made in the nineteenth-century shows weathervanes on both cupolas. (The east cupola was destroyed to build apartments for Miss Cocks, Redland High School's first Headmistress.) At her own expense Martha Cossins continued to employ Thomas Paty to complete the chapel's carvings. She also provided the high-backed settle seats and oversaw the whitewashing of the chapel. The picture over the Communion Table, Vanderbank's copy of Carracci's *Embalment*, was cleaned by a Mr John Simmons, of the Bristol Limners.[31] In 1761 the eagle over the font was carved by Thomas Paty. When the dome was damaged by lightning Martha Cossins paid for new lead covering. In 1762 Martha Cossins died aged seventy-four years and was buried in the family vault in the chapel.[32]

The busts of Martha and John Cossins, carved in 1734 by the sculptor, Michael Rysbrack of London, were removed from Redland Court and placed in the chapel in the niches designed for them. In 1762 Thomas Paty finished the monument to John Cossins and his wife and her relatives.[33] The wrought-iron gates were made by Nathaniel Arthur. On the windowless east wall two blackamoor heads were carved. Several negroes are included on the internal panel designed by Paty and their presence shows how use was made of the slave trade by prosperous Bristolians.[34] The chapel was consecrated in 1790 but was never dedicated to a saint. In 1941 the Parish of Redland became separate from the Parish of Westbury and the chapel became the Parish Church of Redland.[35]

In 1747 Thomas Paty had been employed to add an additional bay to each side of the south front of Redland Court which created more internal space and improved the appearance of the front of the house.[36] The windows are Venetian-style and the central window on each wing has a shell-head niche and originally held lead-based statues of classical Greek figures with outstretched arms. The statues were removed on July 18 1918 and sold for scrap metal for the war effort.[37] Their removal was sanctioned by the Headmistress, Miss Shekleton, who described the statues as 'hideous'! Large antique urns have now been placed in the niches. The connecting structures have two semi-circular ground-floor windows and two plain windows under a cornice.

After the death of John Cossins the estate was left to his wife, Martha. After her death, with no offspring, the property was passed to Jeremy Baker the eldest surviving son of Martha's sister who was a linen draper. A draper would not have the income to sustain the property and despite being left other Bristol properties Jeremy Baker was always in financial difficulties. His death in 1799 revealed a long history of borrowings, misappropriations and final bankruptcy.[38]

Jeremy Baker had entered into an agreement with Sir Jarrett Smith on a mortgage for the property, later transferred to his son, Sir John Hugh Smith, a new family holder of the

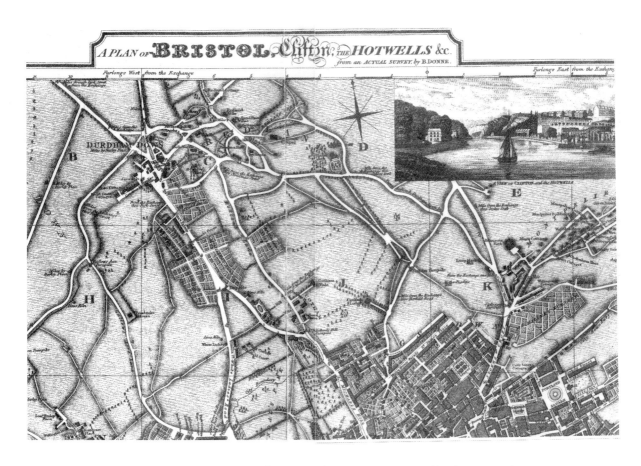

6. Donne's map of Clifton & Hotwells, 1826. This section shows Redland Court and Avenue.
Reproduced by kind permission of the Bristol Record Office

mortgage. The Smith family had married into the Smythe family of Ashton Court who were wealthy speculators. The sale of the property would cover all debts and the residue was to be invested at 3% for Jeremy Baker's children.[39] One of the keys to understanding the development of Redland is the gradual conversion of the Redland Court estate from pasture to residential accommodation. As a result of Baker's financial difficulty the mansion and land were put up for auction in three lots.[40]

Lot 1, purchased for £9,200, consisted of the messuage, the mansion house, and eight acres of land together with other meadow land and the contents of the house. Lot 2 was the wooded area. Lot 3 included the Great Stable along with outbuildings and six acres of land

and was bought at the cost of £1,650 and £1,200 by a gentleman already living in the buildings. The gentleman was Slade Baker, the brother of the Rev. William Baker, who as the eldest grandson had inherited the latter.[41] Lot 1 was sold to George Hunt, acting for Henry Seymour, and by 1800 Seymour was in full legal possession. In 1811 Henry Seymour, Junior, sold Redland Court, Lot 1, and Lot 2, the wooded area, to Sir Richard Vaughan for £13,000.[42] From 1800 onwards the property was seen as a much sought-after residence for a prosperous trader. By comparing the list of fields to be sold in 1799 with the map of 1811, on which all fields are named, it is apparent that the estate had not been reduced in scope and although perhaps sold in separate lots they were back together in 1811 as an estate under one owner.[43]

After the purchase of Redland Court in 1811, extensive, clumsy alterations were made internally to corridors and wings. The Tudor oak panelling appears to have been used all over the house and in many unusual places and along corridors. The installation of running water meant cutting into walls and passageways. The 1811 boundaries of the Redland Court were not the same as shown later in the 1841 map as land had been purchased at the Cotham end of the estate and at the Coldharbour Farm end.[44] This would account for the value of the estate at the time of Sir Richard Vaughan's death in 1833 as £27,645, an increase of £14,000 or so. For the third time bankruptcy saw the estate passed to a group of merchants willing to invest in property. They included William Edwards of Bristol and James Evan Baillee of Inverness. Part of the land was parcelled out for building sites as the area became residential. In December 1829 James Baillee bought Redland Court for £25,000.[45] On the Westbury and Stoke Bishop Tithe Map of 1841 Redland Green is shown as common land and there were fifteen owners for the remaining 90% of the land. The tithe map makes it clear that Redland and Cotham were two distinct settlements separated by fields and the Redland Court estate went as far as Cotham Brow.[46]

In 1841 James Evan Baillie (Baillee), until his death in 1863, owned the largest area of Redland, namely the Redland Court estate of one hundred and sixty-six acres. John Cossins's chapel now belonged to the trustees and comprised forty acres of surrounding land. Sir Thomas Fremantle owned another thirty-nine acres, the trustees of John Sweet, thirty-seven acres, Arthur Palmer, Senior, thirty-four acres and William Henry Warton and his wife, Catherine Innys, twenty-two acres. Descendants of other families, Hugh Vaughan and the Rev. James Taylor held smaller acreages of land. Although

Baillie was the largest land owner he was living in London and was probably not aware of the development of the land for residential accommodation.[47] At this time the mansion house was lived in by William Edwards, who, like Baillie, was one of Vaughan's creditors.

After Baillie's death his executors auctioned off some thirty-four acres of the estate, again to sort out debts, and in 1864 plans were drawn up by Sturge and Sons to convert the land for residential use. These areas are now known as Cotham Brow, Zetland Road and Redland Road. The Sturge family were to have close links with the Redland High School. Miss Elizabeth Sturge was a member of the School Council from 1896-1917. One of the purchasers was William Coates, a builder, who had built houses from 1858 to 1860 in Hampton Road and who continued in 1875 to build more houses in Redland Road.[48]

In 1863 Evan Baillie and other members of the family succeeded to the property. In 1864 the mansion and ninety-one acres of land were sold to William Edward's son, George Oldham Edwards for £25,730.[49] George Edwards, a wealthy banker, married Emily Way, the daughter of the Vicar of Henbury, when she was twenty years of age and he was sixty and they

7. 1929. Rear courtyard, Redland Court. Various changes to windows and doors. Note the below-ground cellars and faceted stone surrounds to vents

came to live at Redland Court. After his death in 1883 she married her lover, Greville Smyth, and moved to Ashton Court.[50] George Edwards was succeeded by his son William Herbert Greville Edwards in 1883.

The development of Redland as a residential suburb began in the 1840s and was more or less complete by 1914.[51] Homes were needed for the upper-middle classes, lawyers, bankers, professionals, as well as cottages for workers. Cottages built in the 1850s with wooden-beamed ceilings exist amongst the more substantial semi-detached stone villas and two-storey terraces. There is only one 'street' in Redland, Wolcott Street, constructed in the 1860s where terraced houses front the pavement. There were also substantial gentlemen's residences with large and well-maintained grounds. Many have been demolished having outgrown their usefulness as residential homes or educational institutions such as the Redland Teachers' College which was housed at Redland Hall. Fortunately, Redland Hill House remains and is home for the Bristol Steiner School.

In 1874 the building of the railway in the Redland area to connect with the docks at Avonmouth led to a request in 1884 by the Redland High School Council for a Redland passenger station to enable girls from outer areas to attend the school and by 1885 this was set in place.[52]

Land which fronted roads, or could have access though lanes and boundaries of fields, was more suited for housing development although a boundary did not automatically ensure the construction of a road. Sometimes land owners entered into an agreement perhaps building down the middle of a plot and having a rear entrance through a lane.

Edwards, with ownership of surrounding fields, was able to make a better decision in planning curved streets around Redland Court and when ownership passed to James Dole this

led to a more regimented layout of roads for twentieth-century houses.[53] James Dole had paid £12,250 for his purchase of the mansion and land and this amount would indicate that it was not the extensive property it had been at the time of George Edward's ownership.

In 1880 the Rev. T. G. Rose, formerly the Minister of Clifton Down Congregational Church, founded a school for girls at 27 and 28 Redland Grove and the houses were purchased in 1882 by a School Council of which the Chairman elect was the Rev. William Prideaux, Vicar of St Saviour's, Redland and the Vice-Chairman, Mr Urijah Thomas. Miss Elizabeth Cocks was appointed as Headmistress.[54] In 1884 James Dole sold Redland Court to the Redland High School Council for £5,500.[55] He had retained a large amount of the surrounding land for development of houses in a fast-growing residential area near the centre of the city of Bristol. Both of these enterprises supported each other, land sales brought property developers, more upper-class and middle-class homes brought families, and girls needed to be given an equal opportunity to be educated in the manner given to boys.

NOTES
1 Kingsley, N., 2001. *The Country Houses of Gloucestershire. Vol. 1. 1500-1660.* 2nd ed. Chichester: Phillimore Press, p.247.
2 Charlton, J. and Milton, D., 1951. *Redland 791-1800.* Bristol: Arrowsmith, p.25.
3 ibid. p.24.
4 ibid. p.26.
5 ibid. p.26.
6 ibid. p.27.
7 ibid. p.30.
8 ibid. p.33.
9 ibid. p.33.
10 ibid. pp.36-37.
11 ibid. p.39.
12 ibid. p.40.
13 ibid. p.41.

14   Wikipedia, n.d. Images of England. *In: Wikipedia: the free encyclopaedia* (online). Available from: http://www.image-sofengland.org.uk. (Accessed 28/12/2009)

15   Malpass, P., 2010. *The Development of Redland.* Unpublished manuscript. p.1.

16   Wikipedia, n.d. Images of England. *In: Wikipedia: the free encyclopaedia* (on line). Available from: www.image-sofengland.org.uk. (Accessed 28/12/2009)

17   ibid. p.1.

18   Charlton, J. and Milton, D.M., 1951. *Redland 791-1800.* Bristol: Arrowsmith. p.42.

19   Ison, W., 1952. *The Georgian Buildings of Bristol.* London: Faber and Faber. p.169.

20   Bungay, J., 1982. *Redland High School, 1882-1982.* Council of Redland High School. p.1.

21   Charlton, J. and Milton, D.M., 1951. *Redland 791-1800.* Bristol: Arrowsmith. p.42.

22   Allen, M. and Ellis, S. 2010. *Nature Tales, Encounters with Britain's Wildlife.* London: Elliott and Thompson. p.254.

23   Wilkins, H.J., 1924. *Redland Chapel and Redland.* Bristol: Arrowsmith, p.22.

24   Charlton, J. and Milton, D.M., 1951. *Redland 791-1800.* Bristol: Arrowsmith. p.44.

25   ibid. p.44.

26   Wikipedia, n.d. Redland Church. *In: Wikipedia: the free encyclopaedia* (online). Available from : www.about-bristol.co.uk/red-02.asp Redland Church. (Accessed 14/04/2010)

27   Wilkins, H, J., 1924. *Redland Chapel and Redland.* Bristol: Arrowsmith. pp.23-24.

28   Charlton, J. and Milton, D.M., 1951. *Redland 791-1800.* Bristol: Arrowsmith, p.39.

29   Wikipedia, n.d. John Vanderbank. *In: Wikipedia: the free encyclopaedia* (online). Available from: http://en.wikipedia.org/wiki/John_Vanderbank. (Accessed 11/09/2010)

30   Wilkins, H.J., 1924. *Redland Chapel and Redland.* Bristol: Arrowsmith, p.27.

31   ibid. p.40.

32   ibid. p.40.

33   ibid. p.41.

34   Morris, S. and Mowl, T., 2002. *Open Doors.* Bristol: Redcliffe Press. p.38.

35   Wikipedia, n.d.Redland Church. *In: Wikipedia:the free encyclopaedia* (online). Available from : www.about-bristol.co.uk/red-02.asp Redland Church. (Accessed 14/04/2010)

36   Charlton, J. and Milton, D.M., 1951. *Redland 791-1800.* Bristol: Arrowsmith, p.47.

37   Redland High School., 1914-1930. *Headmistress' Reports.* Redland High School Archive. BB018.

38   Charlton, J. and Milton, D.M., 1951. *Redland 791-1800.* Bristol: Arrowsmith. p.53.

39   ibid. p.54.

40   Malpass, P., 2010. *The Development of Redland.* Unpublished manuscript. p.6.

41   Charlton, J. and Milton, D.M., 1951. *Redland 791-1800.* Bristol: Arrowsmith. p.55.

42   ibid. p.56.

43   Malpass, P., 2010. *The Development of Redland.* Unpublished manuscript. p.6.

44   ibid. p.7.

45   Charlton, J. and Milton, D.M. 1951., *Redland 791-1800.* Bristol: Arrowsmith, p.57.

46   Malpass, P., 2010. *The Development of Redland.* Unpublished manuscript. p.1

47   ibid. p.3.

48   ibid. p.7.

49   ibid. p.8.

50   Redland High School. 2002. *Old Girls' Newsletter.* p.13.

51   Malpass, P., 2010. *The Development of Redland.* Unpublished manuscript. p.1.

52   Redland High School. 1893-1898. *Council Minute Book.* Redland High School Archive. BB043.

53   Malpass. P., 2010. *The Development of Redland.* Unpublished manuscript. p.10.

54   Shaw. M.G., 1932. *Redland.* Bristol: Arrowsmith. pp.16-17.

55   Bungay, J., 1982. *Redland High School 1882-1982.* Council of Redland High School. p.9.

PART TWO

1

THE EDUCATION OF GIRLS

In 2012 Redland High School celebrates 130 years of historical development. From humble beginnings and the acquisition of Redland Court this school has experienced many changes in the education of girls. The social history of Redland High School draws on factual information from the School's archives and provides an insight into these changes.

The School was confronted with the same problems over successive generations; maintenance of an historic building, in its early days lack of specialist facilities, financial constraints, staff/student ratio, teachers' salaries, choice of becoming private or public, effect on numbers following the development of other schools in the district. The success of girls in achieving university entrances, senior positions in government departments, hospitals, schools, universities, leaders in the community and overseas performers in sport, art, music, drama are consistent throughout Redland High School's history.

In 1868 the Schools Inquiry Commission stated, 'Almost all private schools rest, in some degree, on social distinctions'.[1] Women's social position in Victorian society impinged upon and influenced the shape and form of female education.[2] The upper-class woman, a 'lady', had servants, took the 'grand tour', was governess-educated and seen as a 'cultured' person. The majority of middle-class women could never attain the level of the 'cultured lady' because their husbands' income was not at a financial level to support a 'lady of leisure', although they had the help of a maid and assumed a 'ladylike' stance. The middle-class woman was not an income-earner but gave freely of her time for charitable organizations, helping the poor, attending church regularly and organising Sunday schools. This involvement with the world beyond her home gave her the freedom to demand more from life, to be educated and socially accepted in the company of her husband's friends.

In contrast to the prescriptive ideal of femininity upheld for middle-class women the ideal supported by the middle-classes for women in the 'lower' orders was the concept of '*the good woman*'.[3] Chaucer's *Legend of the Good Woman* was written in defence of women who were true and loving.[4]

Hastow nat in a book, lyth in thy cheste
The grete goodnesse of the Queen Alceste,
That turned was into a Dayesyes;
She that for her housbonde chees to dye,

And eke to goon to helle, rather than he,
And Ercules rescowed hire, padre,
And brought hir out of helle again to blys?

Alceste was that '*good woman*' the ultimate apotheosis of wifely duty. The Daisy flower is virtuous since it opens to light and closes to darkness. Chaucer might have chosen a rose which was fashionable at the time. Instead he chose the English daisy and the symbolism was adopted by the Redland High School in the choice of a flower motif for its emblem. The School's motto 'So hateth she derknesse' is taken from a line in this palinode, *For fere of nycht, so hatith she dirknesse,* a form of poem in which the poet retracts a derogatory remark written in an earlier poem. A staff member's proposal for the motto is discussed later.

The good woman of Chaucerian derivation was a home-loving housekeeper, thrifty, providing comfort. She was virtuous, chaste, happy, loving, and provided a service to men and their offspring. By the middle of the nineteenth-century an influential domestic ideology was established within the dominant middle-class culture.[5] These social class differences between women were to shape the form and content of women's education although not without a great deal of opposition from men and a continuous struggle by women.

The Schools Inquiry Commission, set up in 1868, had castigated the education of girls implying educational standards were falling behind those of boys.

The state of middle-class female education is on the whole unfavourable. It is characterized by want of thoroughness and foundation, want of system, slovenliness and showy superficiality, inattention to rudiments, undue time given to accomplishments, and those not taught in a scientific manner; want of organization…The purely intellectual education of girls is scarcely attempted, it is a complete failure.…Music and singing are considered more important than a knowledge of arithmetic or history, or cultivation of the mind.[6]

The findings of the Taunton Commission (named after the Chairman) were important for women's education and they commended the work by pioneers in the field, Miss Frances Buss, a student at Queen's College, 1849, who founded the North London Collegiate in 1850, and Miss Dorothea Beale, Headmistress of Cheltenham Ladies College founded in 1857, who set the pattern for the development of 'Secondary Schools solely for girls'.[7] Two points were overlooked by the Commission, firstly there was no model to follow, no precedent, and secondly, the initial desire was to give girls a boy's education.[8] Women teachers in this early period of development although receiving the best education available to them through family and home schooling and completing the highest level of further study available were not trained as 'teachers' in the manner of the masters at the boys' schools. Ironically it was the men of the clergy who wanted 'education for their daughters' and were the most liberally minded of the male population. Eventually 'emancipation' was on its way.

The more liberal approach to education offered to boys appealed to socially mobile girls of the upper and middle classes who wanted to undo gender stereotyping. By the 1870s head-mistresses had adopted a broadly based curriculum to include the subject areas of English, English literature, scripture, history, geography, French, German, Latin, natural science, science, mathematics, aesthetics, music, and drawing. There was a growing interest in replicating boys' performances in drill, gymnastics, tennis and cricket and the belief in the more liberal education which made a man 'better and nobler' might also fit a woman for home duties or entry to university.[9]

In Bristol, prior to the 1700s, benefactors had set up charity schools for boys and girls where they received the barest elements of schooling. The Red Maids Institution, founded in 1634, was by far the richest of the endowed schools for girls and they could stay until the age of eighteen years. By 1875 a firmer education policy with an enlarged curriculum saw the number of girls at the Red Maids School reduced to eighty pupils with a leaving age of fifteen years.[10]

The Bristol School Board was inaugurated in 1871 where the political divide was also a religious divide. Six hundred pupils in a Bedminster Church School, St Luke's, were taught in a main hall and two side classrooms.[11] By 1870 eighteen thousand Bristol children were registered at church schools with another one thousand five hundred children from working-class and middle-class families registered at private fee-paying schools or Dame schools. Sunday schools were said to be an attempt at social control by the middle-classes over the poor. The 1870 Forster Act allowed fee-paying schools to exist alongside Board schools.[12]

In December, 1871, the Board of Education's policy was set up as follows:

1. Mixed classes with women teachers for children up to the age of seven years.
2. Segregated classes for children over seven years.
3. The Bible to be read but no denominational teaching.
4. A broad curriculum.
5. Headmasters to be responsible for corporal punishment.
6. Leaving age thirteen years, with some exemptions from ten years to thirteen years.
7. Fees three pence per week up to Third Standard and four pence above. Remission of fees for those unable to pay.[13]

In 1880 the Mundella Act left the minimum leaving age at ten years requiring children to stay at school until thirteen years of age if they failed to reach the local standard of proficiency required for the award of a certificate.[14]

NOTES
1. Avery, G., 1991. *The Best Type of Girl, A History of Girls' Independent Schools.* London: Andre Deutsch, p.1.
2 Purvis, J., 1991. *A History of Women's Education in England.* Buckinghamshire: Open University Press, p.xiv.
3 ibid. p.6.
4 Perceval, F., 1998. *Chaucer's Legendary Good Woman.* Cambridge: Cambridge University Press, p.1.
5 Purvis, J., 1991. *A History of Women's Education in England.* Buckinghamshire: Open University Press, pp.6-7.
6 Redland High School Council, December, 1887. *High Schools for Girls.* Redland Court. Redland High School, p.1 (nyc).
7 Ollerenshaw, K., 1967. *The Girls' Schools.* London: Faber and Faber, p.15.
8 Avery, G., 1991. *The Best Type of Girls, A History of Girls' Independent Schools.* London: Andre Deutsch, p.54.
9 Hunt, F., ed., 1987. *Lessons for Life, the Schooling of Girls and Women, 1850-1950.* Oxford: Blackwell, p.6.
10 Avery, G., 1991. *The Best Type of Girls, A History of Girls' Independent Schools.* London: Andre Deutsch, p.33.
11 Gibson, C., 1997. *The Bristol School Board 1871-1903.* Bristol: Bristol Branch of the Historical Association. University of Bristol, pp.1-2.
12 ibid. p.2.
13 ibid. p.8.
14 ibid. p.12.

nyc – not yet catalogued.

2
1882 THE FOUNDING OF THE REDLAND GIRLS' HIGH SCHOOL

The Rev. T.G. Rose, formerly the Minister of Clifton Down Congregational Church, proposed setting up a school in the Redland district for his eldest daughter who aspired to become a writer and for two girls living in Chesterfield Road and Brunswick Square. Clifton High School for Girls, opened in 1878, was considered too far away as no trams, buses, or railway operated from Redland to Clifton.

The Rev. Rose joined with the Minister of Redland Park Church, the Rev. Urijah Thomas, and approached the University of London to recommend a teacher. Miss Elizabeth Ann Cocks, born in the London area and schooled in France and Germany, was selected. She was one of the first women students to pass the Cambridge Women's Examination, the highest award open to women at that time.[1] The Minister's offer was accepted by Miss Cocks and she commenced the teaching of four pupils in September 1880. Numbers 27 and 28 Redland Grove were acquired for the school.[2]

The Rev. Rose taught mathematics, science, Latin and scripture. Miss Cocks and an assistant taught English, needlework, and drawing, the latter considered necessary for the development of manual and aesthetic skills.[3] There was a need for girls to obtain the educational and academic achievements parallel with boys giving them entry to university with a chance of becoming a teacher or to enter the professional field.[4] In 1882 the Rev. Rose formed a Council and announced his school as being an 'established school'. The Rev. W. Prideaux, Vicar of St

Saviour's, Redland, was elected Chairman and the Rev. Urijah Rees Thomas as Vice-Chairman.

MISS ELIZABETH ANN COCKS
(Headmistress 1882-1907)

In 1882 Miss Cocks was formally appointed as Headmistress in charge of forty-six pupils.[5] To leave a secure second mistress appointment at the established Devonport High School for a proposed school and a Headmistress's position, which at the time of appointment only had four pupils, was courageous and enterprising. Some pupils had been schooled at home by a governess, others had attended Dame schools, some were Junior pupils at local Board schools, St Saviour's in Chandos Road, St John's on Blackboy Hill, St Nicholas' at Westbury-on-Trym. Younger pupils were enrolled at private Froebel Kindergartens in the Redland and Clifton areas.[6]

Boys with an average age of four years were admitted to the Froebel Kindergarten at Redland High School to give them a preliminary taste of schooling before they entered day, or boarding, preparatory schools. Some boys had sisters at the school who were entered in order to continue their education beyond the age of thirteen years. High-achieving students were invited to stay on at school as pupil/teachers, receiving a meagre salary which helped to pay school fees and the promise of entering university to become a qualified teacher. Their names were entered in the Admissions Record.[7] Pupil/teachers in the

8. Miss Elizabeth Ann Cocks, the first Headmistress
(1882-1907)

Board schools saw it as an upward move onto the social ladder. The first pupils registered in May 1882 were Ada Rose, aged sixteen years, who stayed until 1883, Nora Browne and Edith Carver, both aged fourteen years, who stayed until 1884. Girls lived at Redland and in the suburbs of Cotham, Montpelier, Bishopston and Westbury Park. Boarders came from the outlying suburbs of Brislington, Fishponds, Stapleton.[8]

Two sisters and two other girls, daughters of clergymen, entered the school on the recommendation of the Rev. Rose. Ethel Simcock entered as a pupil in May 1882 and re-entered as a pupil/teacher in July 1883. Gertrude Jones, daughter of the Rev. R. Jones, also entered as a pupil/ teacher. The Rev. Prideaux, Chairman of the Redland Girls' School, sent his son to the Kindergarten for three months.[9] Edith Bancroft lived at Totterdown some distance away from

Redland and entered Redland High School in 1883 and returned in 1891, as did many Old Girls after her, as a member of the staff. Their experience at Redland High School helped in their applications for headmistress's positions.[10] In 1884 another clergyman's daughter, Christine Lambert, became a pupil/teacher. As an encouragement to stay for three years parents were entitled to a rebate of 5%.[11] In some circles encouraging girls to be 'educated' and eventually 'married' was tantamount to producing 'clever' sons!

The term *high school* implied further education *at a higher level* and had been used by the School Boards to set up public mixed schools for pupils with ability some of whom had been awarded full scholarships or part-fee exemption. The name *high school* was borrowed by private schools and the argument was seen later as not significant for 'general' education as the term 'high school' was being used for: *Private property, private schools which are not conducted in the interests of the public nor governed by public trustees.*[12]

Some privately-funded high schools dropped the name 'high'. The house mistresses of Winchester High School felt that a school with the name lost upper-class pupils and that their own social standing was at stake. The school became the Winchester School for Girls in 1914.[13] The 1880s saw pioneer high schools giving girls the opportunity to enter the highest level of examinations though some private schools were wary of examinations and prizes. The examinations were marked by men and even this showed a gender bias for some subjects where a feminist point of view might be overlooked. Girls were to be seen as courteous and respectful of men who interviewed them for university entrance. Later, when school uniforms were introduced, this mark of respectability and courteousness was instilled by those schools who oversaw public behaviour away from the school of girls wearing an identifiable school uniform. A Redland High School girl was expelled for not wearing her white gloves in public, although the term 'expelled' merely meant a day's non-attendance.

On 28 April 1882 the Redland Girls' High School Company was formed under the direction of the Rev. Urijah Rees Thomas with support from friends. It was a limited liability company and shares were offered to selected people in multiples of £1. Miss Cocks, as a share holder, subscribed £105. The bank passbook showed £145 in credit.[14] In forming a company for a *public school*, Redland High School followed the lead set by Clifton High School. The 'Articles of Association' empowered these schools to open, at discretion, additional schools in Cotham and other suburbs.[15]

On 1 May 1882 at the first Council meeting, Miss Cocks asked permission to purchase classroom desks, clocks and books to commence a teachers' library and a collection of chemicals which had belonged to the Rev. Rose. In December 1882 Miss Cocks obtained permission to appoint a master to teach chemistry and another to teach drill and a lady to teach dancing.[16] Employment of men as headmasters and members of staff was universally accepted. Miss Cocks, a dynamic five-foot lady with power later to appoint her own members of staff, gradually over the years replaced male teachers with females. She was one of a number of women who were able to organise and work out their own methods and form their own traditions although the difficulties were overcome with help from Council members as benefactors and a dedicated staff.[17]

In April 1883 Canon John Percival, ex-Headmaster of Clifton College, became President of the Redland Girls' High School, a position he held until 1918. He was a great supporter of the 'education of women' and in 1883 formed the 'Association for the Promotion of the Higher Education of Women'. Miss Emily Sturge, a Suffragist, was an elected member of the Bristol Schools' Board. This was a public position rarely offered to women. Miss Emily Sturge was appointed to the Council becoming Vice-President. Her sister, Elizabeth was instrumental in obtaining a generous portion of the Canon Gamble estate for a new science building. The appointment of a woman as a Councillor was radical.[18] Emily had an interest in science and in 1886 gave a scholarship to a Redland girl for study at the Merchant Venturers' College, which merged in 1909 with the University College established in 1876 and the Bristol Medical School established in 1893 to form the University of Bristol which received its charter in 1909.[19] Emily Sturge died at the age of forty-five years when thrown from her horse which took off and hit a cart near Long Ashton.[20]

The School was examined every term by Mr Tait, a Master at Clifton College, who later became a benefactor for the Redland Girls' High School. Eventually the examination became an annual event until the 1900s. Redland Girls' High School was non-denominational although a reading from the Bible was part of the morning assembly. The parents of one pupil asked if their daughter could be excused from any religious teaching. Scripture lessons were taken by Miss Cocks for every Form year. Council discussions were taking place on finding larger premises and knowledge of the impending sale of Redland Court was brought to the Council's attention.[21] Many of the new high schools began in Georgian town houses, or Queen Anne-style residences. Queen Anne architectural features using red brick were adopted for the design of many schools after 1906. Town properties did not have the grandeur or the large, green garden space of Redland Court with its attractive cedar trees.

The first public Prize Giving for the Redland Girls' High School (this was the first name for the school) was held on 30 July 1883. The Mayor, Mr J. D. Weston, gave a prize of two guineas to the 'best' girl in the school from a total of seventy-one girls. Two girls had passed the Cambridge Junior Local Examination in the previous December. One girl had gained a Distinction in Scripture and another received a prize for Freehand Drawing in the examination set by the South Kensington Department of Art.[22]

'Freehand Drawing' required a freely-drawn, linear outline of an object without the use of instruments. The eye followed the shape of the object and the hand holding the pencil drew a continuous line without the pencil leaving the paper. Shading was added later. In 1887 Mr J. Parkyn was appointed as an external art tutor. He had trained at the Bristol School of Art and held the post of Second Master. Women did not commence teaching the subject area of art until the late 1880s. 'Drawing from the unclothed figure' was open to men only. Female students were offered drawing classes using a female model and the class was for women only.[23]

A piano was hired for singing lessons. In April 1894 the Council gave permission for 'a superior piano to be hired for the use of a pupil of special promise'. Piano and violin lessons were taught externally with 25% of the fees going to the school. The fee for a term's piano lessons was one guinea (£1 1s 0d.) and violin lessons were two guineas (£2 2s 0d.).[24] The Council was aware of a bigger catchment area if a railway station could be established at Lovers' Walk within distance of the school and in 1884 they sent a formal request to the Great Western and Midland Railways.[25] The land was owned by Mr Dole who had owned Redland Court. He also sent his daughters to Redland in 1885-1889 and he asked for a rebate in lieu of their staying for four years.

Miss Cocks's report at the second Prize Giving in 1884 announced there were 113 pupils, 88 in the main school and 25 in the Kindergarten. 'Kindergarten' was the name given to the Junior School which was held in a rented house in Grove Park. A Fifth Form was commenced and the following year became the Sixth Form. There were more accolades as Redland Girls' High School was now seen as benefitting the City of Bristol.[26]

In 1883 when I entered as little new pupil there were about fifty girls. There was a Kindergarten Class under Miss Baker, a devoted and enthusiastic Froebelian.... The Fifth Form was created for the first time that year.
Edith Bancroft, pupil, 1883-1888.[27]

Historically, many early childhood educators supported the idea that children should be trained to be productive. Several educational reformers opposed the cultural imposition theory through their beliefs that childhood is an important period of human growth. A German educator, Friedrich Froebel (1782-1852), a pioneer of early childhood educational reform, believed the first learning experiences of the very young are of crucial importance in influencing not only their educational achievements but also the health and development of society as a whole.[28] Miss Cocks' education in Germany may have stimulated her interest in the Froebel methodology which led her in 1883 to establish a Froebel Kindergarten/Junior School several years before the Froebel Educational Institute in London was inaugurated in October 1892.

ACQUISITION OF REDLAND COURT MANSION

In November 1884 Redland Court was purchased for £5,500. Mr Craik, an architect, was appointed to make the necessary alterations. Finally, on 12 May 1885 the Staff and seventy or eighty pupils walked into their new home.

On the opening day of the summer term the great migration took place under the Headmistress's guidance explored the long and narrow passages, the winding stairs, the panelled rooms, the darkened cellars... the long gilt mirrors of the main corridor, the crimson corded silk of the library.... the beautiful oak staircase, the fine proportions, columns, lintel of the entrance hall, three marble mantelpieces, with their Italian carvings and the great iron gates also from Italy ... the elms around the Dutch garden...the fine stables bearing a clock with gilded numbers...I remember Latin lessons in the untouched stable, painted boards bearing the names of Bob and Jerry. Our Matriculation Chemistry class met in the hay loft.

Edith Bancroft, pupil, 1883-1888.[29]

On 19 May 1885 a grand opening ceremony was held, 'a conversazione', to show the three main rooms, namely, the reception room, the library, and the drawing room. All opened onto the front entrance hall. The reception and drawing rooms were painted grey, the panels being edged with pink and gold. On the swing doors which shut off the central block from the wings were long mirrors framed in gilt.[30]

The 'conversazione' was reported on 20 May 1885 in the *Western Daily Press*. No mention was made of the presence of women and attention was only given to the male Council members and dignitaries. The Rev. W. Prideaux spoke of 'men learning to welcome women as their compeers in education'.[31]

On 28 July 1885, the first Prize Giving under the new banner of the Redland High School for Girls, Redland Court, was held in a marquee on the terrace. In her report Miss Cocks said:

We hardly know how to rejoice enough over having become the possessors of Redland Court... enabled us to organise tennis and cricket clubs and other games. My co-workers and I are looking for great results from these outdoor sports. We

anticipate that the daily increasing energy which we see developing in physical exercise will aid the girls in attaining a higher standard of energy and courage in mental work.[32]

Matching athletic prowess with academic studies was another way of matching girls' education with that of boys. There were five pupil/teachers during the period between 1885 and 1889 who were employed to teach Junior and Kindergarten pupils. The occupations of fathers who could afford the fees and who genuinely wished their daughters to be educated ranged from ministers of the church of various denominations, an architect, chartered accountant, chemist, dental surgeon, doctor, naval commander, army major, professor of music, surgeon. As the school prospered and more of the community were involved the occupations of the girls' fathers included, an artist (A.W. T. Armstrong, RBA., RWA., member of the Bristol Savages), bank manager, builder, civil engineer, coal merchant, miller, commercial traveller, farmer, jeweller, leather merchant, sub-inspector of schools, naval outfitter, oil distributor, police constable, poor-rate collector, printer, railway officer, rope maker, tailor, teacher, tutor, wine merchant. There is one female provider listed as dressmaker.[33]

The 1882-1894 Register contains the names of the first 800 pupils, and included boys who attended the Froebel Kindergarten/Junior School. In 1886 there were enough pupils to establish a Senior, Middle, and Junior School. Other developments included a Social Evening Society and a Literary and Debating Society. The Senior School girls acted *As You Like It*, and in the following year, 1887, produced *The Merchant of Venice* and in 1889, *Much Ado About Nothing*. All productions had costumes and sets made by the girls.[34]

In 1886 Mr Gilmore Barnett, a solicitor, joined the Council and became involved with the School's finance and building committees.

In that year a Redland High School girl passed the London Matriculation which resulted in the Council giving £5 for the commencement of a reference library.[35] A shortage of textbooks, particularly for English literature and poetry, resulted in girls spending much of their time copying poems from volumes containing the complete works of Coleridge. In 1887 the Prize Giving was again held in a marquee on the front terrace and numbers had risen to two hundred and two. Another girl had passed the London Matriculation and one girl had passed the first examination for women at Oxford University.[36]

The development of Sweden's 'Ling's Calisthenics' under the direction of Miss Theodora Johnson was very popular with the girls and had begun as a form of drill at boys' schools and in

9. c.1888. Sixth Remove standing on the terrace steps of Redland Court

the Services. Later it was modified to include dancing and movement and formed the basis of all future gymnastic programmes. The girls collected £11 to buy more gym apparatus to be used in conjunction with their calisthenics classes.[37] Visits to the Clifton swimming baths were made on Mondays and a regulation swimming costume was introduced. By 1888 an omnibus, at a fee, was available from Temple Meads Station exclusively for girls attending the Redland High School for Girls.[38]

The sixth Prize Giving was held in 1888 and Miss Cocks reported three girls had gained the London Matriculation and two girls the full Higher Certificates of the Oxford and Cambridge Joint Board Examinations. (Note: the first Prize Giving was held in 1883. Subsequent Prize Givings were counted back to 1882, the year of the commencement of the School.) Edith Bancroft had gained an Exhibition to Cardiff University College and another girl had been awarded the Winkworth Scholarship set up with a legacy from the first Headmistress of Clifton High School enabling the recipient to attend the Bristol University.[39]

Miss Cocks took the Senior girls to Paris for a week in 1890 to view the Paris Exhibition and the Eiffel Tower which had opened in 1889. The holiday was organised by Cooks Tours and the girls rode around the Paris streets in various modes of transport including carriages, Chinese hand-drawn carts, and tiny tramcars driven by mules. Their visit included riding for the first time in a lift installed in the Eiffel Tower.[40]

In 1892 the Prize Giving was honoured by Lady Aberdare, one of the pioneers of 'higher education for women' and who had attended the Conference of Women Workers held in Clifton. Details of the Prize Giving were printed in the *Western Daily Press*, on 10 November 1892. The opening paragraph reflects the male attitude at the time by mentioning 'awarded certificates in the Oxford and Cambridge Joint Local Examinations in Music and Drawing'. These would have been seen as 'genteel' subjects for girls only and in a longer following paragraph is a far more reaching accolade reporting that a Senior pupil was the ONLY girl in England to gain a 'Distinction in History'. In her speech Lady Aberdare stressed that girls were achieving high results because they really wanted and earnestly desired to distinguish themselves.[41]

The clock with the gilt numbers was transferred to the west turret. In 1887 the front hall had been paved and two rooms had been added to the top of the east wing for Miss Cocks's private residence.[42] The additional storey was designed by the architect, Mr Craik, and fitted well into the design of the existing house. He had also submitted plans to the Board of Trade for an assembly hall/ gymnasium in the stable area. The galley above the stables had been converted to a Sixth Form study and chemistry laboratory. The pillars supporting the galley remain today although there was talk at the time for the pillars to be finished with an ornamental capital. By 1894 money had been spent on apparatus for teaching physics and mechanics and five Senior and three Junior Scholarships were offered by the Council to study technical science.[43]

The girls had requested a cricket pitch and willingly helped to roll the surface and raised money to finish levelling the areas below the terrace. In the 1890 school magazine, an article was entitled 'Our Athletic Sports'. Members of the Tennis Club were reminded they had more to do than merely pat balls into the air and rejoice when they fell on the other side of the net and the Cricket Captain reminded girls that a cricket ball in motion is not a subject but is there to be attacked![44] In 1891 Dr Walker Dunbar gave a lecture on 'Physical Training for Girls' which resulted in an improvement in winning games against other schools. A victory over the Clifton High School was well deserved as that team included a daughter and a niece of the famous cricketer, W. G. Grace, a medical

10. 1898. School hockey team.
Hockey was first played at the school in 1892

practitioner. In 1892 hockey was played for the first time and the Captain wrote in the magazine, 'for those who look upon hockey as a dangerous game, no blood has been spilt or terrible wounds received, as yet'.[45] In 1895 an asphalt tennis court was laid in the area beneath the terrace in addition to the two grass tennis courts already established on either side of the terrace.

At the 1892 Prize Giving, the Chairman, Canon Prideaux, announced that The Redland Girls' High School Company had been voluntarily wound up and in its place a new Company had been registered as, The Redland High School for Girls.[46] Along with this new beginning was co-operation with the Local Education Authority who had donated £500 to the building of the hall, and £200 per annum for science teaching, leading to scholarships.[47] In 1893 the Board of Trade expected their contribution to be taken up by scholars who would continue with advanced studies.[48]

In 1892 Mr Edward Leonard, who had trained at the Bristol School of Art, became the Art Master and later became Secretary to the Council. He designed the cover for the school magazine showing the entrance gates.[49] The entrance fee paid by pupils for the Drawing Certificate Examination, organised by the Royal Drawing Society of Great Britain, known as

11. 1892. Drawing for the front cover of the 'School Magazine' by Mr Edward Leonard, Art Master and Secretary to the Council. The drawing was also used for the front cover of the 1932 'School Magazine'

12. Drawings of natural and manufactured objects, *The Book of School Handwork, Vol. I*, 1900

'Ablett's' was one shilling and six pence, rising to two shillings, or two shillings and sixpence if more than one examination was taken. Mr Thomas Ablett was later to change the content of the drawing examination through the introduction of 'Pattern, Design and Colour' which sought to introduce the use of water-colour paints and pastels. In 1906 when the fourth successive art teacher, Miss Rands, was examined by the Inspector of Schools she was criticised for not using colour and for only teaching pencil drawing for the drawing examination.[50] Areas beyond the school curriculum were encouraged and Professor Chattock of Bristol University College was invited to talk on 'New Photography'.[51]

On 23 March 1893 the School was given a 'Certification of Incorporation' and shares were now transferred as debentures. The bank balance was £578. 7s 8d due to the generosity of Mr Gilmore Barnett and enabled projects to go ahead.[52] The girls were concerned over the proposed dimensions of the tennis court. It was made apparent to the Council that areas at least six foot at the ends and four feet at the sides were needed to make a reasonable playing area beyond the court itself. Money was not to be wasted on unsatisfactory outcomes. Money was available for the old clock to be repaired and placed in the proposed new hall.[53]

In March 1893 tenders were called for the building of the new hall, after the appointment of the architect, Mr Craik, in November, 1892.[54] The Town Council had pledged £500.[55] Mr Tait gave £500, and Mr Gilmore Barnett gave £560. Further monies came from fees, £870, and the balance of £450 was paid by Mr Tait.[56] Incoming fees of £400 covered the 1894 overdraft of £452 12s 0d.[57]

The hall built by the Cowlin Building Company was opened in September 1894. Mr William Cowlin had died suddenly in 1890 at the age of fifty years and the business was transferred to his sons. His daughter attended

Redland High School from 1885-1891. The Council was asked if the school shares owned by Mr William Cowlin could be transferred to his widow.[58] The design and construction blended well with the historic building. The original pillars and ceiling were painted yellow, the walls a delicate green, and the dado, dark blue.[59] Use was made of building materials from the old stables and the floors were laid with the original floorboards.[60] Later, the girls complained about sitting on the rough floor and they were allowed to bring cushions. Criticism by the Board of Education's inspectors concerning the lack of facilities when the first Government Inspection was carried out in 1906, was indeed cruel when so much effort and financial contributions had been made by dedicated Councillors.

The Redland Old Girls' Club was formed in October, 1893 and in 1909 became the 'Old Girls' Guild'. By 1919 the Guild had one hundred and fifty members.[61] Gordon House had been leased to the School for the Kindergarten/Junior School. The Junior Headmistress, Miss K. Baker, wanted to conduct the school for infants as an independent venture and asked for the fees in lieu of her salary, less 25% to be given to the school.[62] This was not acceptable to the Council. It did not prevent her from staying for many years and receiving a salary. At the end of 1895 the subject of the behaviour of boarders, of which there were thirteen, came to the attention of the Council which saw the dismissal of the boarding-house mistress who had allowed the girls too much freedom on social evenings. The Rev. Prideaux defended Miss Hall and said she had made a successful business. It was decided to dismiss her and to pay her £150 and the Council would take over the lease.[63]

Any independent high schools, so called because they were independently funded and not dependent on the Boards, were established with private funds and later became charitable trusts. 'They have nearly always been pinched for funds: they have patched and contrived,

added here a little, there a little, sometimes taking what their advisors have considered appalling financial risks, mostly doing things in the cheapest possible way and rarely able to build on a large scale; few, as will be seen, have not experienced grave financial crises. Many arose through efforts made by women with determination and vision to realize their own dream of what girls' education should be like'.[64]

The Council was always looking for sources of income and even small amounts of interest on debentures were welcome and also new purchasers. Wealthy benefactors, often Council members, were willing to cover overdrafts and even to pay the rates. Mr Gilmore Barnett contributed over £1,000 to enable the accounts to be in credit.[65] In 1899 the Council changed banks from Lloyds to the Metro Bank of England and Wales because Lloyds refused to hold the overdraft.

In 1893 Miss Cocks's salary was £83 6s 8d per annum and the average salary for a teacher was £32 per annum. Miss Bancroft's salary commenced at £28 6s 8d per annum and was increased to £33 6s 8d after gaining a BA at London University. She was the first 'Old Girl' to take this degree when London was the only university open to women graduates. Mr Edward Leonard, the Art Master, was engaged externally and he was awarded £16 3s 9d per annum. Salaries were paid from the income from the fees and if the number of pupils dropped there was a need to economise. In 1894 there was a drop of £74 in the income from fees. Miss Cocks refused a salary increase and even the accountant, Mr Wilberforce Tribe, who stayed with the school for many years, was willing to drop his salary from £73 8s 4d to 60 guineas, (£63 0s 0d).[66]

The cost of maintaining an old building was an expense which could not be overlooked. It was reported in 1894 that the left-hand side of the terrace steps was dangerous to use and the steps were closed until they could be repaired.

SENIOR SCHOOL

Work for year ending July, 1891.

FORM	SCRIPTURE	HISTORY	ENGLISH LIT. AND LANG.	GEOGRAPHY	NAT. SCI.	SETS	FRENCH	GERMAN	LATIN	MATHS
VI	St Luke	English 1485–1660 or Roman 72 B.C. To 180 A.D.	Morris's Historical Grammar Chaucer's Prologue	None	Physics (Mechanics Heat & Light) Electricity and Magnetism	1	Louis XIV (Voltaire) Le Misanthrope Le Medecin Malgre lui (Moliere)	Peter Schlemihl (Chamisso)	Livy 1	Arithmetic. Euclid and Algebra Trigonometry Statics
V	St Luke	English 188–1760	Morris's Grammar Shakespeare's Henry V and Macaulay's Clive & Warren Hastings	None	Physics (Mechanics and Heat and Light)	2	'Unseen translation' and anthologie des poetes Francais	Undine (De la Motte Fouque)	Virgil Euclid IX	Arithmetic Euclid and Algebra
IVA	St Luke	English 1066–1485	Morris's Grammar Shakespeare's Julius Caesar	None	Physics (Light)	3	Le Conscript (Erckmann Chatrian)	Karze Erzzahlungen (Schmidt)	Ecloge Latinae (Frost)	Arithmetic Euclid Algebra
						4			Abbot's Via Latina	

Lessons are also given in Singing and Drawing.

Some choice of Subject allowed in the higher Forms.

13. Senior School. Work for year ending July 1891

The quote to repair the steps was £50 and was not carried out until 1896. Another expense was the demand for apparatus for the teaching of physics and mechanics. A new piano was needed for the proposed assembly hall and quotes and a comparison with hiring or buying and exchange of an old piano belonging to Miss Cocks were tediously debated. A final purchase was made from the Co-op at a price of £18 for a new piano, supplied by the Bristol Piano Company, being the cheapest arrangement after quotes from established companies such as Duck and Son, later known as Duck, Son and Pinker.[67] Economising was suggested. There was to be no increase in the lease of the house for the Kindergarten. Certificates were to replace prizes. Oil and coal were to be purchased in bulk. Cuts were to be made in printing costs, although there was discussion on advertising for new pupils and boarders. Half-penny stamps were to be used instead of penny ones! Although suggested, it was not possible at this time to offer a 'free place' for a girl from a poor family.

Cash was needed to pay the architect's fees of £10 12s 0d. Mr Tait had advanced £250 for commencement of the hall with a promise of a further payment of £250. Mr Wilberforce Tribe, the accountant, pointed out that even in debt the new hall at a cost of £1,500 would be considered by the bank as an asset and even the gardener's cottage had a value of £200. He said he was looking for a loan of £4,500 at 3.5% interest.[68] In 1897 an advertisement was placed in the local papers which resulted in seventeen new pupils enrolling for 1898. Prior to the advertisement boarders' numbers had dropped from sixteen to eight. In 1898 seventy-seven pupils came from the district of Redland; twenty-six from Bishopston; twenty-three from Cotham; fifteen from Clifton.[69] A meeting was held in 1893 to discuss the sharing of a Swedish gymnastics teacher with the Clifton High School for Girls but this proposal was rejected as Miss Cocks was travelling to London to recruit staff and had asked the bank for an overdraft of £500. She intended to use the money for salaries of potential staff with the promise of repayment through school fees.[70]

Requests for return of fees were carefully considered and two parents were sent letters concerning non-payment of fees with the threat of a court appearance. One parent, a doctor, managed to avoid an appearance through the payment, as a token gesture, of one term's fees. In 1895 the bank overdraft had risen to £800 and again Mr Tait advanced £2,000 for a second mortgage. A potential staff member, Miss Smith, MA (London), asked for a salary of £150 which the Council rejected. She was offered employment at a lower salary with a suggestion she have two free afternoons. She did not accept the offer.[71]

Members of the staff accepted appointments on a year's probation and their permanent appointment depended on the school's success in the examinations. In 1895 Mr Edward Leonard, who taught drawing, resigned to take another position. On June 13 1895 the School's Education Committee recommended the appointment of Miss Katherine Cocks, a niece of the Headmistress.[72] She was living at Redland Court in the apartment belonging to Miss Cocks and in the 1891 census her occupation is listed as 'Teacher of Drawing'. Katherine Cocks had attended Redland High School from 1883-1888 and her name is the first on the Honours Board (situated behind the stage in the Assembly Hall) and shows she was awarded a *Distinction in Drawing in the Higher Certificate Examination, 1887*. She left Redland High School to train for

14. c.1904. Miss Cocks and Staff.
Canon Percival on the right

the Art Teachers' Certificate at the South Kensington Department of Art and was one of the first women to receive this award.[73]

At the Council Meeting, 22 October 1896 Miss Katy (Katherine) Cocks submitted two designs for an examination certificate along with her suggestion for a motto derived from Chaucer's *Legend of the Good Woman*. Chaucer's words were, *So hateth she dirkness* (alternative spellings, *derkness, derknesse*). The designs were rejected but the motto proposal was referred to the Council's Education Committee. Katy Cocks chose to alter Chaucer's word from 'hateth' to 'loveth not', which may have been a Feminist way of expressing the word 'hate'. 'Hate' was too strong a word to be used by ladies of the Victorian period. The motto submission read *So loveth she not derkness*.[74] The school motto when finally carved above the rear doors in the Assembly Hall, reads, *SO HATETH SHE DERKNESSE*. 'Derknesse, 'Darkness', meaning: 'sin' or 'virtuousness'.

In November 1896 the School featured in an article printed in the magazine, *Punch*, entitled, 'A Bishop's Ideas on Ladies Ideals'. He had criticised the wearing of waistcoats and other male clothing by girls which brought further comments in the *Daily Telegraph* newspaper on his wearing of lawn sleeves and an apron. At the next Prize Giving Bishop Percival said he would never refer to women's clothing again.[75]

In July 1897 the School celebrated Queen Victoria's Diamond Jubilee and for the music concert six girls performed on three pianos. Also in that year Redland High School was second in England for results in the Oxford and Cambridge Joint Board Examinations.[76] In 1898 a Miss Dahl arrived to teach 'Swedish Drill' and remained in the school for many years. It was decided to make the first day of July as the selected day for a yearly Commemorative Service. In 1898 a school orchestra was set up by Mr Harold Bernard who also stayed at the school for many years. The Music Department was pleased to hear of Alice Cardell gaining her L.R.A.M. Also in that year the distribution of pupils was as follows: from the district of Redland, seventy-seven; Bishopston, twenty-six; Cotham, twenty-three; Clifton fifteen; Bristol, eighteen. The total number of pupils was 188. The number of boarders had dropped from sixteen to eight in the previous year although seventeen new pupils had enrolled in 1897.[77] In 1899 the fees per term for the Senior School were: pupils aged eleven to fourteen, £4 4s 0d, over fourteen years, £5 5s 0d. Boarding fees for a year were £42 0s 0d.[78]

Queen Victoria visited Bristol in 1899 and Mr Tait gave the school a Union Jack to fly from the flagpole.[79] Some girls were given the opportunity to see Queen Victoria as she passed through the streets. In 1900 the girls collected money to reinstate the bell from the original Redland Court and to install it for use for morning assembly.[80] 1900 saw the death of Miss K. Baker, Headmistress of the Junior and Kindergarten since 1883. Her place was taken by Miss Ida Deakin who stayed for twenty years.[81] In 1909 Miss Deakin established the Froebel Kinder-garten Student Training programme for the Higher Certificate of the National Froebel Union.[82] Some of these student/teachers boarded at the boarding school. In May 1901 the Rev. Urijah Rees Thomas died and was honoured as being one of the first founders of the School. During 1901 the Gordon and Wolverton Houses in Clarendon Road were bought and the boarding school known as St Margaret's commenced.[83] The boarders attended St Saviour's Church of England for Sunday services. Mr Gilmore Barnett took over the role as Chairman of the Council.

Miss Cocks was fully aware of the circum-stances of owning and maintaining a beautiful historic building and relatively large grounds which had several 'Cedar of Lebanon' trees. The large tree in the terrace side of the house was particularly impressive and early photographs show children gathered under its shady, low branches. Many etchings of the day include this magnificent tree in the composition of the picture. In the late 1700s the landscape gardener, Capability Brown, had imported some seeds of the Lebanon Cedar and was responsible for the trend to include these magnificent trees in the grounds of eighteenth-century houses. However, there was no comprehensive plan by the Council to retain the landscaped gardens as there was a need for tennis courts and a cricket pitch. Stately elm trees surrounded the garden.

15. Kindergarten. Boys and girls, under the Cedar of Lebanon, c.1885/6. Note the girth of tree

Miss Cocks gave the names of 'Fradubio' and 'Fraelissa' to two trees near the Dutch garden.[84] In 1888 the Council had expressed their dissatisfaction with the general neglect of the grounds by the caretaker/gardener.[85]

In 1901 Mr Tait donated a Gold Medal to a deserving pupil based upon results in the Higher Certificate Examination or outstanding success of scholarships to universities. The award was called the 'Victoria Gold Medal Award' honouring the late Queen Victoria.[86] A special Honours Board remains on the wall behind the stage in the Assembly Hall and contains sixteen names, dating from 1901-1916, and gold medals were only discontinued when the Great War, as it was known then, commenced in 1914. Gold could not be spared in wartime and were replaced by certificates with the promise of a medal to be presented at a later date.

In 1903 the School celebrated its twenty-first Anniversary and the Staff gave the School the high-backed oak chair, with carved decorations of daisies and school motto, which had been made from timber from the old Deanery. The chair is a copy of one which belonged to The Skinners' Company and the original was held in the Bristol Art Gallery at the time of the 1932 publication on the history of the School written

16. High-backed, carved oak chair
donated by Staff, 1903

by the School Secretary, Miss M.G. Shaw. The girls' contribution of £20, although the amount needed was considerably more, enabled the School motto to be carved into a large piece of oak timber and in 1906 the carving was fitted over the door of the Assembly Hall.[87]

A new art room, along with a science laboratory, was set up in 1903 after the Bristol Education Committee gave a grant of £300. Mr Ablett, from London, was asked to recommend some plaster casts of classical statues suitable for 'Form' drawing. He may have seen a chance to unload some obsolete figures as his London art school's initiatives were moving into the more fashionable modes of figure drawing, 'au naturel'. In turn these classical statues were abandoned by more progressive and future art teachers and by the 1940s only one plaster cast remained in the art room. Donations to set up the art room and the purchase of these casts were given by the Staff, Old Girls and friends in South Africa along with a gift of £100 from Mr Edward Robinson. Two girls won scholarships to the Royal College of Art.[88]

The School worked zealously for soldiers fighting in the Boer War in South Africa. Their fund-raising efforts resulted in the collection of £35, equivalent to £3,000 today. The money was to be used by General Baden-Powell for the relief of women and children in the town of Mafeking. In 1904 Baden Powell wrote a personal letter of thanks to the girls and Staff of Redland High School. It is amazing that this letter has survived as it was available when Miss M. G. Shaw wrote of its existence in 1932 and appears to have been torn up at some later stage. After professional restoration, at a cost of over £700, the letter, the envelope and photograph are now carefully stored in the School's archival collection. As an antique it is priceless and would be well-sought after by a collector.[89]

In 1906 Redland High School installed its first telephone at a cost of £6 with a further £1 for an extension to Miss Cocks's private residence.[90] In the 1880s the Staff wore tightly fitted, long frocks over bodies encased in corsets and Miss Cocks's black gown had an extended train which gave her a commanding presence. Girls complained of high collars poking into their necks and the problems of keeping long hair in place with combs and ribbons. The Edwardian era still demanded corsets and school girls could only be free of these when they participated in the new form of gymnastics. For this activity the gym tunic was introduced and many years later became the gymslip and adopted by government grammar schools as a school uniform. Private schools then developed their own uniforms, their own dress code. Skirts and coats used special materials, such as tweeds and woollen plaids, and were only available to a particular school. Hats with cockades and hat bands were also part of the school uniform. To some degree, in the private schools, uniforms levelled out any social differences which might occur when scholarship children entered as 'free place' pupils.

Travel to the school buildings was mostly on foot. In some cases along muddy footpaths and demands were made to improve these. In 1888 the Secretary drew attention to the condition of Redland Court Road in wet weather and the question of making a footpath was discussed.[91] As this was a private road it was not improved until 1911 and the School was asked to contribute £79 8s 9d. Bicycles were becoming popular and several staff rode bicycles and a bicycle shed was built. The omnibus brought girls from Temple Meads railway station to the School and the eventual opening of the railway station at Redland in 1898 made access available from the outer suburbs of Bristol.

The Staff, all spinsters, stayed in their positions for ten to twenty-five years. The academic qualifications of the Staff appointed by Miss Cocks from the 1890s to the early 1900s were of the highest level. Miss E. Moore was a graduate of Somerville College, Oxford, Miss Helen Drew was a graduate of Newnham College, Cambridge, and Miss Emilie Thackery was a graduate of Lady Margaret Hall, Oxford. Miss Elizabeth Rich graduated in physics and chemistry from the University College of Bristol and returned to teach at Redland High School which she had attended previously. Miss Nancy Evans graduated from the Royal College of Music and taught pupils privately. Mr Ernest Cook was paid £88 per term for teaching science. He had trained at the Merchant Venturers' College in Bristol and the Royal College and went on to become the Director of the Teachers' Training College at Fishponds.[92] A new 'School Prospectus' was produced in July 1900 which drew attention to staff profiles and the illustrated cover showed an etching of Redland Court.

In 1906 at the School's Prize Giving ceremony, Bishop Percival said, *Redland would grow to a strong efficient and most valuable school for that district and children of the 'middle-class' but the school should also look to do something for less privileged children in the form of a city scholarship*. This came to fruition in the next decade. Miss Cocks was a born organizer and her influence was so dynamic a quality that she was able to instil into the School a public spirit and sense of corporate life which continues to the present day.

In 1906 the School had its first inspection although a preliminary visit had been made in 1905. The inspection was conducted by representatives of the Board of Education, Whitehall, London, in order to apply for 'Government Grants' and to offer 'free' places for outstanding girls whose parents could not afford the fees. There were twelve full-time Staff members and three visiting staff and the girls were placed in twelve forms throughout the school. Numbers had risen to 241 in 1902 but had fallen to 225 at the time of the Inspection. The occupations of the fathers included eighteen professionals, several independent traders, farmers and commercial managers.[93]

The fees were as follows: Kindergarten under six years, £1 10s 0d, over six years, £2 2s 0d, eight to eleven years, £3 3s 0d, eleven to fourteen years, £4 4s 0d, over fourteen years, £5 5s 0d. Boarding-house fees for a term were £14. Dancing lessons were £11s 0d, advanced drawing, £1 1s.6d, singing, £2 2s. 0d, instrumental music, from £1 1s 0d – £4 16s 0d.[94]

The Inspectors noted the School was of the 'ordinary' high school type with a large percentage staying until eighteen years of age. 50% of those starting at the School came from private schools. There was concern that the high fees charged by Redland High School were equated with high performance and that in some cases 'cheaper' fee-paying schools might attract pupils away from the School.[95] The Council later reported they were not concerned because Redland High School continued to draw its support from 'that class of society which does not support the "cheaper" schools' and they were not worried about numbers of future pupils.

The Inspectors drew attention to the proximity of the railway station, opened in 1897, and the large garden both of which would serve an increase in numbers in the future and provide space for future buildings.[96] Did they envisage building in front of the house? They noted how much had been achieved although they described the current state of the buildings as neglected and in need of a coat of paint, emphasising that the building was not designed as a school. Were the inspectors viewing the situation in their terms? A school was a school if it had classrooms and facilities, as in the newly built Government Grammar schools. Did they have in mind that the Redland High School in its present form would not succeed and eventually could be taken over? The School Council owned more than two acres of land and special permission would have to be sought from the Board of Education on any plans for its future development.

Redland High School had been set up by private enterprise, in much the same way as the current thrust for so-called 'free schools'. How much influence do Governments have on private enterprise education? In 2010 the Government funded 'free' schools based on evidence that there was a need in the area for a new school. Some educators were worried about the quality of the physical buildings to be provided for setting up a 'free' school.[97] The historic Georgian house had been seen as unsuitable for a school by the Inspectors in 1906. The Council had made enormous progress with developing facilities as far as their budget would allow and the school now had an assembly hall, a library, classrooms and an art room. The inspectors were impressed with the boarding school arrangements for seventeen students, supervised by eight house-staff, of which two were teachers. Boarding schools were usually provided for by the private sector.

The curriculum offered was in accordance with the Education Board regulations. The Inspectors also noted the School was only operational in the mornings and gave longer periods of study for some subjects than the time set by the Board of Education. They suggested two languages, French and German, should be taught along with Latin for girls at the senior level and adherence to Board of Education text books. The Inspectors applauded the teaching of Latin, history, mathematics and science but were critical of the art lessons which only involved pencil drawing and even the drawings were criticised for their inaccuracies! Needlework and drill were subjects limited by facilities and staff expertise and all studies were limited by an inadequate library.[98]

The inspectors continued to press for better premises for the sciences, more classrooms, and more depth in the teaching of some subjects, of which art was one selected for improvement, although they said they had no desire to interfere with the individuality of the school. Fortunately

Miss Cocks was President of the Association of Headmistresses and although she was not in good health she kept Mr Gilmore Barnett informed of procedures. The School could not function without the Board of Education's approval and their policies on 'what constitutes a good education'. These could be seen as providing specialised facilities, a full curriculum, all-day attendance and well-qualified staff. In addition the policy of providing scholarships for the disadvantaged 'bright' girl could be incorporated if the School accepted funding from the local education authority, the LEA. School fees alone would not in the long term provide enough finance to operate the School, make the changes and pay staff salaries.

Owing to her ill health Miss Cocks sent a letter to Mr Barnett of her intention to resign in July 1907 the year the School celebrated its twenty-fifth anniversary. In that year the School took the highest place among girls' schools in England in the Joint Board Higher School Certificate Examination, gaining fourteen Certificates and ten part-certificates.[99] In her farewell speech, 1907, Miss Cocks said, *Success is not due to having all the circumstances in one's favour.*[100] In 1907 the Council advertised for a replacement. Miss Cocks died a year later in 1908 and in the same year Mr Gilmore Barnett also died. The appointed headmistress to succeed Miss Cocks was Miss Emily Shekleton.

NOTES

1   Shaw, M.G., 1932. *Redland High School.* Bristol: Arrowsmith, p.15.
2   ibid. pp.15-16.
3   ibid. p.16.
4   Ollerenshaw, K., 1967. *The Girls' Schools.* London: Faber and Faber, p.18.
5   Shaw, M.G., 1932. *Redland High School.* Bristol: Arrowsmith, p.17.
6   Redland High School, 1882-1894. *Register of Scholars,* Redland High School Archive, AR 013.
7   ibid.
8   ibid.
9   ibid.
10   Bungay, J., ed., 1982. *Redland High School, 1892-1982.* Council of Redland High School, p.15.
11   Redland High School, 1882-1894. *Register of Scholars,* Redland High School Archive, AR 013.
12   Redland High School Council, December, 1887. *High Schools for Girls.* Redland Court. Redland High School, p.3 (nyc).
13   Avery, G., 1991. *The Best Type of Girl, A History of Girls' Independent Schools.* London: Andre Deutsch, p.4.
14   Bungay, J., ed., 1982. *Redland High School, 1882-1982.* Council of Redland High School, p.4.
15   Redland High School Council, December, 1887. *High Schools for Girls.* Redland Court. Redland High School, p.4 (nyc).
16   Shaw, M.G., 1932. *Redland High School.* Bristol: Arrowsmith, p.17.
17   ibid. p.9.
18   ibid. p.18.
19   Wikipedia, n.d. University of Bristol. *In: Wikipedia: the free encyclopedia* (online). Available from: http://en.wikipedia.org/wiki/University_of_Bristol (Accessed 20/4/2010)
20   Sturge, E., 1928. *Reminiscences of my life.* Bristol: Arrowsmith, p.85.
21   Shaw, M.G., 1932. *Redland High School.* Bristol: Arrowsmith, p.18.
22   ibid. p.19.
23   Wikipedia, n.d. Royal College of Art. *In: Wikipedia: the free encyclopedia* (online). Available from: http://en.wikipedia.org/wiki/Royal_College_of_Art (Accessed 12/5/2010)
24   Redland High School, 1882-1894. *Admissions Register of Scholars.* Redland High School Archive, AR 013.
25   Shaw, M.G., 1932, *Redland High School.* Bristol: Arrowsmith, p.20.
26   ibid. p.20.
27   Bungay, J., ed., 1982. *Redland High School, 1882-1982.* Council of Redland High School, p.21.
28   Wikipedia, n.d. Froebel Educational Institute. *In: Wikipedia:the free encyclopedia* (on line). Available from: http:www.froebel.org.uk/ (Accessed 18/02/2010)
29   Bungay, J., ed., 1982. *Redland High School, 1882-1982.* Council of Redland High School, p.10.
30   Shaw, M.G., 1932. *Redland High School.* Bristol: Arrowsmith, p. 22.
31   *Western Daily Press*, May 19, 1885. *School Prizegiving.* Redland High School Archive (nyc).
32   Shaw, M.G., 1932. *Redland High School.* Bristol: Arrowsmith, p.24.
33   Redland High School, 1882-1894. *Admissions Register of Scholars.* Redland High School Archive, AR 018

34 Shaw, M.G., 1932. *Redland High School.* Bristol: Arrowsmith, p.26.
35 ibid. p.26.
36 ibid. p.27.
37 ibid. p.28.
38 ibid. p.29.
39 ibid. p.29.
40 Bungay, J., ed., 1982. *Redland High School 1882-1982.* Council of Redland High School, p.28.
41 *Western Daily Press*, November 10, 1892. Redland High School Archive (nyc).
42 Shaw, M.G., 1932. *Redland High School.* Bristol: Arrowsmith, p.27.
43 Redland High School, 1892-1905. *Council Minute Book.* Redland High School Archive (nyc).
44 Shaw, M.G., 1932. *Redland High School.* Bristol: Arrowsmith, p.33.
45 ibid. p.36.
46 Bungay, J., ed., 1982. *Redland High School, 1882-1982,* Council of Redland High School, p.19.
47 Redland High School, 1892-1905 *Council Minute Book.* Redland High School Archive (nyc).
48 ibid.
49 Shaw, M.G., 1932. *Redland High School.* Bristol: Arrowsmith, p.38.
50 Board of Education, 1906. *Report of First Inspection of the Redland High School for Girls, Bristol.* London: Whitehall. Redland High School Archive (nyc).
51 Redland High School, 1893-1898. *Council Minute Book.* Redland High School Archive. BB043.
52-58 ibid.
59 Shaw, M.G., 1932. *Redland High School.* Bristol: Arrowsmith, p.40.
60 Redland High School, 1893-1898. *Council Minute Book.* Redland High School Archive. BB043.
61 Shaw, M.G., 1932. *Redland High School.* Bristol: Arrowsmith, p.87.
62 Redland High School, 1892-1905. *Council Minute Book.* Redland High School Archive (nyc).
63 ibid.
64 Avery, G., 1991. *The Best Type of Girl, A History of Girls' Independent Schools.* London: Andre Deutsch, p.5.
65 Redland High School, 1893-1898. *Council Minute Book.* Redland High School Archive. BB043.
66-71 ibid.
72 a. 1891. Census. b. Honours board. c. Redland High School prospectus, 1898.

73 Redland High School, 1893-1905. *Council Minute Book.* Archive. BB141.
74 Shaw, M.G., 1932. *Redland High School.* Bristol: Arrowsmith, p. 41.
75 ibid. p.41.
76 Redland High School, 1893-1898. *Council Minute Book.* Redland High School Archive. BB043.
77 ibid.
78 ibid.
79 Shaw, M.G., 1932. *Redland High School,* Bristol: Arrowsmith, p.45.
80 ibid. p.46.
82 ibid. p.46.
83 ibid. p.47.
84 Bungay, J., ed., 1982. *Redland High School 1882-1982.* Council of Redland High School. p.70.
85 Redland High School, 1893-1905. *Council Minute Book.* Redland High School Archive. BB141.
86 Shaw, M.G., 1932. *Redland High School.* Bristol: Arrowsmith, p.47.
87 ibid. p.49.
88 ibid. p.49.
89 Letter from Baden Powell, 1904. Redland High School Archive (nyc).
90 Shaw, M.G., 1932. *Redland High School,* Bristol: Arrowsmith, p.45.
91 Redland High School, 1892-1905. *Council Minute Book.* Redland High School Archive.
92 Shaw, M.G., 1932. *Redland High School,* Bristol: Arrowsmith, p.34.
93 Redland High School, 1888-1917. *Staff Register.* Redland High School Archive. BB 092.
94 Board of Education, 1906, *Report of the First Inspection of the Redland High School for Girls, Bristol.* Redland High School Archive (nyc).
95 ibid.
96 ibid.
97 ibid.
98 Wikipedia, n.d. Free Schools, 19, June, 2010, *In: Wikipedia: the free encyclopedia.* Available from: http www.newstatesman.com/2010/06/schools-teachers-groups. (Accessed 27/06/2010)
99 Board of Education, 1906, *Report of the First Inspection of the Redland High School for Girls, Bristol.* Redland High School Archive (nyc).
100 Shaw, M.G., 1932. *Redland High School,* Bristol: Arrowsmith, p.52.

3
1907-1920 DIFFICULT TIMES, THE FIRST WORLD WAR YEARS

The total exclusion of women from higher education and university entrance had by 1906 become a thing of the past although there was still opposition to the 'Women's Movement' and 'Women's Suffrage'. In 1906 with the militants demanding political equality there were many instances of meetings disrupted with the cry 'Votes for Women'. In 1911 a mass rally for all women, supported by the working classes and graduates wearing their academic gowns, was held in London as a show of how far they had come in their pursuit of equal opportunities for women. However, they were unaware of what lay in store in 1914 when the Great War, as it was known then, broke out. The Militant Suffragists became ardent Militant patriots.[1]

The new Headmistress, Miss Shekleton, appointed in 1907, was to face some difficult times. The School was under the pressure of Inspections from the Board of Education and was also to face four years of a world at war. There were many changes in the Staff and after 1907 disputes concerning salaries as a result of the Burnham award. Shortage of money for improving facilities demanded by the inspectors and the constant repairs to the buildings were a financial burden until an expected legacy turned out to be worth far more than was anticipated.

Until 1908 young children were taught at home schools. Mrs Rumball in Harcourt Road had five pupils and one of these entered Redland High School. A Miss Barnes conducted home classes in Berkeley Square and a pupil, number 1,530 in the School Register had attended the

Froebelheim Kindergarten in Clifton and had a private tutor before entering Redland High School at the age of eleven years. There was a yearly intake of boys under the age of eight years and numbers varied from six to eight boys at any one time. Several enrolments showed children had attended Miss Knight's 'Froebel House' Kindergarten in Coldharbour Road in 1906, 1909, 1910 and up to 1915.[2] Florence Knox, daughter of the Rev. John Knox, Religious Tract Society, had spent sixteen months at the Froebel Institution in Kensington, London and entered Redland High School in 1901, leaving in 1908.[3] Pupil records after 1917 did not disclose

17. c.1900. Redland Court. Girls in summer uniform. Straw boaters with hatband and badge, black stockings and shoes. Staff in long dresses. The Assembly Hall, on the right of the photograph, was built by the Cowlin Building Company and opened in September 1894. Architect Mr Craik

previous schooling as by this time most of the pupils entered from the established Board schools.

Serious schooling had not been the norm and comments were made on what was now expected of pupils attending Redland High School in the way of regular attendance and homework. Education for girls was being taken more seriously by the girls themselves particularly those who were awarded scholarships for entry at Middle School level and who were expected to succeed and to enter a university.

1907 was the first year the School received a regular grant from the Board of Education and in return agreed to admit each year a regular percentage of scholars from the Board of Education's Elementary schools.[4] Enid St John was the first girl to receive a 'free place' and also the first Redland High School girl to be admitted to Cambridge University and later she became a member of Redland's High School's Staff. The formal documentation from the Board of Education was received in 1906 and placed the School on the list as a recipient of grants under Section 32 of the Regulations for Secondary schools.[5]

In 1906 Miss Cocks had asked her own Council's Education Committee to be empowered to draw up a scheme for permanent increase of salaries.[6] This may have been initiated because new appointments were being filled by well-qualified university graduates who expected to commence on substantial salaries. Miss Cocks had retired by the time the School had begun its first full year in 1907 as 'recognised'. Mr Gilmore Barnett, as Chairman, sent a letter to Miss Cocks.

We have long been aware that our school was among the first in the country and we have known that the credit was all your own.[7]

In her farewell speech Miss Cocks announced:

It is justifiable and natural for a public school to feel proud of its traditions as for a family to feel proud of its ancestral glories, but as in the family, so in the school, the desire to bequeath good should be the expression of gratitude for good inheritance.[8]

MISS EMILY SHEKLETON
(Headmistress 1907-1920)

The position of Headmistress was accepted by Miss Emily Shekleton, who, at the age of forty years, had been the Headmistress of Bath High School.[9] She held an MA from Dublin University and was offered accommodation on the school premises in the apartment vacated by Miss Cocks. In the 1911 Census, Miss Emily Shekleton's residence is shown as Redland Court.[10]

In 1908 Mr Gilmore Barnett, the School's Chairman, died, and his loss was felt because he had held the post for twelve years and had guided the School through the good and bad times. He had been more than generous on many occasions giving money and books and his widow was welcomed as a Councillor. He was succeeded by the Rev. John Gamble, later to become Canon Gamble, educationist, as well as fulfilling his church duties. Canon Gamble was to hold the position of Chairman for twenty-one years and was fully supportive of 'Education for Girls and the Sciences'. He made it known he intended to leave some money for the building of science facilities and in anticipation the School planned for what they thought they could afford.

In 1903 Mr Tait generously gave playing fields at Druid Stoke for the use by Redland High School. He said he had bought the land as an investment and even if the land was not used for recreation it could be sold off and the money donated to the School.[11] This investment turned out to be worth several millions of pounds in later years.

In 1908 an arbour was re-discovered underneath the terrace which had been blocked as a precautionary measure to support the steps leading to the terrace. It was remembered by a pupil in 1895 as overgrown with honeysuckle, clematis and roses, with a seat for three people.[12]

In 1909 at the School's Prize Giving the Bishop of Bristol commented on the wonderful views enjoyed from the terrace and he wished his new Palace built in 1898 had the same spectacular view.[13] The Palace was built a little further away on farm land now known as Redland Green and was burnt out on December 2, 1940, by German incendiary bombs and later completely destroyed by a landmine which took out four houses nearby and left a huge crater. All that remains today of the Bishop's Palace is a stone wall.

In 1900 Miss K. Baker had died. She had been in charge of the Kindergarten for eight years and her place was taken by Miss Ida Deakin, an Old Girl, who was also a Froebel graduate. She was to remain in the position for twenty years. Froebel advocated that women had an important role to play in the education of young children and should train as teachers, which in the mid-1800s was unusual.[14] The 1901 Census shows Miss Deakin, a twenty-year old, and Miss Bancroft aged thirty-one, residing at the boarding house at 32 Clarendon Road and they were in charge of nine boarders.[15]

The Kindergarten needed a new Junior School mistress. Miss Deakin recommended Miss Byrne, on an annual salary of £160.[16] In 1909 Miss Ida Deakin commenced the training of student-teachers for the Higher Certificate of the National Froebel Union using the School's established Froebel methodology and an understanding of the Froebel principles of learning.[17] The student-teachers paid fees to attend the course and some even paid boarding fees. Two students graduated in 1911.[18] In 1919 a Court of the University of Bristol had sanctioned an Ordinance associating the School's Kindergarten

Training Department with the Training Department of the University. A letter held in the School's archives from the Teachers' Registration Council stated that under these conditions Redland High School's Kindergarten Training Department would be recognized by the University for the training of registered teachers.[19] The last intake of Froebel Kindergarten teachers who trained at Redland High School's Junior School finished their training in 1940.

In 1910 the School was handed its second Inspection Report issued by the Board of Education, Whitehall, London.[20] A most notable difference was in the high-level qualifications obtained by those applying for teaching positions. This was due to the increased number of girls who had achieved success in their examinations which enabled them to enter universities and to pursue a career in teaching.

The number of pupils had increased by forty-two making a total of 264. In this obvious success the Board of Education recognized good management under a new Headmistress. An improved financial position was due to grants from the Local Education Authority. The School was receiving £761 from the Board of Education and £250 from the Bristol County Borough Council. The amount of free places fixed at 10% was being adhered to as per agreement. There were twenty-one assistant Staff members, six of whom were part-time.[21] Yearly school fees were: under six years-of-age £4 17s 6d. Over six years-of-age £6 13s 6d. Eight to thirteen years-of-age £10 10s. 0d. Over eleven years-of-age £14 5s 0d. Over twelve years-of-age £15 3s 0d. Over fourteen years-of-age £17 6s 6d.[22]

The 'Inspectors' Report' included information on the 'class of life from which pupils were drawn'. The percentages for these were: 33% professional, 1% farmers, 16% for traders and contractors, 21% for clerks, 3% for public service, 1% for domestic service, 3% for artisans and 6% not recorded.[23] The occupations listed are similar to those recorded at the commencement of the School but there is no reference to any ecclesiastical parents.

The new buildings opened in 1904, the date of which can be seen from Redland Court Road, had provided the School with an improved laboratory, art room, classroom and a domestic economy (science) room, library and cloakroom. The Inspectors noted the smaller improvements to classrooms and the assembly hall. The apartment previously occupied by Miss Cocks was now converted to classrooms and residential accommodation ceased.[24]

The Inspectorate envisaged there would be financial constraints as they understood the School was going ahead with the science buildings which they had drawn attention to in their 1906 report. They noted advanced Latin teaching was not offered as it had been in the past and realised the School was in the process of change of staff, subjects offered, and new buildings. It was proposed to move the Junior School and Kindergarten from the Boarding School premises into the main building. The

Inspectors hoped this would lead to more enrolments to support the employment of seven Kindergarten trainees.[25]

Reading between the lines of the 1910 report the Inspectors clung to the traditions they knew through their own schooling and their lifetime's association with education. They refer to 'poetry teaching', rather than 'appreciation'. They had learnt poetry 'by heart' and were able to recite long poems. This traditional approach, to some degree, was still in vogue until the 1960s, albeit the poems were shorter! The Inspectors also commented on the importance of 'the learning of grammar' and 'testing of it', rather than 'good writing' in essays and felt the teacher in question, Miss Andrews, newly graduated and very popular with the girls, was 'doing too much of the work herself'.

The Inspectors praised the work in history and the capabilities of the teacher who was following the more liberal approach to the teaching of 'History in Context'. The number of distinctions awarded in history for the Cambridge Higher Certificate over the previous ten years bore witness to this 'good teaching'. The teaching of geography was seen as thorough with 'good' notebooks and referencing. The purchase of a globe was recommended.[26]

French was taught in the Upper Second and German in the Lower Fourth. The Inspectors found a very high standard in French, again borne out by the high number of distinctions for the Cambridge Higher Certificate which had been achieved in the previous six years but were critical of starting German in the Upper Form. This may have been due to German being offered as an alternative to Latin which in 1910 and in the previous years would have been essential for those girls intending to continue their studies at university. Interest in Latin had been on the increase as a direct result of strong teaching over the years between the first inspection in 1906 and the second in 1910. One pupil was taking Greek.[27]

HEAD MISTRESS

Miss E. Shekleton, M.A. (Dublin), Honour School of Modern History (Oxon.).

ASSISTANT MISTRESSES
*Miss H.M. Wright, Mathematical Tripos (Cantab). Second Mistress.
*Miss M. Andrews, MEd. and Mod. Lang. Tripos (Cantab).
  Miss W. Bayliss, Oxford Higher Local (Women's) Examination.
  Miss G. Blumer, Inter B.Sc. (Lond.).
*Miss I. Deakin, Higher Cert. National Froebel Union. Head of Junior School.
*Miss M. Heath, Cambridge Higher Local (Women's) Examination
*Miss E. Heawood, Hon. School of Mathematics (Oxon.).
  Miss H. Ledgerwood, B.A., (Queen's University, Belfast).
*Miss E. Lees, Hon. Sch. of Mod. History (Oxon.). Third Mistress
  Miss J. Nicol, Honour School of Modern Languages (Oxon.).
*Miss A. Piel, B.Sc. Hons. Gold Medal, (Dublin University).
* Miss E. Smith, Hon. Sch. Mod. Lang. (Oxon.).
* Miss E. Symes, M.A., Classics, (London).
* Miss D. Weekes, Med. and Mod. Lang. Tripos (Cantab). Head of Middle School.

KINDERGARTEN
*Miss I. Mayers, Higher Certificate National Froebel Union.

VISITING STAFF

Dressmaking	Miss Johnson.
Drawing and Painting	Miss L. Rands
Physical Exercise	Miss Dahl
Dancing	Miss Gordon
Class Singing	Mr. R. O. Beachcroft, M.A., Mus Bac., F.R.C.O. Director of Music
Piano	Miss Finlow, L.R.A.M., (Medalist).
Piano	Miss Cove, L.R.A.M., (Medalist).
Piano	Miss D. Clarke, L.R.A.M.
Singing	Miss Hinde (Ex-scholar, R.A.M.).
Violin	Mr Maurice Alexander.
Violincello	Miss Pullen.
Domestic Science	Miss Peters, First Class Diploma, Domestic Subjects.

BOARDING HOUSE, St. Margaret's Clarendon Road. (*situated close to High School*) **HOUSE MISTRESS** Mrs. BARRON For details see Boarding House Prospectus. * SIGNIFIES TRAINING DIPLOMA

18. 1915. School Prospectus. List of Staff

The teaching of mathematics came under criticism because of the inexperience of the Staff. Although highly-qualified they lacked 'good' teaching skills according to the Inspectors who suggested they should meet to discuss strategies for improvement to ensure there was continuity in the learning.[28] In 1916 and 1917 two girls gained distinctions in mathematics and were awarded entry to prestigious universities, indicating the problems were addressed.

The subject of science was well organised by the Senior Mistress who, according to the Inspectors, was not good at communicating with the younger girls and they hoped the appointment of a younger member of the Staff, after gaining experience, would take over the role of the junior science teacher. A very high standard was achieved for physics and chemistry in the Sixth Form. The Inspectors were informed that Nature Study for the Junior School was taken by the Froebel teacher-trainees under supervision.[29] The development of girls studying science and related studies was high on the priority list because this was the main thrust of developing the building programme.

Miss Lilian Rands, the art teacher, who wore fashionable Magyar silk dresses in shades of cobalt and violet in contrast to other teachers who wore long dresses in shades of navy and brown, was appointed in 1903 and employed part-time at four shillings an hour. She was not accepted on the permanent full-time staff until 1917, with a salary of £120 per annum, despite having trained at the Government School of Art in Bristol with further study in Paris and had been awarded the Ablett's Teacher Artist Certificate.[30] A new art room was ready in 1904 although the room lacked any art desks or professional equipment. The girls took the drawing examination set by the Royal College of Art, previously known as the South Kensington School of Art. A voluntary afternoon painting class was held for which a fee of £1 was charged per lesson.[31]

19. 1914. The Art Room (built in 1903). Pupils drawing from the plaster casts of classical sculptures. Donated by Mr Edward Robinson

The Inspectors were critical of the course offered for domestic economy which appeared to be taught by non-qualified and part-time staff and they noted the standard of dressmaking was low.[32] Specialist teaching of piano, violin, harp, and singing, was taken by trained staff. The Inspectors thought the Senior staff member who taught piano was not actually taking on her role as a Director even though she was paid to do so. It is obvious that one of the Inspectors was qualified to examine the subject area of music and had a modernist approach to the teaching of music in schools, with a 'music for everyone' through class singing. He/she was obviously not satisfied with the way music was taught.[33] A new music teacher, Miss Cove, was appointed in 1911 and stayed until the 1940s.

Physical education, for which a gymnastic tunic was worn, was taught by external teachers and limited to twenty minutes of drill with combined year classes of forty or sixty girls.[34] The wall-bars, for which past pupils had collected money, were not being used and the enthusiastic good work in the past seemed to have lost ground following the resignation of the Swedish gymnastics' teacher.

It was reported that the School was well-managed and the Old Girls' Society met three times a year, although by 1910 this was now called the Old Girls' Guild, having changed its name from the original Redland Old Girls' Club. By 1919 the Old Girls' Guild had 150 members.[35] The Inspectors concluded that the future new buildings and the library's acquisition of books, the well-chosen staff, and the increased number of pupils would ensure continued prosperity.[36]

In 1910 building work commenced on the Elizabeth Cocks Memorial Library in memory of the first Headmistress and subscribed to by parents and past members of the school and friends. The memorial tablet presented by the Old Girls' Guild remains over the fireplace.[37] The library was designed by the eminent architect, George Oatley, who later became the architect for the new science wing. He survived many frustrating encounters with compromises until the amount of the Gamble legacy was finally revealed.

A formal opening of the Cocks Memorial Library took place on 29 March 1912 with Dr H. T. Warren, the President of Magdalen College, Oxford, performing the opening ceremony. He had lived in the area of Redland as a child and he ended his speech by saying,

A truly educated person was one who tried to understand the past, the present, and the future.[38]

The library was fully extended through the Gamble bequest and 560 books were given to the School. It was a tradition that a girl on leaving should donate a book to the library. The popular Miss Edwards, a dedicated teacher of English, was initially responsible for setting up the library until a qualified librarian was appointed.[39] Miss Edwards continued to teach English until 1947 owing to a shortage of teachers in the war years.

20. 1915. Interior of the Elizabeth Cocks Memorial Library. Designed by the architect, Mr George Oatley in 1910. Opened in 1912. The plaque over the mantelpiece presented by the Old Girls' Guild

She taught English to girls whose mothers she had taught when they were pupils.

Miss Bancroft, also an Old Girl, was a long-standing member of Redland's Staff who eventually left to become a headmistress and except for her three years at Cardiff University had been with the School since 1883.[40] There was an allegiance to the School by dedicated staff. Dr R.O. Beachcroft had joined the Staff as a part-time singing master and in 1911 the position of Director of Music was assigned to him after the recommendation by the inspectors, a position he held until 1926.

In 1913 Mr Tait died. He had on more than one occasion rescued the School from bankruptcy. He had paid off overdrafts and had invested in the School's company shares. In remembrance of the visit by Queen Victoria to Bristol in 1899 he had given a 'Gold Victoria Medal', to be awarded annually to the 'best' pupil, later decided on through the highest mark in an external examination.[41] The first girl to receive a gold medal was Mary Butlin, the School Captain. In 1914 Miss Shekleton wrote in her report that Ethel Edwards had been awarded the Victoria Gold Medal.[42] All the events in the society calendar were embraced by the School and King George's Coronation was celebrated with lights and the flying of the Union Jack. A list of the Victoria Gold Medal awards can be found on an Honours Board behind the stage in the assembly hall. Gold was not available during the war years and the medals were replaced by certificates. These gold medals are very rare and efforts have been made to trace them.

At the end of 1913 the School's accountant, Mr Tribe, died. He had kept a keen eye on the financial position and also held the position of School Secretary. His place was taken by Miss M. G. Shaw, nick-named MG, after the racing car. She had access to records at that time and published an account of the Redland High School's history up to 1932. In 1914 it was decided to award certificates, not prizes and any

money earmarked for prizes was to be given to the Refugees Relief Fund.[43]

In November 1914 the Headmistress reported there was an urgent need for a piano for the boarding house. A special report was tabled in 1914 on the teaching of music which had been severely criticised in the 1910 'Inspectors' Report'.[44] The appointment of Dr Beachcroft in a part-time position with four teachers working under him was now under scrutiny. The Inspectors reported on the poor response to singing in the lower classes with regard to voice exercises and sight-reading, although they were pleased with the level of instrument playing and an orchestra of twenty-four players.

In 1915 the School was visited for a third time by a team of four women inspectors and two male inspectors. Since their previous visit in 1910 there had been an increase of forty-nine pupils making a total of 294 although pupil numbers dropped by fourteen in 1915.

There were twenty-six members of the Staff of whom fifteen were full-time and eleven were part-time and only two Staff members remained from when the School was last seen in 1910. The Inspectors attributed this to the limited salaries offered. Salary increases could not be given by the Council who were aware of the financial position of the School. The Inspectors recommended Senior staff should be well-paid in order to retain their services. The Inspectors noted the School's financial position had been improved although a £4,000 mortgage remained. The School was following the Board of Education's order to pay off a second mortgage and a loan from the bank. Mr Oatley suggested an increase in the fees could generate more income.

By 1915 the required additions to buildings had been made and the Inspectors congratulated the Council on their achievement. The provision of a domestic room for a domestic economy course included the teaching of cookery and laundry management. The compulsory intro-duction of this course was seen as enhancing the

21. REDLAND HIGH SCHOOL
MISS SHEKELTON, HEADMISTRESS AND STAFF
1914

| Miss Symes MA Classics | Miss Ledgerwood BA | Miss Dobbs Hons. Modern Lang. (Oxon) | Miss Piel BSc. (Hons) | Miss Lees Hons. History (Oxon) | Miss Heath Cambridge Higher Local Temporary. Later taught at Westbury Park Primary School | Miss Cove (Music) L.R.A.M. |

| Miss Deakin Head of Junior School Higher Cert. National Froebel Union | Miss Rands (Art) Bristol School of Art | Miss Wright Mathematics Maths Tripos (Cantab.) | Miss Shekleton Headmistress MA Hons. School of Modern History (Oxon) | Miss Hamilton Hons. School of English (Oxon) | Miss Weekes Modern Languages Tripos (Cantab) | Miss Blumer BSc. |

Miss Shekleton is sitting in the carved chair donated by the Staff for the School's 21st Anniversary

| Miss ? Student teacher | Miss Nichol Hons. Modern Languages (Oxon) | Miss Shaw (School Secretary, author of *Redland 1932*) | Miss Dumble Student | Miss Bayliss Oxford Higher Local |

curriculum offered to non-academic girls without lowering the standard of other courses.[46] The Inspectors noted the time given to physical training was insufficient and recommended the appointment of a full-time member of staff and a longer time than the twenty minutes previously allocated for a lesson.[47]

Religious teaching in the Upper and Junior Schools was taken by Miss Shekleton and in the Middle School by members of the Staff. Six mistresses were appointed to teach English although the Inspectors did not approve of the subject being divided into Literature, Composition and Grammar. They noted a set textbook was being used for an outline of 'Historic Literature'. The teaching of history was much praised and also geography although the Inspectors thought the teaching of geography could be improved with a teaching-aid such as a globe which they had recommended in the 1910 inspection. Even the purchase of a globe was seen as an unnecessary expense!

French, German, and Latin were seen as 'well taught' and the Inspectors noted two girls were studying Greek. The Inspectors would have liked to see more time spent in mathematics lessons and more involvement from the Senior Mistress in the Middle School. The School had continued to achieve a high success rate in examinations in science, notably chemistry, and attributed the success to the enthusiasm of the member of the Staff.[48]

The art curriculum had been thoroughly overhauled as a result of Ablett's new teaching methods and the change in the broader world of Art after the works of the Impressionists and the Post-Impressionists, Cézanne, and Van Gogh had been publicly exhibited. Art teachers could not fail to notice the use of bold colour in these artists' works. The formal drawing of the Royal Drawing Society as an examinable subject was thrown out for a more experimental approach. Given the limited facilities, a small, narrow room and no form of an art desk or suitable equivalent,

Miss Rands made the best of the situation and set up 'Life Drawing' after initial study of the plaster casts which had been given to the School. The Inspectors were critical of the standard of the drawings except for some drawings of birds made at the museum.[49] Miss Rands introduced colour-painting by way of plant studies after her appointment in 1917 as a full-time member of the Staff. She stayed for one further year and left in 1918.

As a result of the inspection Miss Shekleton requested clocks for the classrooms following the comments by the Inspectors concerning length of lessons. She was made aware of the Inspectors' comment about 'staff attitudes not being good' but refused to accept this criticism and in her report she refused to comment.[50] The Inspectors alluded to the School being 'under-staffed' with regard to the standard of work in the higher forms. In July 1915 two months after the Inspectors' visit, Miss Shekleton set about organising a new 'Prospectus' to show the School to the public in the best possible way. A list of the Staff indicated those who had teacher-training diplomas, an important issue for the inspectors who had raised the issue after the 1915 and previous 1910 inspections. The 'Prospectus' was illustrated with photographs of the south and north fronts of the building showing the Assembly Hall and Elizabeth Cocks Library. Interiors of the domestic science room, the science laboratory and the art room were also featured.[51]

We had a nice art room. I have a picture of us working there. Really we were doing prep, but we were hounded out to sit in the art room, with our backs to the camera. They only wanted to photograph the room!
Josephine Norgate, 1912-1916.[52]

A list of the Council shows the President as The Lord Bishop of Hereford, Canon Percival and the Chairman as the Rev. J. Gamble. Due to the new constitutional rules the Council included eight women. In addition to Miss Fry, Council members included the wife of the architect, Mrs Oatley, Mrs Rashleigh, Mrs Edward Robinson, whose husband had given money for the art room, Miss Frances Robinson, Miss Elizabeth Sturge, Miss Wait, Miss Wills. Many of these women became generous benefactors to the school.[53]

The photographs used for the 'Prospectus' show a classroom set up in the room next to the central room of the house and is identifiable through the marble fireplace decorated with garlands and the head of a woman. The Kindergarten was housed in the west wing overlooking the Dutch garden and the room is identified by the windows. The teacher, Miss Mayers, a Froebel graduate, is assisted by three students who were enrolled in the school-based Froebel teacher-training course. Other photographs showed the use of the Assembly Hall where chairs were set out in rows and when used for gymnastics included one vaulting horse, wall bars and ropes suspended from the high ceiling.[54]

The policy of the School was set out under attendances, home work, outside lessons, examinations. Notes for absences were now

23. 1915. Assembly Hall used for gymnastics.
Note the climbing ropes suspended from the ceiling and wall bars on the left

asked for and pupils detained to stay at the school on Wednesday afternoon if their work was reported as unsatisfactory. Homework timetables suggested no girls in the Senior School should be involved with homework after 9.30 p.m. Outside lessons, which previously had included music tuition, were not to be taken without permission. Piano lessons were to be encouraged to be taken at the School.[55]

The Sixth Form took the Higher Certificate of the Oxford and Cambridge Joint Board for Distinction, or the Cambridge Higher Local, or University Scholarship. The Senior Remove Form took the Matriculation Examination, London or Bristol. An Entrance Examination pass was required at all levels before admittance. Pupils under the age of fourteen years, already enrolled, could compete for five scholarships valued at a reduction of half of the school fees. Other scholarships from endowments were Percival, Cocks, Sturge and Gilmore Barnett, valued at £15 each, and were tenable for one year for girls staying in the Sixth Form for a second year. Five scholarships, as a result of an examination, were offered at half-fees to new entries under the age of fifteen years. Copies of previous examination papers could be obtained for a shilling. 'City of Bristol' scholarships for

22. 1915. Classroom in the central part of the house.
Identifiable through the marble fireplace and the classical head of a woman

'free' places, usually numbering about four or five per year were also available. The School offered a half-fee scholarship to two boarders.[56]

The Inspectors thought the fees were quite high. There was a rise of between £3 and £5 per year from previous years. 11% of pupils' fees were paid by the Government Education Department through the offer of 'Free Places'.[57]

The 'Prospectus' made parents and girls aware of the strict rules. No pages of exercise books were to be torn out. A fine of three pence was imposed if ink was spilt on a desk. Outdoor-shoes were to be changed on entering the premises and there was to be no running in the corridors or leaning against the walls. Writing or passing notes in class was strictly forbidden. All items were to be marked with the owner's name and a fine of a half-pence if found in the lost property cupboard or one pence if unmarked. Only textbooks were allowed to be brought to school and parents could sell textbooks back to the school if no longer needed.[58]

There were arrangements in place for the reporting of infectious disease in the boarding house and strict rules were in place regarding removal of an infected pupil.[57] Miss Shekleton was available every Monday from 2.45 p.m. to 4.30 p.m. to receive parents after an appointment had been made.

Academic successes continued and Kathleen Cole was the first Redland girl to complete a medical degree, MB, ChB, at the University of Bristol, as it was known later. An increase in school numbers to three-hundred saw the Senior Remove become the Matriculation Form and the Sixth Form for Post Matriculation study, with the Lower Certificate Examination discontinued

24. 1915. The Sixth Form with Miss Emily Shekleton (Headmistress 1907-1920). A uniform was now established; long, side-opening skirt worn with various styles of blouse and tie

with no external examinations before the Matriculation year.[59] 'Bye' students were those who were admitted to specialised courses, cookery or secretarial work.

At the end of 1916, the net balance in the School's account was £215 3s 2d. The number of pupils had risen to 314 which included thirty-two boarders and six boys in the Kindergarten.[60] Later in 1917 it was decided to take two extra bedrooms in a house opposite the boarding house because of the increase in the number of boarders.[61] Most pupils walked, bicycled, or caught the tram to reach the school. The train station at Redland had been operational since 1899 and brought girls to the school from outlying suburbs. Fuel was rationed in the war years and only given to essential duties.

With the possible exception of one or two doctor families, and even some of them did their rounds in a carriage, I can remember only one family with a car until after 1918.
Elizabeth Baker 1913-1923.[62]

Electric light was installed in the main building. A basket-ball had been purchased as an intro-duction to the popularity of netball as a sport for girls.[63]

Life was completely changed with the outbreak of war in 1914. In that year a Head-mistresses' Conference was held at the School which was a great honour.[64] The war saw an end to taking summer holidays at English coastal resorts or at the northern French resort of Deauville or on the southern French Rivera and 'holidays at home' with activities in art, crafts, music and drama were offered. In 1917 the Council proposed to take out an insurance policy for the school buildings against air-raids. London had been attacked and this new form of warfare was at the time an unknown threat.[65] The girls were shown films of the action in France and during the war.[66] By January 1918 there were 328 pupils including thirty-four

boarders and four boys, an increase of fourteen pupils since 1915.[67]

The School became involved in helping with the war effort and some Belgian refugees were supported through acceptance of their children at Redland. Other charities, such as the Star and Garter Fund, were subscribed to through donations of clothes, silver foil, silver thimbles, metals, and even horse-chestnuts which were used for preparing gunpowder. The girls knitted and sewed accessories, useful socks and scarves, and they even adopted a prisoner-of-war. As part of the war effort the Council decided to sell the eighteenth-century lead (smelter) statues which were positioned in the wall alcoves on the terrace side of the house.[68] In an early etching of Redland Court one of the statues depicts a three-quarter size male figure with outstretched arm. There was a rumour the school buildings might be taken over for a hospital.[69]

The war was having an effect on the number of senior girls who were leaving early and not staying on or delaying their entrance to university. In 1917 another Old Girl, Miss Rees, who had completed her BSc. was appointed for a probationary year at a salary of £120 per annum.[70] Miss Enid St John was appointed to teach science and she stayed for many years.

W. Lewis Fry loaned pictures for the library and the gardener suggested planting valuable timber on the estate. A typewriter was purchased for secretarial work. Despite the upheavals and losses of male family members, friends, and two fathers of girls, successes continued with one girl in 1916 becoming the top student in the whole of England in the Cambridge Higher School Certificate and led to her wining an Open Scholarship to Newnham College.[71]

The new Board of Education for regulations on salaries was set up in 1917. The scale was as follows:

Class A Heads of Departments, £150-£200, with increments of £10 per annum.
Class B Graduates, £120-£180, with increments of £10 per annum.
Class C £120-£160, with increments of £7 10s 0d per annum.
Class D Junior mistresses (non graduates) £100-£120, with increments of £7 10s 0d.
Miss Andrews, Senior English teacher, received £145, and Miss Rands, Art Mistress, received £140 per annum.[72]

The School showed an interest in developing the arts and a lecture by the well-known art historian, John Ruskin, was arranged. Miss Fitchew, the new art teacher, was appointed on a salary of £160 per annum.[73] Miss Fitchew took extra sketching, on Durham Downs, paid for privately and organised visits to the City Museum. She was an accomplished draughts-woman and her pen and ink detailed drawings of John Cossins's gate and the Georgian staircase are extremely competent.

Music tuition fees had increased to two guineas (£2 2s 0d) per term. The School decided to deduct only 15% of the fees instead of the 25% paid previously to the Music teachers as piano lessons were now taught at school.[74] Dr Beachcroft, Director of Music was in charge of the choir.[75] Mr Alexander was in charge of the orchestra and stayed until 1946.

On 30 October 1917 the foundation of the School House system was established, which had been suggested by the girls. Many were aware of the existence of 'Houses' at their brothers' schools. At the Godolphin School a pupil in 1915-1919 recalled that 'the house was the motive of every effort and the crown of every achievement'. A house win for a sport resulted in the ceremonial drinking from a sports' cup by members of the House.[76] 'Houses' also had a house master, or mistress, and songs, slogans, flowers, house colours, mascots, and were named after benefactors, or even towns. As one

25. Pen and ink drawings of Cossins's gate and Redland Court's internal west wing staircase. Drawn by Miss Fitchew, art teacher, appointed in 1918. Reproduced from the 1926 School Prospectus

pupil recalled, 'All us little Juniors have to slave away to get STUPID good house-marks for the Seniors'.[77] Four House names were chosen and named after past Councillors. They were assigned colours and flowers.

GILMORE BARNETT HOUSE
House Colour: Blue
Flower: Forget-me-not
Motto: 'Play up, play up, and play the game'

Mr Gilmore Barnett came from a Bristol family and at one time lived in the Georgian House in Great George Street which has been open to the public for many years as an example of the interior decoration of an eighteenth-century home. He attended Clifton College when Dr Percival was Headmaster and became a solicitor interested in public health, serving on the Council for twelve years. In 1902 he became Chairman of the School, resigning in 1904. He died in 1908. Mr Gilmore Barnett gave substantial amounts of money when times were hard and also donated many books to the library.

PERCIVAL HOUSE
House Colour: Purple
Flower: Purple and white heather
Motto: 'Nil Desperandum'

Dr Percival was the Headmaster of Clifton College. After retiring he joined the Council although his career in the Church continued and he become Bishop Percival of Hereford which kept him away from Council meetings. He continued to support the school, especially on matters concerning the 'education of girls'.

TAIT HOUSE
House Colour: Green
Motto: 'Remember'

Mr Tait, a Master at Clifton College and the first Inspector, gave the School the playing fields at Druid Stoke and had also been a great benefactor in times of financial troubles, paying off mortgages and donating gold medals for the best academic performances.

URIJAH THOMAS
House Colour: Red
Flower: Scarlet Pimpernel
Motto: 'Work while it is called today'

The Rev. Urijah Rees Thomas was one of the original founders of the School and was the Minister of the Congregational Church in Whiteladies Road. He had an interest in the Bristol Help Society which gave meals to poor children and he also involved the girls in helping with such a worthy cause. He too was supportive of the 'education of girls'.

Many years later GAMBLE HOUSE (colour: yellow) and the ELIZABETH COCKS HOUSE (colour: pale silver) were added. As one Redland girl wrote, 'The Houses have made concrete many a girl's sense of *esprit de corps*, and have given her a definite part to play in her quarter of the big whole'.[78] Due to the appointment of a full-time physical education teacher in 1917 there was a great interest in the inter-house sports carnivals and gymnastic performances. There were also inter-house drama competitions and swimming competitions. Sisters were allocated the same house.

The Minute Book of Urijah Thomas House, donated by one of the girls, now housed in the School's archives, with its red leather cover and gold lettering, is a comprehensive study into the *esprit de corps*.[79] At the first House meeting the girls were given a wooden button covered with red ribbon, called 'scarlet' and were shown a photograph of their founder which was always displayed in the entrance hall. A House mistress was appointed and a decision taken to write a House song based on the 'Soldiers' Chorus' from *Faust*. There was discussion on a suitable motto and it was decided to use the Rev Urijah Thomas's own motto, 'Work while it is called today'. Urijah Thomas House was the first to ask for its own notice board and the rest of the Houses followed.

The first inter-house sports were hockey and netball, followed by cricket and tennis. Drama and music were also competitive house initiatives and Urijah Thomas House was the most successful in the music competitions for several years which were judged by outside professional musicians. Knitting for the Red Cross, and sales of work were also encouraged and the money donated to the Prisoner-of-War Fund. In 1919 fête money raised by the Houses was given to pay for the restoration of the parapet.

The winning of House shields was coveted and the most prized was the House Conduct Shield which Urijah Thomas House held for the first years of its inception.

Two notable members of the Urijah Thomas House in the 1920s were Margaret Harrington, a scholarship girl, House Captain, and Beryl Corner (to become Dr Beryl Corner, OBE, MD, BSc, FRCP (Lond.), DSc, FRCP Ch, Councillor, Chairman of the Governors, President of Redland High School Council).

Beryl Corner was appointed Secretary of Urijah Thomas House after her return from the country in 1920, after an absence of three years, eventually leaving in 1928. She was the wicket-keeper for the inter-house cricket matches. In 1923 new commercially-made house buttons of red cotton were introduced and cost two-pence each.[80] The interest in inter-house sports was mainly due to the appointment of a full-time physical education teacher from the Bedford Physical Training College on a salary of £130 per annum.[81] The School benefitted for many years from the recruitment of teachers trained at this

26. 1915. Form IVB, Uniform was not compulsory, although wearing of blouse, tie and skirt had been introduced

institution. The House songs were very popular, remembered years later after girls had left school, and discontinued after the 1940s.

Council members were concerned about girls' education, although in the early days they were also interested in investing their money in what was a private company with shares and dividends. However, they were more than generous in their donations of money to a cause because the returns on their long-term investment would only benefit them if the cause was successful. The educational initiative in the first quarter of the twentieth-century came from the private sector where there was a certain amount of independence and no talk of a national curriculum or involvement with the Board of Education.[82] However, it all came down to 'money'! Entering agreements with the Boards and accepting money for buildings and promises of scholarships and guaranteed enrolments of 10% of all pupils also dictated conforming to the Board's levels of 'what constitutes a good level of education' which included well-qualified staff, 'good' teaching methods and suitable buildings.

Class sizes were between twenty and twenty-four pupils.[83] In January 1917 the net balance in the bank was £215 3s 2d.[84] By 22 March 1917 the balance had dropped to £174. 7s 2d. By 17 May 1917 the net balance had risen to £610 13s 0d. The annual profit was £717 6s 11d and was due to an increase in the number of fee-paying pupils.[85] By October 1917 there were 356 pupils, with thirty-three boarders and the bank balance stood at £843 16s 9d.[86]

Savings amounted to £407 7s 5d. There were available funds for outside-painting and maintenance at a cost of £95.[87] The renting of extra rooms for the boarding school led to a suggestion to move the Kindergarten into the boarding-school's premises.[88]

Miss St John and Miss Rands, the art mistress, were accepted as regular members of staff after their probationary year.[89] The Staff were considered to be well paid.

By July 1917 higher salary scales were introduced.
Class A (second mistress) from £180-£250, increments by £15.
Class B Graduates from £120-£180, increments by £10.
Class C Graduates from £120-£160, increments by £7 10s 0d.
Class D Junior Mistress, non-graduate. £100-£120, increments by £7 10s 0d. [90]

In 1917 there was a national outbreak of meningitis and two girls at the school died and another pupil died from a defective gas-heater.[91] A shortage of coal led to complaints about working in cold buildings.[92] Throughout England there was an outbreak of influenza which affected staff and pupils. A solution was to purchase smaller, efficient grates. Fuel rationing also affected the boarding-school's heating system.

In 1918 there had been five cases of measles in the boarding-school and twelve in the school and by 1920s attention to health had become obsessive.[93] Boarding schools were to appoint a nurse and a 'school health certificate' was essential if girls returning were to be cleared of contact with contagious diseases. The School arranged a health lecture by Lady Barrett for parents and if the parents agreed was to be given to the girls later.[94] The whole issue of girls having healthy bodies with free-flowing garments, especially when performing sport or gymnastics, came with the abandonment of the corset after the Edwardian period. The free-movement classes conducted by Miss Dahl finished when she left in 1918 and her equipment was given back to her and she was paid for the more permanent fixtures.[95] By 1918 there were 372 pupils with the increase mainly in the Junior

School. Miss L. Oatley, daughter of the architect, Mr George Oatley, was employed to help in the Junior School.

The next period in the history of the School brought the most radical of educational changes. The Board of Education, developed from the School Boards, sought to improve the under-privileged, 'bright', pupils' chances of receiving a secondary education. By 1918 eight out of ten places were to be offered as Junior City Scholarships at Redland High School, with the fees paid by the Education Authority.[96] This 'takeover' by the 'State', with its wider implications, led one Secretary of State for Education in the 1980s to say that he wished it had never happened. *'If I could move back to 1870 I would have taken a different route'.*[97] Scholarships were offered to officers' daughters who had lost their fathers in the war.[98]

The School Board agreed to pay the £400 grant per annum but even this was not enough to consider the raising of salaries. Staff continued to ask for increases, up to and over £20 per annum. There were several issues to consider. First, there was general uncertainty about future changes to society after the war ended, and secondly, the School was carrying a heavy financial burden with the combined courses expenditure exceeding the £400 grant. Only ten girls continuing with advanced studies were fee-paying and to encourage more girls to stay on, more funding for disadvantaged girls was requested.[99]

At the beginning of 1918 school numbers were 372, with thirty-one boarders and five boys.[100] Following the directions set by the Board of Education school numbers rose by another twelve and included thirty-six boarders. By July 1918 the School had £1,226 16s 7d in credit and by October 1918 this had been reduced to £1,163 0s 6d.[101]

On 7 November, 1918 Canon Gamble announced the loss in France of a son of a fellow Councillor and the tragic event was close to the declaration of the end of the war, on 11 November, 1918. There was much excitement when the end of the war was announced by Miss Shekleton and many girls were crying. At the Armistice Service the School sang the hymn 'Praise the Lord, ye heavens adore him'.[102] Several girls had lost their fathers and the word 'deceased' was entered in the register and in some cases a girl had to leave owing to financial difficulties.[103] A war-effort letter was received from the King.

In 1918 Madame Farquhar, French-born, was appointed to teach French.[104] The appointment of a married woman was unique at that time, although after seven years she left to have a baby but returned to the School years later, staying until the 1940s. Textbooks were bought from the Scholastic Trading Company in Bridge Street.

The shop closed down in 1945 and the supply of textbooks was taken over by Georges's Bookshop in Park Street. The Inspectors had requested that standard textbooks were to be purchased.[105] A decision was reached to share the mathematics and staff facilities at Colston's Girls' High School and physics and chemistry at Redland, using the new well-equipped laboratory, alternating yearly.[106]

Redland had a strong Science side from early days and was I believe, one of the few girls' schools to take physics in Public Examinations. We shared our Higher Certificate work with Colston's Girls' School..... The Sixth Form enjoyed the room now allocated to the Headmistress.....we bicycled to the games field at Druid Stoke, to cheer our team on with wild yells....money for prizes was given to the Red Cross during the war.
(Margaret Harrington 1914-1922).[107]

Margaret Harrington had been awarded a 'free place' and she returned to Redland High School as a student-teacher, under the title of 'teacher exhibitioner'.

After the end of the war, the Council discussed the use of old Army huts as temporary buildings for science, as a partial rebuilding on a small scale which would involve borrowing money. Mr George Oatley, the architect, was asked to draw up plans, although he disagreed with the proposal, following the estimated costs of £2,250 for the science room and £1,690 for the physics room and the laying of a foundation stone for when the promised legacy for a new building would occur.[108] The death of Canon Gamble, the School Chairman, changed these temporary plans as the large bequest, recorded at a Members' AGM, was, £20,000.[109] The Council did not expect the legacy to be so considerable and plans were drawn by Mr Oatley, the architect, for permanent laboratories and classrooms.[110] The School became 'a school' in the true sense of the word, although it took another two decades before the new buildings were finally completed and opened in 1930 after Mr Oatley had become Sir George Oatley following his success in designing buildings for Bristol University.

Increased numbers in the Senior School through the offer of 'free places' led to an increase in the Junior School and Kindergarten as parents became aware of a shortage of places for their children if they waited until Senior School entry. Available money for improvements rested on pupil numbers and income from fees. In 1918, Miss Daltry, a National Froebel teacher, was appointed to the Kindergarten and Miss Byrne became the Head of the Junior School.[111]

In October 1917 the School was £843 16s 9d in credit which enabled them to purchase tables and six chairs for the Kindergarten.[112] The increase in numbers had led to overcrowding in the small, square-panelled room, a legacy from the Elizabethan Manor, in the west wing overlooking the Dutch garden. The cellars in the west wing were used as a cloakroom and there was a mysterious iron ring in one of the large

stones in the passage way which was said to have been used to secure highwaymen caught on Durdham Downs. They were temporarily imprisoned and later tried by the Lord of the Manor at the Redland Manor House.[113]

A suggestion had been made to move the Kindergarten back to the boarding house and to look for other premises for the boarders.[114] In November 1918 the Council was given the opportunity to purchase 19 Clarendon Road. The market price was £575 and the School was prepared to offer £550.[115] The School already had a mortgage on the boarding house.[116] Due to objections to the use of 19 Clarendon Road for a school, the offer was rejected and the Kindergarten moved into the boarding house as a temporary measure to solve the overcrowding in the main part of the school buildings.

A General Election took place on 14 December 1918 resulting in a Coalition Conservative Government and was the first where all adult men and women aged thirty and over could vote. In December, 1918, the School's net balance was £1,653 7s. 6d and became a deficit when cheques to the value of £1,847 15s 8d were paid out.[117] Once again the School relied on pupil intake and the 1919 incoming fees

In 1918 a school uniform was becoming fashionable partly due to the uniforms which had been part of women's wear in the war. In 1914 it was suggested the head prefects put up their hair and wear white, silk blouses and long, navy-coloured, serge skirts which fastened at the side. On wet days long-legged boots fastened with eyelets and laces were worn and on entering the school building were changed for indoor-shoes which had been made compulsory. By the 1920s long skirts were replaced by navy and later dark-green, pleated gym tunics which initially followed the pattern of the gym teacher's uniform, green, with a velvet neckline, as worn by graduates from the Bedford Physical Training College.[118] The white, silk blouse, for which there was no standard pattern, was replaced later

1. Redland Court, built in 1735. Purchased by the Redland High School for Girls in 1884.
Photographer, Vickie Howard, b.i.i.p., 2010

2. Entrance gate. John Cossins's 'Coat of Arms' includes the 'Golden Lion of Cossins'.
The ram's horns signify fecundity, rebirth, renewal and rejuvenation.
The five goat horns represent the five planets where the goat of lust is attacking the heavens.
Photographer, Vickie Howard, b.i.i.p., 2010

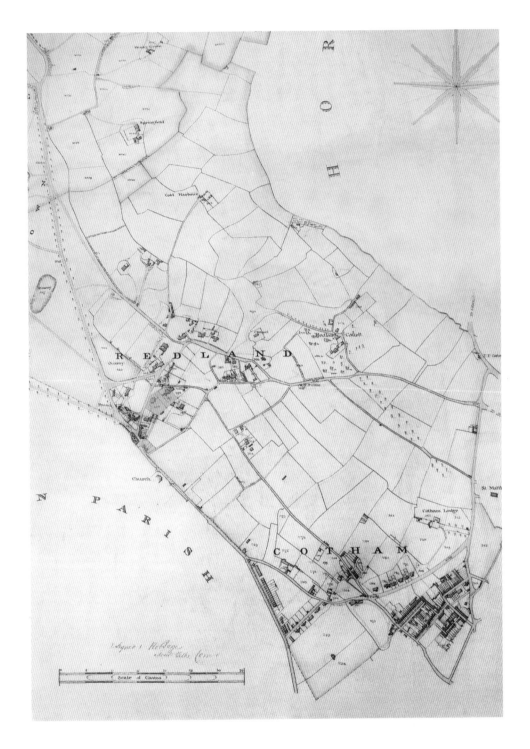

3. Map of the district of Redland, 1841.
Shows Redland Court, Redland Chapel, Turnpike gate on road (Redland Road).
Bristol Record Office as supplied by Dr P. Malpass (School of the Built Environment, UWE)

REDLAND COURT.
The Seat of   Sir Richard Vaughan,
To whom this Plate   is inscribed by J & H S Storer

4. Lithographic print of a drawing by Storer, 1825, showing Redland Court as a residence for
Sir Richard Vaughan. (Colour has been added to the original black and white print)

Note the 'Halley's Comet' weathervane on the East wing. The Comet was sighted in 1761 and the
weathervane was installed by Martha Cossins in memory of her husband's death in 1759.
The East cupola and weathervane pulled down when accommodation built in c.1886 for Miss Cocks, the first
Headmistress. Now seen on the West Wing, or may be one of a pair originally on the East and the West wings.

Also note the figure, with outstretched arm, in the alcove.
Two metal figures were removed to help the war effort in the First World War.
The figures were described by Miss Shekleton, the second Headmistress, as 'hideous'.

5. *Above*: Oil painting of John Cossins, first owner of Redland Court.
Below: Oil painting of Martha Cossins, wife of John Cossins.
Painted by John Vanderbank (1649-1739) *Photographer, Heather Kent, 2008*

6. West wing, interior staircase, Redland Court. *Photographer, Heather Kent, 2008*

7. Coloured pencil drawing. Redland Chapel, built for John Cossins in1743. Drawn by R. Farnsworth, c.1940s. Donated to Redland High School by Jenny Allen-Williams in 2006.
Photograph courtesy of RHS School Development Office, 2010

8. Weathervane, showing Halley's Comet, West cupola.
Photographer, Vickie Howard, b.i.i.p., 2010

by a white, cotton blouse. Black shoes and stockings completed the uniform. Pupils wore bow-ties, ribbons, and striped ties. When a standard pattern for the blouse was established the 'male' form of the tie was worn. All shoes had to be changed on entering the building and house-shoes and gym-shoes were kept in the cloakrooms. There was no standard coat. Hats were compulsory, black felt in winter and white straw in summer, complete with hat band. White gloves were to be worn at all times although at the end of the war years these were said to be difficult to acquire. Later, the school blazer was introduced, dark-green with a logo on the pocket, initials of R.H.S. surrounded by daisies. A plain, white dress was to be worn for occasions and prize giving, and later, a 'best' dress of silk, with a circular pattern of daisy flowers, was introduced.[119]

At the opening of the school year in January 1919 enrolment numbers were 382 and included thirty-five boarders and a loss of seven pupils from the previous year. There were several instances of unpaid fees or requests for half-fees due to loss of income through a war injury, or death, of a father. There was a balance of £1,365 9s 10d. with an outgoing of £969 8s 10d. Interest of £17 was added from debentures.[120] It was decided to increase the fees for piano lessons from £1 11s 6d to £2 2s 0d. The School would only deduct 15% instead of 25%.[121] Outgoing expenses in 1919 were more than the balance of the bank account, however by the end of the financial year the School had made a overall profit of £541 15s 9d.[122] Women were now accepted on the Council to form a Ladies Committee.[123]

Following the death of Dr Percival nominations were called in June 1919 for the office of President of the School Council. There were two candidates, the Master of Bailliol and the President of Magdalen College.[124] The Master of Bailliol, Dr A. L. Smith was elected.[125] An annual meeting of members was held at the end of every year and the first meeting was recorded in the Share-holders' Minute Book in 1913. Members were circulated information on the work of the school, numbers of students, and progress in examinations, entrances to universities and success at those universities. Details were given of passes in the Royal Drawing Society's Examination and number of works selected for hanging in the Society's Spring Exhibition. Two to four works were selected annually from the Redland High School for Girls. Membership of the Council was fairly stable in the period of Miss Shekleton's position as Headmistress and members of the Council were also representatives from the Board of Education. Mention was made of the dignitaries who presented the prizes at the Annual Prize Giving. The health of the girls was also reported as it related to the flu epidemic of 1920. In 1921 news of the illness of Miss Shekleton was received.[126]

The Council was aware of the power of the Inspectors since the school was part of the Direct Grants Scheme and knew they might close down certain subject areas if it was seen that conditions did not meet the necessary standards of 'good practice'. Council members were aware of the need for three new science rooms and their proposal for buying huts for that purpose were rejected by the Inspectors. Temporary buildings in wood, weatherboard with felt roofs could be built for £740.[127] At the Council meeting, 17 July 1919 the Council received notice that the temporary buildings were not acceptable and they would need to rethink the whole project to make it acceptable to the Inspectorate. Quotes were given as £2,750 for a science room, £1,690 for a physics laboratory, with a further £870 for the inclusion of central heating.[128] It was agreed to take out a loan for £4,000 and to lay a foundation stone to indicate the Council's intentions to the Board of Education that they were serious about providing facilities for science education at

Redland High School. The Council were not about to be bullied into dropping this subject area when such hard work had gone into the establishment of science for girls.

By the autumn of 1919 the National Union of Teachers had endorsed a new structure for determining Elementary Teachers' salary scales, nationally, under the Burnham scale. Miss Deakin, as Headmistress of the Junior School and Kindergarten, received a Board of Education increase as she was an Elementary Teacher. No woman teacher whatever her experience or qualifications would ever receive more than four-fifths of a male teacher's salary on the same grade.[129] At Redland, teachers' salaries ranged from £240-£250 per annum for the position of Headmistress, to £180-£230 for a Second Mistress, £170-£200 for a Head of Department, £150-£180 for a Senior School teacher and £120 for a Junior School teacher.[130]

Eventually in March 1920 a mass rally was held at the Albert Hall organised by women teachers in London and the National Federation of Women Teachers, NFWT, for representation on the Burnham Committee to press for equal pay for women and the setting up of the National Union of Women Teachers, NUWT.[131] The issue of salaries was discussed with staff at Colston's and Clifton and the three schools felt they should appeal to the Board of Education.[132] Staff demanded a 20% increase. Miss Deakin's salary was only £210 per annum and for the amount of work involved in the Kindergarten Teacher-Training Award was inadequate. It was felt that a teacher with a first class honours degree should expect to receive a salary of £360 per annum.[133]

The school magazine, which had lapsed since its inception by Miss Cocks in 1890, was revived in 1919 by Miss Bancroft, an Old Girl, who had returned as a teacher. In 1919 a ninety-foot well found under the floor of the Secretary's office was concreted over.[134]

In October 1919 the School's bank balance was £1,888 9s 4d. Outgoings were £1,392 6s

3d.[135] A major expense for the School was the insurance of £25,000 for buildings and £7,000 for the boarding-house. Legal insurance was £7,000.[136] The School purchased an ex-Army hut for the playing fields at a cost of £45 with a further £100 to be paid for construction, later paid by Miss Fry. School numbers had increased to 383 with forty-one boarders and fourteen pupils in the Kindergarten which included six boys. In addition there were four student-teachers employed in the Junior School under the Froebel Training Award.[137]

In January 1920 Council members were informed of Miss Shekleton's retirement on health grounds. By 1920, after the resignation of Miss Shekleton, headmistresses' salaries increased three-fold.[138] Although tiresome, with Inspectors' recommendations for buildings and equipment, the great advantage of 'recognition' by the Board of Education inspectors was that it attracted well-qualified staff who expected to receive salaries according to their qualifications and experience.[139] In May 1920 the Staff

27. 1919. Cicely Wilson. Captain of Percival House

received a £10 incremental increase which was equal to the Bristol scale of teacher adjustments.[140]   A new Staff member who applied to teach mathematics expected a salary of £320 per annum based on her eighteen years of experience.[141]   A decision was made to increase the boarding fee by £6 a term and school fees would also be raised. The yearly fee for under seven years of age, was £9, seven to ten-year olds £15, over ten years, £18, and over twelve years, £21.[142]

In October 1920 an advertisement for a new Headmistress was placed in the Bristol newspapers and a larger announcement circulated in education journals.

ADVERTISEMENT FOR POST OF HEAD-MISTRESS

GOVERNING   The school was formed as a Company precluded from paying Dividends and is governed by a Council of fourteen members including representatives from the Local Education Authority. The President of the school is the Master of Balliol, Dr A.L. Smith and the Chairman is the Rev. J. Gamble, B.D.
STATUS The school holds a good position among the Girls' Public Schools of the County and is in receipt of Grants from the Board of Education and the Bristol Education Committee.
NUMBERS (October 1920) 385 pupils in the school, with nine pupils in the Kindergarten.
BOARDERS The boarding-house is close to the school. Forty boarders and ten Housemistresses.
STAFF Twenty-one Assistant Mistresses and a visiting teacher.
SALARY From £600 rising to £800
WORK The School is divided into Junior, Middle and Senior School. Advanced courses in Science, Mathematics taken in conjunction with Colston's Girls' School. There is a Kindergarten Training Award affiliated to the University of Bristol.[140]

Eight applications were received. Miss E. Edghill, MA Classical Tripos (Cambridge) was the successful applicant with Miss C.M. Taylor, a New Zealand graduate, as a second choice.[143]

Many tributes were paid to Miss Shekleton, or 'Shecks', as she was affectionately known, as it appears she was very close to the girls and although tall and dignified in contrast to Miss Cocks she was just as dynamic and approachable. In 1921 owing to the illness of Miss Shekleton, the public Prize Giving was cancelled. Prizes and certificates were presented privately to the winners. Shareholders were kept informed of the School's progress through the annual general meetings and examination results were listed for their information as well as successes by former pupils at Cambridge, Oxford, and Bristol Universities.[144]

Miss Edghill was unable to commence until the summer term of 1921 and the position of Acting Headmistress was given to Miss St John in September 1920.

NOTES

1   Sturge, E., 1928. *Reminiscences of my life*. Bristol: Arrowsmith, pp.60-61.
2   Redland High School, 1895-1917. *Register of Scholars, 800-2,428*. Redland High School Archive. AR 010. pp.84,94.
3   ibid. p.110.
4   Shaw, M.G., 1932. *Redland High School*. Bristol: Arrowsmith, p.53.
5   Redland High School, 1903-1917 *Council Minute Book, No.3*. Redland High School Archive, p.16 (nyc).
6   ibid. p.16.
7   Bungay, J., 1982. *Redland High School, 1882-1982*. Council of Redland High School, p.40.
8   ibid. p.40.
9   Shaw, M.G., 1932. *Redland High School*. Bristol: Arrowsmith. p.53.
10 Government Census, 1911.
11 Bungay, J., 1982. *Redland High School, 1882-1982*. Council of Redland High School, p.44.
12 ibid. p.23.
13 Shaw, M.G., 1932. *Redland High School*, Bristol: Arrowsmith. p.54.

14 Manning, J.P., 2005. 'Discovering Froebel: A Call to re-examine his Life and Gifts'. *Early Childhood Education Journal,* 32 (6), pp.372-373.

15 Government Census, 1911

16 Redland High School, 1903-1917. *Council Minute Book, No. 3.* Redland High School Archive (nyc).

17 ibid.

18 ibid.

19 Shaw, M.G., 1932. *Redland High School.* Bristol: Arrowsmith. p.54.

20 Board of Education.. 1910. *Inspection Report.* London: Whitehall. Redland High School Archive. p.4 (nyc).

21 ibid. pp.4,5.

22 ibid. p.2.

23 ibid. p.3.

24 ibid. p.5.

25 ibid. p.5.

26 ibid. p.6.

27 ibid. p.7.

28 ibid. p.8.

29 ibid. p.9.

30 Redland High School, 1888-1917. *Staff Register.* Redland High School Archive. BB 092.

31 ibid.p.9.

32 Board of Education, 1910. *Inspection Report.* London: Whitehall. Redland High School Archive. p.9 (nyc).

33 ibid. pp.9,10.

34 ibid. p.11.

35 Bungay, J., 1982. *Redland High School, 1882-1982.* Council of Redland High School. p.231.

36 Board of Education, 1910. *Inspection Report.* London: Whitehall. Redland School Archive. p.12 (nyc).

37 Redland High School, 1917-1933. *Minute Book, No. 3.* Redland High School. Archive p.1. BB140.

38 ibid. p.2.

39 ibid. p.8.

40 ibid. p.41.

41 ibid. p.11.

42 ibid. p.12.

43 Redland High School, 1914-1930. *Headmistress Reports.* Redland High School Archive. BB018.

44 Board of Education, 1914. *Inspector's Report.* London: Whitehall. Redland High School Archive pp.1-3 (nyc).

45 Board of Education, 1915. *Inspection Report.* London: Whitehall. Redland High School Archive. p.5 (nyc).

46 ibid. pp.10-11.

47 ibid. pp.6-10.

48 ibid. p.10.

49 ibid. p.10.

50 Redland High School, 1914-1930. *Headmistress Reports.* Redland High School Archive. BB018.

51 Redland High School, 1915. *Prospectus.* Archive p.2. SP17.

52 Bungay, J., 1982. *Redland High School, 1882-1982.* Council of Redland High School. p.59.

53 Redland High School, 1915. *Prospectus.* Archive p.3. SP17.

54 ibid. p.14.

55 ibid. p.13.

56 ibid. p.14.

57 ibid. p. 9.

58 ibid. p.13.

59 Redland High School. 1917- 1933. *Council Minute Book, No. 3.* Redland High School Archive. BB140.

60 ibid. p.2.

61 ibid. p.17.

62 Bungay, J., 1982. *Redland High School, 1882-1982.* Council of Redland High School. p.81.

63 Shaw, M.G., 1932. *Redland High School.* Bristol: Arrowsmith. p.60.

64 ibid. p.59.

65 Redland High School, 1917-1933. *Council Minute Book, No.3.* Redland High School Archive. p.1 BB140.

66 ibid. p.2.

67 ibid. p.3.

68 ibid. p.41.

69 Redland High School, 1914-1930. *Headmistress Reports.* Redland High School Archive. BB018.

70 Redland High School, 1917-1933. *Council Minute Book No 3.* Redland High School Archive. BB140.

71 ibid.

72 ibid.

73 ibid.

74 ibid.

75 ibid. p.15.

76 Avery, G., 1991. *The Best Type of Girl, A History of Girls' Independent Schools .* London: Andre Deutsch, p.116.

77 ibid. p.117.

78 Bungay, J., 1982. *Redland High School, 1882-1892.* Council of Redland High School.

79 Redland High School, 1917. *Urijah Thomas Minute Book.* Redland High School Archives. BB017.

80 ibid.

81 Redland High School, 1917-1943. *Staff Register.* Redland High School Archive. BB023.

82 Avery, G., 1991. *The Best Type of Girl, A History of Girls' Independent Schools.* London: Andre Deutsch. p.125.

83 Redland High School, 1917-1933. *Council Minute Book, No.3.* Redland High School Archive. p.1. BB140.

84 ibid. p.8.

85 ibid. p.8.

86 ibid. p.11.

87 ibid. p.12.

88 ibid. p. 13.

89 ibid. p.15.

90 ibid. p.4.

91-96. ibid.

97 Chitty, C. 2004. *Education Policy in Britain.* Basingstoke: Palgrave Macmillan. p.6.

98 Redland High School, 1915. *School Prospectus.* Redland High School Archive (nyc).

99 Redland High School, 1917-1933. *Council Minute Book, No.3.* Redland High School Archive. BB140.

100 ibid.

101 ibid.

102 ibid.

103 ibid.

104 ibid.

105 Bungay, J., 1982. *Redland High School, 1882-1982.* Council of Redland High School. p.79.

106 Redland High School, 1917-1933. *Council Minute Book, No.3.* Redland High School Archive. p.4. BB140.

107 Redland High School, 1913- 1958. *Shareholders' Minute Book* Redland High School Archive. p.72. BB139.

108 Redland High School, 1917-1933. *Council Minute Book, No.3.* Redland High School Archive. p.29. BB140.

109 ibid. p.30.

110 ibid.

111 ibid.

112 ibid.

113 ibid.

114 ibid.

115 ibid.

116 Redland High School, 1995. *Old Girls' Newsletter. Rosalind Franks Memories.* Redland High School Archives. (nyc)

117 ibid.

118 Redland High School, 1917-1933. *Council Minute Book, No.3.* Redland High School Archive. p.54. BB140.

119 ibid. p.56.

120 ibid. p.59.

121 ibid. p.63.

122 ibid. p.67.

123 ibid. p.67.

124 Redland High School, 1913-1958. *Shareholders' Minute Book.* Redland High School Archive. BB139.

125 Redland High School, 1917-1933. *Council Minute Book, No.3.* Redland High School Archive. p.63.

126 ibid. p.66.

127 Kean, H., 1990. *Deeds not Words.* London: Pluto Press. p.90.

128 Redland High School, 1917-1933. *Council Minute Book, No. 3.* Redland High School Archive. p.63.

129 Kean, H., 1990. *Deeds not Words.* London: Pluto Press. p.83.

130 Redland High School, 1917-1933. *Council Minute Book, No. 3.* Redland High School Archive. BB140.

131 ibid.

132 Shaw, M.G., 1932, *Redland High School.* Bristol: Arrowsmith. p.68.

133 Redland High School, 1917-1933. *Council Minute Book, No. 3.* Redland High School Archive. BB140.

134 ibid.

135 ibid.

136 Avery, G., 1991. *The Best Type of Girl, A History of Girls' Independent Schools.* London: Andre Deutsch. p.128.

137 Redland High School, 1917-1933. *Council Minute Book, No 3.* Redland High School Archive BB 140. p.83.

138 ibid p.83.

139 ibid. p.93.

140 ibid. p.95.

141 ibid. p.96.

142 Redland High School, 1913-1958. *Shareholders Minute Book* Redland High School Archive. BB139. p.39.

143 ibid.

144 ibid.

4
1921-1926 WOMEN TEACHERS AND THE BURNHAM SCALE

By the end of September 1919 the National Union of Teachers (NUT) had endorsed a new structure of determining Elementary Teachers' salaries nationally, known as the Burnham Scale. The fight for equal pay was not yet won and women teachers, who by 1919 had replaced the loss of men teachers, would not receive more than four-fifths of a male teacher's salary on the same grade.[1] In March 1920 women teachers from Bristol assembled at Oxford and walked to the Albert Hall, London, for a mass rally.

The National Union of Women Teachers (NUWT) had some success with the Local Education Authority. Progress was marred when the Geddes Report asked for a national 5% cut to support the unemployed and the NUT agreed.[2] By 1920 the NWTU was not fighting for political acceptance, as in the Suffrage Movement, but was seen as a 'new order', a threat to male teachers and there were campaigns to undermine their activities. There were also comments about spinsters being in charge of young girls and it was suggested senior schools should incorporate 'motherhood' into their curriculum. A shortage of eligible men for marriage, due to the tremendous loss of young male lives in the 1914-1918 war, was the reason behind many spinsters becoming teachers. Teaching children made up for their own loss of not being married and not having children of their own. In many respects this was the reason behind a band of very dedicated teachers staying in the same school for many years.

At the end of 1920 Redland High School Council learnt of the £30 salary grant awarded to Redland's staff. The financial position of the School was not good and there was talk at Council meetings of taking out a mortgage to cover the overdraft. A decision was needed on the Junior Advanced Certificate and it was decided to leave this until Miss Edghill's arrival. An overdraft of £675 3s 11d did not deter the Council from paying the trainee-teachers' fees of three guineas each to attend lectures at the Bristol University as part of their Froebel teacher-training conducted at the School.[3]

The effects of the 1914-1918 war were still being felt and the School adopted a school in one of the devastated areas of France, Gouy sous Bellone.[4] In the December holidays of 1920 some pupils and staff, including the art mistress Miss Fitchew, went on an art tour to Italy the first of many art tours offered by the School in later years. The Council approved the new Burnham Scale of salaries but they were not in a position to uphold them until the Local Education Authority granted them the money. The Council also agreed to the payment of the maintenance of the boundary wall, fencing, and the painting of the office before Miss Edghill's arrival. On 17 March 1921 the Council welcomed Miss Edghill to the School.[5]

MISS ELLA MARY EDGHILL
(Headmistress 1921-1926)

Miss Edghill, MA (London) Classical Tripos Class 1 (Cambridge), had previously held the post of Headmistress of the King's High School, Warwick. She was interested in the historical aspects of Redland Court which though appreciated by former headmistresses was really seen by them as providing a building in which to operate a school rather than its merits as a classified heritage building. The large Cedars of Lebanon planted in the eighteenth-century became as important to Miss Edghill as the building itself and she set about maintaining the grounds with the respect they deserved. In Miss Cocks's era a caretaker/gardener came with the property and except for general maintenance was not involved in appreciating the early landscaping. The Dutch garden had remained relatively free from any changes and Miss Edghill took an interest in restoring it in an Elizabethan formal geometric pattern with low, box hedges.

In her first Prize Giving Miss Edghill reported:

The Redland High School girls grow up in such an

28. 1932. Junior School pupils in the Dutch garden

atmosphere that when the time for leave-taking arrives, they set off along the road still possessed of the inspiration that comes from contact with places of ancient beauty.[6]

Miss Edghill was entering a new epoch for the education of girls which had now transcended the sexual and class barriers. In 1884 a remark was made that *high schools* are here to stay. St Paul's School had fostered the mixing of social classes, which resulted in some parents selecting schools where there was less of a class barrier and others selected a school in a particular residential location.[7] The Cheltenham College did not have examinations until 1916 and if girls wished to continue to universities they received special coaching.[8] Examinations were not just about learning facts about wars but involved discussion on the cause and effect of wars. Historically, the education of girls in some areas began with girls attending classes in the Mechanics Institutes and listening to lectures and then proceeding to High Schools in the large cities, Leeds being an example.[9]

Girls were now competitive academically and in sport. School sports classes were compulsory and matches took place between schools for hockey, netball, cricket and tennis and internally via the School's inter-house competitions. In 1922 the courtyard at Redland was asphalted to make a playing area for netball which had become a popular girls' sport. Arrangements were made with Colston's Girls' High School to share their playing field within walking distance of the school premises. The fields at Druid Stoke were too far away for weekday travel. Extra tennis courts were hired at considerable cost from the Redland Lawn Tennis Club, also within walking distance. A second gymnastic teacher on a salary of £225 per annum was appointed in 1923.[10]

The Bristol Town Council had given the School a grant of £3,200 which enabled the School Council to implement the Burnham

Salary Scale and eligible staff received two-thirds of the first year's award. Miss Cove, the music teacher, received an increase of £30 as she had passed her L.R.A.M. She had previously been placed in the 'non graduate' category.[11] Payment of the Burnham Award was mandatory. The Council became involved and attempted to evade awarding the Burnham Scale by stating they would only pay the award if staff had qualified from Cambridge or Oxford with First Class Honours Degrees. Miss Edghill reported that Second Class Honours were still 'good' and those staff with this qualification deserved the award and increase in salary. Her request was later dismissed by Council. Teachers were themselves asked to appeal any decisions which went against them. The argument was, municipal schools would not have Cambridge or Oxford graduates and yet graduate teachers in those schools would be given the award.[12]

In September 1921 it was found necessary to increase the fees as building repairs to the dangerous parapet were urgently needed.[13] In December 1922 two of the School Houses, Gilmore Barnett and Urijah Thomas, raised the money to have the parapet restored.[14]

Yearly fees were: Under 8 years, £12 12s 0d. 8-11years, £15 15s 0d. Over 11 years, £18 18s 0d. Over 12 years, £22 1s 0d.[15] The bank overdraft was £986 18s 1d.[16] Pupil numbers were 379 with forty-one boarders and eight Kindergarten trainees. The Council expressed their concern over outstanding fees and said the School was at fault because they had no ruling about collecting these. A request for the offer of a 'free' boarding place could not be offered to a deserving pupil because of the tight financial position. The School could not cover parents' requests for exemption of the recent increase in fees which the School had found necessary to introduce. A request from two nuns from the Sacred Heart Community for reduced fees for entrance as Kindergarten trainees was also rejected by the Council.

On the 21 July the bank overdraft had risen to £1,368 17s 4d.[17] A new Head of the Junior School had been appointed on a salary of £250 per annum as she held a BA degree. Requests were coming to Council for two Honours Boards in the Assembly Hall and apparatus at a cost of £40 for the science department.[18] As in the past overdrafts were only reduced when fees were paid and by October, 1921, the bank overdraft was considerably reduced to £447 1s 10d. Although Redland was sharing Colston's playing field and the arrangement suited both parties this was not the solution to finding a permanent playing field nearer to the school for Redland's use only. The Council were asked to investigate if some farm land on Redland Green could be made available. At the Council meeting the Rev. F.G. Benskin, a Councillor, noted the Victoria Gold Medal had not been presented during the war years and three medals had been awarded but not actually given and he wondered if these should be presented.[19] There were some changes to Council at the end of 1921 as Canon Gamble was invited to take up an appointment as the Dean of Bristol Cathedral. His place was taken by Dr Franks and a long association between Redland High School and the Franks family was commenced.[20] The bank overdraft at the end of 1921 rose to £1,556 9s 5d and was only reduced to £270 15s 5d in March 1922 though payment of fees.[21]

In 1922 Redland High School was inspected for the fourth time by the Board of Education. The Inspectorate consisted of five men and two women. The Council was asked to include women as one-third of the Councillors. The Staff consisted of twenty-one regular members and three occasional members. The number of pupils remained at 387 and could not be increased due to the staff/student ratio, which the Board of Education placed at too high a proportion of staff, which was justified by the small size of the classrooms which only held a limited number of pupils. The School had received a grant of £3,250 from the Bristol City Council when numbers were at their highest.

Yearly boarding fees were £61 and laundry an extra £3 per term. Extra subject fees per term were: dancing, £1 5s 0d, gymnastics, £1 10s 0d, art (painting) £3 3s 0d, violin, cello, solo singing, £11 0s 6d, piano from £7 17s 6d rising to £11 0s 6d. Membership of the orchestra was £1 2s 6d.

120 girls were over the age of sixteen and thirty-five had proceeded to university or other higher education institutions. The Inspectors were pleased to hear that since 1918 thirty-two girls had left Redland High School to become teachers.[22]

The Inspectors noted the time given to the 'usual' subjects in the curriculum was satisfactory although in some classes there was mediocrity and in others keenness and alertness. The Inspectors attributed this to 'lack of discipline'. The years at war with Germany had seriously affected young people's lives and the Victorian strict family life which their parents had experienced was no longer maintained. The shared advanced courses in mathematics and science with Colston's Girls' School were seen as providing a high level of education, resulting in entrance to universities, although the number of girls attending from Colston's was twice the number of girls from Redland. It would appear that most of the subjects offered at advanced level were well-taught by experienced teachers, although the study of English Literature was restricted by being related to the historical development of the novel rather than a broader approach to reading contemporary works. The Inspectors reported 'their [the girls] intellectual curiosity requires stimulating by every means'.[23]

The teaching of history appeared comprehensive and chronologically studied as a pupil moved through the curriculum; however the Inspectors thought more attention could be paid to local history and the ancient east. The Inspectors from London would have noted the

School was housed in an historic building which in itself would have provided information on local history and more pupil involvement with the past.[24]

Lessons in geography were seen as relating to the local environment. Teaching aids, maps and illustrations were not as readily available as in other schools and the Inspectors recommended purchase of these. In the area of languages the Inspectors were full of praise for the teaching of French and German, although they noted that piano lessons nearby were seriously disturbing![25]

The subject area of mathematics was taken by two Staff members, recently appointed, one in 1920, and the second in 1921. Both had substantial academic qualifications and pupils gained a high level of credit passes in the examination. This was not the case in the lower forms where basic arithmetic was seen as weak because of poor practice.[26] Since the last inspection there had been a complete change in the science staff and the changes were being felt as new alternatives were offered although opportunities were limited because of the lack of facilities, an issue which was being addressed by the Council. The Inspectors suggested giving up the domestic subject room to science studies.[27] By the 1920s there was no subject area of domestic training, later called domestic science, as the curriculum followed the boys' model. In some schools needlework and dressmaking were seen as women's subjects. Some enterprising teachers wrote their own handbooks on cooking and home maintenance.[28] It was several years later before the subject area of home, or domestic, science gained respectability. The Inspectors' view was that science was becoming a more important subject in girls' schools if they were to compete against the boys and needed to include it in their curriculum.

The time allocated to art lessons had been increased to one hour for each form although the Inspectors did not consider this enough time

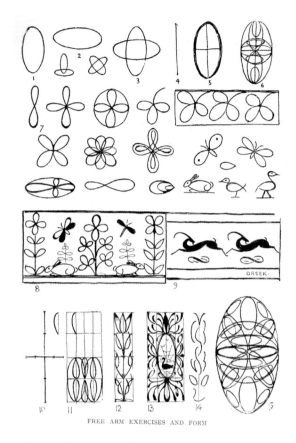

29. Ablett's new art syllabus. Free arm exercises and form design exercises.
The Book of School Handwork, Vol 1, 1900

to produce artworks. They were concerned about uninteresting objects presented for the girls to copy and paint without any quality of outcome. More quality drawing and study of pattern and illustration were needed to enhance the art curriculum.[29] In 1922 the Inspectors were exceptionally critical and alluded to the high standard of work which the School had previously produced and now needed a stimulus. They hoped the input of a new head-mistress, appointed that year, would help the School to regain its prestige as a high-achieving school.

At the end of 1921 debts of £11,995 had been reduced to £6,800. Fees had been raised in 1921 and the net increase was nearly £1,400 from the previous year. With the sustainable numbers the

Inspectors noted the School should have no difficulty paying its way.[30] This was a different attitude to their opinion in 1911 and later in 1915 when pupil numbers had dropped due to the effect of the war.

The need for a science laboratory was a major concern and alternative schemes were drawn up as to how much the School could afford. The Council expressed concern about the Inspectors' comments made in 1911 and again in 1922 of the sharing of the subject areas of science and mathematics with another school which they considered unsatisfactory. If these subject areas were dropped from the curriculum the School might miss out on retaining its position as a Public School and might have to be closed down. This was a cause for concern for the Council because they feared the sale of the house and the two acres of land would be handed over to the Education Authorities for the building of a Government Grammar School. In June, 1922, two quotes were obtained for a timber building to house a science laboratory, one of £1,200 4s 10d and one of £1,102 4s 10d.[31] There was discussion on the safety issues of a wooden building and suggestions were made of an asbestos roof covering. The architect, Mr George Oatley, was brought into the discussion and was asked to develop plans for this building. As a Councillor of the School he did not support the proposal as he was against spending money on temporary buildings.

Miss Edghill began a 'Leaving Scholarship Fund' which was later converted into the Shekleton Memorial Scholarship with £1,000 to be used as £50 a year for three years and awarded to a girl proceeding to one of the universities. The Old Girls pledged £300 a year towards the fund.[32] In 1922 Miss Edghill's salary was set at £700 per annum, with yearly rises of £50 and a maximum set at £800. The School showed a profit for 1922 of £1,130 and suggestions were made of using the money to set up a domestic science room and the purchase of a globe (at last!) and a set of encyclopaedias which had been suggested by the Inspectors.[33] If the number of pupils was less than the previous year the Town Council Grant was also reduced. From receiving £3250 in 1922 the School now only received £2,925.

After 1922 Miss Edghill introduced the compulsory wearing of a school uniform. Green blazers, green pleated tunics or skirts were to become the regulation dress with a standard blouse, pointed or rounded collar, and an optional green tie.[34] Two parents protested over the compulsory wearing of a uniform. The old-style navy gymslips had been optional.[35] Indoor shoes were also a compulsory requirement.

There was concern over the health of Miss Deakin as it appeared she was suffering from deafness.[36] In 1922 Miss Ida Deakin retired from the position of Head of the Kindergarten and Junior School.[37] At the beginning of 1923 the

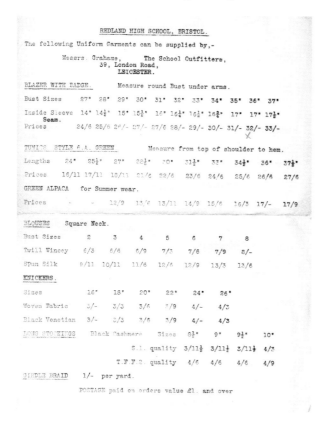

30. 1930. Price list for school uniform

Council formally requested the payment of school fees in advance and applicable also to music fees. There was to be a full term's notice of withdrawal of a pupil, or fees would apply.[38] School numbers were static at 378 and there could be no increase in the Junior School as accommodation was limited.

All expenses were carefully considered although the Council had to comply with the cost of cutting trees in the School grounds when branches were falling over into Clarendon Road. However, the Council sanctioned a new carpet for the Staff Room and also two fire-extinguishers.[39] Repairs to the roof, at a cost of £18 10s 0d, were an essential item for the Council to consider payment.[40] Pupil numbers were extended to 390 and fees from new pupils enabled the purchase of tennis nets and desks.[41]

The boarding school had actually made a profit of £160 and the total profit for the year, 1923, was £1,738 4s 1d. The Council was aware of the 'look of the school' and admitted the whole interior needed a coat of paint. The question of the accommodation for the Kindergarten was a priority and it was suggested an old railway-carriage could be purchased for the purpose of a classroom and could be placed underneath the library window.[42] This was not purchased and instead an ex-Army portable building was for sale and duly purchased. A parent complained of her child being cold in the temporary classroom. This ex-Army hut was eventually moved to a location below the terrace and became the music room for many years and singing voices breathed out smoke on cold days!

The architect, Mr George Oatley, had reported on the crumbling condition of the outside walls of the main building. He rejected the notion of plastering and rendering. The School was fortunate in having the services of a knowledgeable architect, whose daughter was on the Staff. Also, a crack in the wall of the boarding house needed repairing and the staircases in the house needed strengthening as they were not designed for continuous traffic. The staircases were supported in an appropriate way at a cost of £7 16s 0d and were under architect supervision.[43] Miss Edghill's understanding and love of things 'old' probably helped to bring the necessary sympathetic repairs to the attention of the Council and Mr Oatley. The Council had received news of some land available for a sports field, at a cost of £1,300 but the priority was for the repair of the building which was quoted at £1,165 4s 5d and seen by Miss Edghill as more important than a playing field.[44] In 1923 this amount was quite a considerable cost. The repairs also included work on the balustrade, the urns and the cornices. Any restoration of the historic building would have the approval of Miss Edghill, who probably considered 'heritage' preservation above the needs of sports teams.

In 1923 the Council asked for a new valuation of the buildings to accommodate the bank's £4,000 mortgage arrangements.[45] The main buildings were valued at £27,630, the new buildings, £5,750, the boarding house £7,895 and furniture £2,300. A personal client had been found to take over the mortgage but wanted 5.5 % return which was more than the bank's 4.5%.[46]

In 1924, seven girls, four with distinctions, had passed the Bristol Higher Certificate, twenty-nine girls had passed the Cambridge School Certificate, three had passed the Froebel Kindergarten Training Award, Part 1, and five had passed Part 2.[47] Miss Edghill had made it her decision to select the candidates for the Entrance Scholarship Free Places.[48] The Burnham Award was still causing problems especially for Staff who had alternate qualifications to a University degree, namely the art mistress, and it was up to the Council to work out where her placement lay.

In 1925 Redland High School students gained some excellent exam results. Leslie Sweet won an Open Scholarship in History at Lady Margaret Hall, and was the first Redland girl to win one of the State scholarships. Seven girls had passed the Higher Certificate of the University of Bristol, twenty-nine had gained the Cambridge School Certificate, four with Honours and there were five Distinctions. Seven Froebel students had passed Part 2 of the National Froebel Higher Certificate.[49] Five former pupils had distinguished themselves at Oxford, two at Cambridge, one at Bedford College, London, and over thirty at Bristol University. Miss Shekleton had died in 1924 and at the Old Girls' request it was decided to name a scholarship in her honour and the award to be known as the Shekleton Memorial Scholarship Fund. In 1926 the first girl to receive the award was Rosalind Franks, the daughter of the Rev. R.S. Franks, the Principal of Western College and later Chairman of the Council, after Canon Gamble's death. The interest on the fund enabled £50 a year to be allocated for a scholarship.[50]

In 1924 the School was given a crystal wireless set by an unknown benefactor and electric light was installed in the boarding house at a cost of £60.[51] 1924 saw the death of two Councillors including the President, the Master of Balliol.[52] They left a small legacy which enabled a few repairs and improvements to be made. The President's place was filled by the Bishop of Liverpool.[53] The School was now showing a profit and it was decided to use this to reduce the mortgage. Money was available for gym equipment and Miss Edghill's passion for improving the look of the school with new trees bought and planted.[54]

Miss Edghill expected strict discipline. Six girls were under scrutiny and there was even more pressure not to expel them if they were scholarship girls. The Staff were asked to keep an eye on them and they could only be dismissed if the Staff agreed. Expelling the girls was the last resort.[55] During Miss Edghill's first year the School was associated with the Save the Children Fund and the School Houses adopted children from Europe and contributed to their well-being. This tradition was continued for many years.[56] Decisions were made through a Senate consisting of Senior girls who held responsible positions. Another interest was membership of the League of Nations which sought to bring peace to the world and continued years later when it was renamed the United Nations. Through Miss Willey, who was involved in the League of Nations, girls at Redland were brought into the arena of politics and international affairs giving them a much wider view of the world than a previous generation.

In 1926 the School produced Shakespeare's *The Taming of the Shrew* with costumes and scenery made by the girls. At the request of an Old Girl a School song was written by a staff member, Miss Hazlehurst, and later in the same year it was set to music by Mr Smith, the music teacher, and sung for many years at the School's Prize Giving and special occasions.

And so we sing who do delight to wear the yellow, green and white, So hateth she derknesse.[57]

In 1926 the School learnt of Miss Edghill's resignation to take a Headmistress' position at St Felix, Southwold, a school situated in open country renowned for country walks and an outdoor life style and would appear to have suited Miss Edghill's interest in landscape and nature.

In March 1926 an advertisement was placed in newspapers and educational journals for the position of Headmistress at Redland High School. Miss C.M. Taylor, a New Zealand graduate, was interviewed and duly appointed.[58] This was her second application as she had been the second choice at the time of Miss Edghill's appointment. During the five years while Miss Edghill was Redland's Headmistress, Miss Taylor was the Headmistress at the Northampton School for Girls.

NOTES

1   Kean, H., 1990. *Deeds not Words*. London: Pluto Press, p.84.
2   ibid. p.99.
3   Redland High School, 1917-1933. *Council Minute Book, No.3*. Redland High School Archive. BB140. p.100.
4   Bungay, J., *Redland High School, 1882-1982*. Redland High School Council. p.73.
5   Redland High School, 1917-1933. *Council Minute Book, No.3*. Redland High School Archive. BB140. p.103.
6   Shaw, M.G., 1932. *Redland High School*. Bristol: Arrowsmith. p.72.
7   Avery, G., 1991. *The Best Type of Girls, a History of Girls' Independent Schools*. London: Andre Deutsch, p.57.
8   ibid. p.63.
9   ibid. p.63.
10 Redland High School, 1917-1933. *Council Minute Book, No.3*. Redland High School Archive. BB140. p.152.
11 ibid. p.103.
12 ibid. p.114.
13 ibid. p.107.
14 ibid. p.139.
15 ibid. p.104.
16 ibid. p.107.
17 ibid. p.108.
18 ibid. p.115.
19 ibid. p.120.
20 ibid. p.127.
21 ibid. p.128.
22 Board of Education, Bristol C.B, 1922. *Report of the Inspection of Redland High School for Girls, Bristol*. Redland High School Archive. p.1 (nyc).
23 ibid. p.3.
24 ibid. p.8.
25 ibid. p.8.
26 ibid. p.9.
27 ibid. p.10.
28 Avery, G., 1991. *The Best Type of Girl: A History of Girls' Independent Schools*. London: Andre Deutsch, p.60.
29 Board of Education, Bristol C.B.. 1922. *Report of the Inspection of Redland High School for Girls, Bristol*. Redland High School Archive. p.12 (nyc).
30 ibid. p 4.
31 Redland High School, 1917-1933. *Council Minute Book, No.3*. Redland High School Archive. BB140. p.129.
32 Shaw, M.G., 1932. *Redland High School*. Bristol: Arrowsmith. p.73.
33 Redland High School, 1917-1933. *Council Minute Book, No.3*. Redland High School Archive. BB140. p.130.
34 ibid. p.125.
35 ibid. p.128.
36 ibid. p.134.
37 Shaw, M.G., 1932. *Redland High School*. Bristol: Arrowsmith. p.74.

38 Redland High School, 1917-1933. *Council Minute Book, No.3.* Redland High School Archive. BB 130. p.145.
39 ibid. p.148.
40 ibid. p.149.
41 ibid. p.150.
42 ibid. p.156.
43 ibid. p.162.
44 ibid. p.165.
45 ibid. p.163.
46 ibid. p.165.
47 ibid. p.172.
48 ibid. p.172.
49 Redland High School, 1913-1958. *Shareholders' Minute Book.* BB 139. p. 51.
50 Redland High School, 1917-1933. *Council Minute Book, No 3.* BB 130. p.164.
51 Redland High School, 1917-1933. *Council Minute Book, No 3.* Redland High School Archive. BB 130. p.181.
52 ibid. p.181.
53 ibid. p.181.
54 ibid, p.179.
55 ibid. p.181.
56 Bungay, J., 1982. *Redland High School, 1882-1892.* Redland High School Council. p.73.
57 ibid. p.78.
58 Redland High School, 1917-1958. *Shareholders' Minute Book.* BB.139. p.60.

5

1926-1940 THE WALL STREET CRASH 1929 AND THE OUTBREAK OF THE SECOND WORLD WAR 1939

Prior to her appointment at Northampton Girls High School Miss Taylor had been a Staff member of St Paul's Girls' School. At St Paul's work came before play and a girl was not allowed to be in a sports team if her work was failing.[1] Redland High School was now in the hands of a headmistress who would demand high standards. Discipline was very much about saying 'please' and 'thank you', keeping to one side of the narrow corridors, always walking, and no running on the stairs. Miss Taylor's advice to the girls was:

You must always aim higher than you think possible otherwise you will obtain little.[2]

Even up to 1926 there was still a marriage bar requiring teachers to resign or to be sacked on becoming married. Women had a 'choice' in keeping a job and staying unmarried, or to marry and lose their livelihood which was harsh after their efforts to enter university and to gain a qualification which accounted for intelligent women deliberately choosing a single life.[3] The Staff at Redland were all spinsters except for Madame Farquhar. The relationship between female teachers may have been more than finding a partner to live with or to share a house together for companionship. These issues were never spoken about in the twenties and thirties. Miss Taylor had outside science interests, considered a male subject area, and she wrote and published papers on scientific research. Redland High School for Girls was fortunate in

having staff with wider interests and embracing these into flexible teaching programmes. These forms of 'open ended acquisition of knowledge' were to set an educational model for learning which was unique at that time.

The failure of the banks and the Wall Street crash in 1929, with sellers of stocks and no buyers, also flowed on into the general economy producing out-of-work employees and creating a new poverty. There had been much development and growth after the end of the war in 1918 and an air of optimism for the future, particularly in the emancipation and education of girls. Electric light, telephones, cars were only a few of the new improved life-style for the middle-classes. Difficult economic times lay ahead in the 1930s and cuts needed to be made in the number of staff employed at Redland High School as pupil numbers were also on the decline. Europe was about to be thrown into turmoil as Germany set about re-arming. In 1936 two women teachers, one of whom was an Old Girl of Redland High School, were in Germany for the Olympic Games. As they crossed the road one of the teachers cut across the corner of the marked crossing. Two armed guards, Brownshirts from the German army, were waiting on the pavement and immediately arrested the young teacher for the offence but may have selected her because of her Jewish facial-features. The second teacher pretended she was not with her companion and went immediately to the British Consul to secure her friend's release from the local police station where she was being held. It was a lucky escape and foretold of worse to come. Germany's involvement with the Spanish Civil War from 1936 to April 1939 also heralded a new warfare tactic, the aerial bombing of cities and civilians.

Miss Taylor's Headmistress' position at the end of her career took her into the outbreak of the Second World War and the unenviable situation of running a school in a country which was once again at war with Germany, a war involving the whole world.

MISS CLARA MILLICENT TAYLOR
(Headmistress, 1926-1940)

Miss Taylor, MA, a graduate from Victoria College, Wellington, New Zealand had continued her academic career at Cambridge involving research with William Pope, a distinguished research-chemist. In 1912 she accepted a teaching post as a chemistry teacher at Clapham High School, London. This was an inspired step into a subject area dominated by male teachers. The story of her life and her teaching career were the subject of a paper entitled, 'Clara Millicent Taylor, 1884-1940', by Professor Ian Rae of the Faculty of Science at Monash University, Australia, and appeared in a publication *Chemistry in Britain* produced in

31. c.1930. Miss Clara Millicent Taylor
(Headmistress 1926-1940) and Staff

1991.[4]

While Miss Taylor was Headmistress of Northampton School for Girls she published a book, *The Discovery of the Nature of Air and its Changes during Breathing*.[5] In March 1926 before her appointment to Redland High School her paper, 'The Transference numbers of Sodium and Hydrogen in mixed Chloride Solution', received in August 1925 was published in the *Journal of American Chemical Society*. This interest in science and Miss Taylor's personal research may have been one of the reasons she was selected by Redland's 'non-traditional' Council. Science education for girls had always been a priority for the development of the Redland High School to gain a prestigious place in the list of high schools.

Miss Taylor's salary of £650 per annum was based on her five years' experience as a headmistress. The School's financial position was healthy and stood at £5,823 3s 10d. Outstanding payments were £1,316 11s 3d. Mr George Oatley, the architect, recommended that the large urns should be restored at a cost of £90 and a further amount of £185 for the sustaining of the walls of the main house.[6] The School received a grant from the Local Education Authority of £1,400 and use of the grant came to the attention of the Director of Education who asked the question, 'Is the grant being used towards payment of loans?'[7] Even if this situation was played out as purported the use of grants which ultimately went on improvements was seen by the Council as increasing the value of the property.

During 1927 legacy money from Miss Hilda Wills, a former Councillor, enabled improvements to the garden and shrubs were cleared away to show the Italian wrought-iron gate with the coat-of-arms of the Cossins family. Visitors now had a clear view of the school buildings from the avenue of trees, known as Lover's Walk, which was originally the carriageway leading to Redland Court.[8] The carriageway had been mapped out for building lots until Mr George Thomas and a few other public-spirited citizens made an agreement with the owner, Mr G.O. Edwards, and later owners, that the best parts of the avenue were to be preserved. Also Mr Francis Fry and his brother donated four acres around the railway area to the Bristol City Council for a public park. Finally in 1884 it was reported to the Council that Mr W. H. Edwards, son of Mr G. O. Edwards, had executed a conveyance to the Corporation, *of that part of the Avenue which extended from Redland Road to the railway bridge for perpetual enjoyment of the public.*[9]

£1,000 was set aside as a reserve fund for emergencies. Repairs were needed to a chimney stack, replacing of glass in the porch and the thinning of trees. Miss Wills' legacy also enabled tennis courts to be built at the playing fields at Druid Stoke and the building of a new pavilion to replace the ex-Army shed.[10] In 1927 Miss Alice Gardner died and bequeathed a sum of money for continuation of the Classics Prize, a prize she had generously given while serving on the Council.[11] A new classics teacher was to be appointed and the position had been left open until the arrival of Miss Taylor and was awarded to Miss Bailey, MA First Class (Manchester) and she remained in the position for many years.[12] The School now had 368 pupils, fifteen Kindergarten, Froebel trainee-student teachers, and thirty-four boarders.

In 1926 Dr Beachcroft had resigned as Director of Music and Mr Smith was appointed. In December 1926 the prizes and certificates were presented by the Vice-Chancellor of Cambridge University. Six girls had taken the Higher Certificate of the University of Bristol and one girl had gained a Distinction in French. Thirty-one girls had gained the Cambridge School Certificate, thirteen with Honours and six Distinctions. Seven pupils had gained the Froebel Higher Certificate, Part 2. An ex-pupil had been made a Fellow of Newnham College.[13]

In 1927 Phoebe Ashburner studying French at Somerville College was awarded a Clothworkers' Scholarship valued at £80.[14]

At the end of 1927 the School gave a successful performance of Shakespeare's *Twelfth Night*.[15] In 1927 numbers had dropped to 343, a drop of twenty-five pupils, with thirteen Froebel student-teachers. In 1927 the Board of Education issued a circular indicating they may, if they chose to do so, cease giving Direct Grants and schools would have to rely solely on grants from their Local Education Authority.[16] The School Council was still challenged over its use of the Board of Education's grant and was further accused by the Town Clerk of Bristol who had noted the 'improvements' to the building's stonework. Finally a grant of £1,400 was approved by the Local Education Authority.[17]

As a result of the 1922 inspection, the School had received a written report by the Board of Education's Inspector of Domestic Subjects. Girls' schools had fought hard to establish themselves and were reluctant to include purely feminist subjects in the curriculum and domestic economy as a subject area, as it was first known, was moving into the field of charity work in hospitals.[18] Domestic science, as it was later labelled, still bore the stigma of being a non-academic subject suitable for those 'being fit for nothing else'.[19] It was to take another thirty years before the subject area took on any significance. However, there were girls at Redland who did not wish to strive for entrance to university. Their parents wanted the best for their daughters and they paid the fees for their daughters to receive a 'good' education. Miss Taylor was fully supportive of any incentives for girls to achieve in whatever field of study and she endorsed the move to employ a well-trained domestic economy teacher. The subject area had been introduced many years before but was dropped as the classroom was urgently needed as a science laboratory. The forthcoming Gamble legacy which was rumoured to be used for building science facilities would release a room for the subject area of domestic economy.

In 1928 Miss Taylor requested a visit to New Zealand for 'personal reasons'. She was questioned by members of the Council as to the nature of these but refused to give any details and she implied it was because of family commitments.[20] Miss Taylor was absent for a term although at that time the only mode of transport was by ship and travel to New Zealand and return to England took three months. In her absence Miss Edith Willey, an experienced history teacher, acted as Headmistress which enabled her to apply later for the position of Headmistress of Leeds Modern Girls' School set up to meet the increasing demands of the 'education of girls'.[21] Miss Willey met Beryl Corner's parents to discuss their daughter's future and at Miss Willey's suggestion Beryl Corner was persuaded to study medicine, a field in which she became famous for establishing a children's hospital in Bristol. In 1928 Miss Taylor and P. K. Thomas published a book entitled *Elementary Chemistry for Students of Hygiene and Housecraft* and a second publication entitled *A Junior Dictionary for Domestic Science Students*.[22]

In 1928 the School Council entered into an agreement with the Canal Corporation enabling them to borrow £2,000 with the proviso it would be paid back if the company was wound up. The School was in debt again because of a drop in numbers and non-payment of fees due to sickness on a nation-wide scale in 1928. The Boarding School had made a loss of £81. Savings were made on the dismissal of gardeners and garden costs. Miss Fry, one of the women members of Council, was concerned that financial problems and the recent borrowing should have been more widely debated. Two Staff members were leaving the mathematics and science departments.[23]

Were the financial problems the reason for Miss Taylor's absence? Was she thinking about

returning to New Zealand to take another appointment? When she returned there was a very low morale in the school. Mr George Oatley recommended raising the fees to overcome the financial problem. Council suggested an advertising campaign. Miss Taylor was confronted with complaints of the heating of the art room, constant reminders of the need for art desks, requests for more blackboards and improvements needed for the floor of the Assembly Hall. For the latter Miss Taylor suggested gym-shoes to be worn at all times! Two new Staff members arrived to fill the vacancies, Miss Engledon for mathematics and chemistry and Miss Patch for science. The latter was to stay until the 1950s and was well remembered for her photographs of the School and Staff. School numbers were now down to 336, thirty below the numbers in 1926. Sickness also affected the Staff and Miss Fitchew, the art teacher, was given a term's rest.[24]

In 1928 the National Froebel Federation visited Redland to assess the teacher-training course conducted at the School. They were now looking at presenting awards at 'A' level for the 'best' students. Miss Byrne, Head of the Kindergarten, had resigned and the National Froebel Inspectors were anxious about future developments of the teacher-training course to be offered under a new member of the Staff, Miss H. Phillips, to be appointed in 1929. Their report presented in March 1929 made it clear that no opportunity had arisen, or seems likely to arise, of overcoming 'a serious weakness' in the classroom accommodation for practice-teaching provided by the School.

The training department, and the preparatory department of the School are accommodated in a house which is primarily a boarding-house presided over by a house mistress, who probably, and quite naturally, tends to regard the students as intruders. Miss Phillips manages her pupils and her trainee student-teachers as well as anyone could in the circumstances, but satisfactory teaching and training, especially of the best modern type, are not possible in the conditions under which she works.[25]

At the end of December 1928 the Council had defended its position saying the School was unique and could not be equated with any other school and the Board of Education should not make demands on them. The Council were planning a science building and an estimated £7,000 was needed initially and a loan of £10,000, and further financial help making a total estimated cost of new buildings at £23,000 in the long run. The Council was optimistic that they would receive an amount of £10,000 from Canon Gamble's estate.[26]

In February 1929 the Chairman, Canon Gamble, died. His scholarliness and integrity concerning girls' education gave Redland the acclaim it deserved. He had always promised to leave a legacy for higher education and in particular he requested it to be used for developing 'Science for Girls'. Miss Elizabeth Sturge, a Councillor, was responsible for administering the unexpected £20,000 legacy. At one stage the Council thought some of the money could be used to buy a house for the Junior School. Fortunately, Miss Sturge steered the school through the legal proceedings which stated the money was to be used for 'higher education'.[27] The School also received Canon Gamble's Queen Anne desk for the library and over 500 books from his library. In March 1929 the Council elected a new Chairman, the Rev. R.S. Franks, Principal of Western College. The Rev. Franks had been on the Council since 1921 and had two daughters who had attended Redland High School. In 1929 the Old Girls gave an oak reading desk (lectern), to match the carved chair and table, in memory of Miss Helen Drew a former member of Staff who died in 1927 while Headmistress of Colston's Girls' School.[28]

In 1929 some of the girls in the Senior School visited the Italian and the Persian Art Exhibitions in London. In 1931 they visited the Continent and in 1932 Miss Perrott and Miss Yonge took twelve girls to the 'World Explorers' Camp' in Germany.[29]

In 1935 Miss Yonge and Miss Gill took girls to the Rhine Gorge area staying in youth hostels and became aware of the Hitler Youth Movement and the hatred of the Jews.[30] This visit was to have an impact on Miss Gill who bravely took on the adoption of a Jewish girl whose parents were ultimately to lose their lives in the Holocaust.

From March through to December 1929 there was much debate at Council level concerning the plans for the new science building. Some of the Council were still thinking along the lines of 'a suitable building for science' costing between £7,000 and £10,000. The architect, Mr George Oatley, became frustrated with the constant changing of his concept of providing a complete science wing to include a chemistry laboratory and a physics laboratory with an additional preparation room and cloakroom. He had even suggested a flat roof which would one day allow for a second-storey. He also submitted plans for two classrooms and a below-ground cloakroom on the east wing. He estimated all of these buildings could be built for up to £20,000.[31] Legal proceedings take time and 1930 was to pass before the money became available and enabled tenders to be called. Miss Taylor also reminded the Council that a new gymnasium was needed and any new developments should not be built on an area of the school grounds which would negate the construction of a modern gymnasium.

The problem of the housing of the Junior School and Kindergarten was also discussed. A house in Woodstock Road was for sale at £2,800. The house was inspected by the School's architect, Mr George Oatley, and he said it would make four classrooms. He suggested the

Council make an offer of £1,500. Mr Oatley stressed that money from the Gamble bequest should not be, and could not be, used to purchase this house. Finally, the School's offer was rejected on the grounds that the house was worth more as a residence and that permission had not been granted to use it for school purposes.[32] The same house came on the market many years later and was purchased for the School's Sixth Form.

In 1930 economic measures were taken to reduce the Staff by one full-time and two part-time teachers enabling the school to have one teacher for gymnastics. This had been found necessary and was recommended by the Inspectors owing to an increase in the time allotted for the subject. Another cost cutting measure was the non-teaching of German in the curriculum. Some of these measures were as a result of the decline in numbers. When income from fees dropped, which paid teachers' salaries, cuts were made to the number of staff employed. The School could not afford luxuries. However, through the generosity of the Council and a good friend of the School, a large grand-piano was purchased for the hall and the price negotiated from £110 to £75.[33]

By July 1930 discussion took place concerning the termination of the boarding-school, St Margaret's, which was making a loss. In October, 1930 it became obvious that there was no likelihood of a building grant from the Board of Education now the Gamble bequest was known to them. Councillors were still asking if savings could be made on the proposed science buildings, enabling the release of money for School purposes, namely the housing of the Junior School and Kindergarten which would be homeless if the lease was not renewed on the boarding house property.[34]

In 1930 prizes and certificates were distributed by Miss E.H. Major, Mistress of Girton College. The records of the Shareholders' AGM show there was a drop in the number of girls taking the Higher Certificate of the University of Bristol and the decline in the number of girls taking the Cambridge School Certificate followed on with only four girls taking the Higher Certificate in 1932. However, the numbers of girls taking the Cambridge School Certificate had doubled by 1932.[35] The Wall Street Crash of 1928-9 had its effect on schools which relied on numbers attending and payment of fees in order to function.

Until 1931 the Sixth Form had occupied the central room of the main building leading on to the terrace. Miss Taylor was responsible for changing the large room into a study and reception room for the use of the Headmistress, a tradition which has continued. New furniture had been purchased on her arrival as previous furniture had belonged personally to Miss Edghill. Once again necessary repairs were needed and the school was forced to raise the fees by two guineas, (£2 2s 0d) to gain an extra £1,000. There was a mortgage on the School's buildings of £4,000 and £3,631 owed to the bank. No endowments could be offered except for the established leaving scholarships.

At the beginning of 1931 the two driving forces behind the managed use of the Gamble bequest were Miss Elizabeth Sturge and Mr George Oatley. They convinced the Council, who had been arguing about the needs of the School in housing the Junior and Kindergarten and portioning out the inheritance, that the greater part of the money should be used to build a science block and additional classrooms and any remaining money was to be used in conjunction with the Shekleton Memorial Fund to provide scholarships for girls proceeding to Bristol University, as the university, itself had not directly benefited from any part of the legacy.[36]

In March 1931 tenders were called for the proposed science wing and the new classrooms. Eleven tenders were submitted and ranged from £15,461 to £19,350. The tender was given to Stone and Company who had premises in

32. 1931. Work commencing on the Gamble Science buildings, classrooms and cloakrooms. Architect, Mr George Oatley. Builders, Stone and Company. Opened in October 1932 by H.R.H. Pricess Alice

Redland Road. Their tender submitted was £17,242 which was in the middle range.[37] £14,000 of the legacy was available for immediate use in October 1931.

In 1930 the Froebel Inspectors reported the accommodation for the Junior School and the Kindergarten was inadequate and sharing the premises with the Boarding School was unsatisfactory despite the falling in the number of boarders which eventually saw closure. The boarding school, under the name of St Margaret's, the name derived from Marguerite, the daisy flower, was set up for girls from outside Bristol. St Margaret's boarders had their own uniform and a green blazer edged with yellow braid. The name 'St Margaret's' was embroidered on the badge pocket and on Sundays the boarders wore their uniform to St Saviour's Church in Chandos Road.

In 1931 the Froebel training was inspected by Mr T. Raymont MA and assisted by Miss E.R. Murray from the National Union of Froebel Teacher Training, London. In 1931-2 the National Froebel Union reported on their inspection and although acknowledging the excellent results were considering making a public announcement on the closure if better accommodation was not provided or was promised in the near future.

Whether the National Froebel Union should be recommended to continue to include this Training Department in their list of institutions approved for the purpose of Certificate A is one of the most difficult of the problems with which I have had to deal since the inspection was started.
T. Raymont, January, 1932.[38]

Mr Raymont was critical of the Governors failure to remedy the serious deficiency of accommodation which had been reported on three years previously. On receiving this report the Council agreed to inform the Staff of their intention to find suitable accommodation. Mr Raymont was concerned for students who had began the course and had passed level B but would not be able to complete if the training course closed.

On a more optimistic note the School celebrated its Jubilee Year in 1932. A film was made of the School's activities, photographs of the Middle School's production of the Robin Hood Pageant recorded the occasion and the School Secretary, Miss Shaw, wrote and published a book on the history of the School. Miss Bailey produced *Iphigenia in Aulis* and costumes were designed by Miss Cove and Miss Fitchew.[39] The Old Girls held a supper for the occasion and invited Miss Bancroft. In 1932 the Shakespeare Memorial Theatre was opened in Stratford-on-Avon and Redland High School was one of a number of Bristol schools to be part of a joint schools' visit travelling by train.

At the Council meeting held 25 May 1933 a letter was received from Mr George Oatley, architect, now Sir George Oatley, who had been knighted for his designs and building of the new Bristol University. In his letter he stated that his firm now had a partner, Mr Ralph Brentnall, whom he said would take over the responsibilities concerning the new Science building and any future buildings for Redland High School.[40] School numbers were now 360. Miss Moxley, a Froebel-trained teacher, with creative talents in art, poetry writing and theatrical costume-making and who stayed for a number of years, was appointed as Head of the Junior School which was now housed in the main building, in Rooms 1 and 2 and those above. In 1933 a circular, number 1,428, was sent by the London Education Authority with a request for schools to reduce the number of staff in Secondary schools. In 1930 the average age of girls leaving Redland was seventeen years. Taking in 10% of 'free' places the school was criticised for concentrating on specialist staff and an extravagant use of them for small classes.

The school uniform had remained as a three, box-pleated, dark-green tunic, with a regulated

33. 1932. School Jubilee, 50th Anniversary. Middle School, Robin Hood pageant

34. 1932. School Jubilee, 50th Anniversary, Senior School, 'Iphigenia in Aulis'

hemline, which was examined in the gym class. The tunic was used for sport and gymnastics as well as for everyday wear. Some of the older-style panama hats were cut down to make them shallower and the cut hidden by the hat band. This practice continued through the war years when panama and velour hats were hard to come by and use was made of old ones. The wearing of a uniform was made compulsory and girls wore black stockings and black, lace-up, or bar-strap shoes, a navy, gabardine raincoat and a green blazer with a pocket-badge of a circlet of daisy flowers and the letters RHS embroidered in yellow stitching.

In 1934 the gymnastic tunic was replaced by a dark-green pinafore dress with an extra wrap-around skirt for participating in sport.[41] The skirt was later adopted as the main uniform for Senior girls and the pinafore for Middle and Junior pupils, together with a white, long-sleeved blouse, dark-green tie, green woollen pullover with white, yellow and green striped V-neck, brown stockings, brown regulation-style shoes and indoor sandals. The school uniform was supplied by Marsh in Whiteladies Road and Clarks' shoes and sandals by Massingham's Shoe Shop in Whiteladies Road. Mr Massingham's daughter had attended Redland High School. There was little competition from other suppliers and the fabric used for the skirts and tunics could not be purchased from warehouses.

Finally, black stockings were replaced by brown stockings, lisle, not silk, or fawn-coloured knee socks, and in summer, white ankle-socks. The summer dresses were dark-green cotton with white cuffs and collar and for special occasions a shantung silk, light-green frock, with cream collar and cuffs. As these were made of tussore-silk they were unobtainable in the 2nd World War years when silk supplies from Japan ceased. They were too 'special' to be thrown away and some girls wore them in the war years as a day-time dress. The green, silk dress replaced the white dress worn on special

35. 1933. Senior School pupils. Uniform, box-pleated dark-green tunic. Girdle worn at the hip-line, 1929, and in 1932 at the waist-line. Black velour hats with hatband and badge, black stockings and shoes. Dark-green blazer with pocket badge of circlet of daisies. Navy-blue raincoats

occasions. One of these tussore-silk dresses was made into a dance tunic when the subject area of dance was introduced in 1947.

Redland continued to share staff and facilities for mathematics and science. Pupils bicycled to Cheltenham Road to reach the Colston's Girls' High School, an experience they found strange leaving the comfort of their own school. Chemistry was taught at Redland and biology at

36. 1937. Sixth Form pupils outside Miss Taylor's study

Colston's. Assemblies were held in the Assembly Hall which held the gym equipment, wall bars, climbing ropes from the ceiling, and moveable exercise-bars fitted to the walls. All of these remained in place until the new gym was built in 1965. The Sixth Form sat on chairs at the rear of the Assembly Hall and the Staff sat on chairs in the original stable area beyond the pillars.

The new science buildings and classrooms were officially opened in May 1933, although parts of the building project had been completed two years previously and rooms were already in use.[42] Dr Franks, Chairman of the Council and his father, Lord Franks, President of the Council, were amongst the distinguished guests. Professor Winifred Cullis of London University delivered the address in which she said,

No person today could be adequately or properly educated who had no knowledge of the natural sciences. Teaching of that kind was one of the broadening and steadying influences in the world. The world is crying out for the truth, a clear, cold, reasoned judgement and that is the sort of spirit I hope will be engendered in these laboratories.[43]

In 1933 the Council was sent an advance notice of a forthcoming inspection which had been delayed because of the impending building plans. The last inspection had taken place in 1922. In June 1933 the Board of Education sent its Inspectors to visit. They noted that the School's numbers had dropped from 385 to 336 but were on the increase again and had reached 360. Girls from the Junior School had to pass a written examination in mathematics and English before entering the Senior School. Failure to pass meant repeating a year and trying again or withdrawal. Free places for the Senior School were offered by the Local Authority. The Inspectors noted that out of the 130 girls who had left during the previous three years nearly a third had entered universities with a view to becoming teachers.[44]

The School still had a mortgage of £4,000 on the school buildings at the rate of 4.5%. For a number of years expenditure had exceeded income and the School was showing a debit balance of £3,631 owed to the bank. The Inspectors noted that the Council intended to increase the fees thus raising £1,000 per annum. They hoped increased numbers would also boost the income. The School was supported with a grant from the Board of Education for £2,422 and the Local Authority of £1,550.[45] Thirty-three girls were holding free places, twenty-two of which were Government-aided and eleven were through the Governors, part-fees or assistance, and amounted to donations of £200 per annum. Leaving exhibitions were provided for through the Gamble and Shekleton bequests.[46]

The Inspectors noted the new buildings funded by the Gamble bequest and were praise-worthy of the science, geography, biology (latter two shared) laboratories and the new classroom and additional facilities for a dining-room and new kitchen. However, they thought the furniture for the classrooms, desks for the art room and equipment for the domestic science lessons were inadequate and some re-decorating was necessary to make existing classrooms lighter in appearance. More tennis courts were needed and the netball court needed re-asphalting. The library appeared to be functioning well and the Dewey system of cataloguing had been introduced.[47]

The Staff were considered to be well-qualified and of an above-average quality.

The Inspectors were concerned that pupils were not reaching the stage of the School Certificate Examination early enough and suggested that the School should be re-organised on the basis of a five-year course thus reducing the number of year classes and increasing class size, with the goal of all those in their fifth year taking the School Certificate Examination.[48]

The Inspectors' comments on the Junior School echoed those of the previous inspection of 1929. The Kindergarten was still housed in the boarding school and they suggested knocking down a wall to convert two small rooms into one to accommodate the twelve children. They were reasonably pleased with the organizational aspects of the teaching and the help by the Kindergarten trainees but were more critical of the work being done in the Junior School now housed in the main building. Children entered the Junior School from other Pre-Schools or Junior Schools and the level of their work, particularly in arithmetic was criticised by the Inspectors, although the 'happy' atmosphere belied any incompetency.[49]

The teaching of Scripture was still part of the curriculum, even at a non-denominational school, and was taken by the class mistress, not by Miss Taylor who wished to revise the content of the syllabus and was in the process of doing this.

The teaching of English was highly praised at all levels as was the teaching of history and geography. The Inspectors attributed this to the dedicated and highly-qualified staff in these areas of study. The new buildings had made a substantial improvement in courses offered, although a suggestion was made to provide a room for the subject area of history, with

37. 1934. Payment of fees

illustrations and teaching aids. French and Latin were also seen as being 'well taught' with Latin results in examinations reaching credit level for twenty-one out of twenty-two candidates. Mathematics and science examination results were also improving.[50]

The Inspectors noted the School now possessed an optical lantern for slides, a micro-projector, an epidiascope and a Kodascope.

These were expensive items at the time and were the cutting edge of technology which all Secondary Schools were expected to acquire for presentation of source material such as enlarged photographs and drawings which supplemented the use of textbooks. Many of the Staff used their own photographs of places they had visited to enhance geography and history lessons.

The Inspectors were pleased to see two periods for art were now in place for the Senior girls and only a few of those taking art for the School Certificate entered 'drawing' as a subject for examination. The work done in class appeared 'neat' but not 'exciting' and a suggestion was made for pupils to take 'voluntary' art study which would set 'free' any potential talent. Domestic science was yet to be developed now that the new science wing would release a suitable room and could replace the smaller subject area of needlework, which in turn would be incorporated into the new syllabus.

Class music was taken by a member of the Staff who had been at the school for 22 years and she was assisted by the Director of Music, part-time and visiting music teachers specialising in piano and instrumental tuition. The School possessed six pianos of reasonable quality and generally music played an important part in school life with a music club and inter-house music competitions.

Physical education was reported as being limited by the lack of facilities and had not kept pace with modern thought and progress. Athletic children were not suffering although their capabilities were not being developed and attention was needed to develop the posture and health and well-being of many of the children. These commitments were beyond the capabilities of one teacher and the cut made in staff numbers for physical education had been unwise. Swimming had been introduced as a voluntary activity and was yet to be developed throughout the school. Changing into correct

dress for physical education was not possible because of a lack of changing rooms with showers and the present arrangement of removing a tunic or skirt met with disapproval from the Inspectors.[51]

In concluding the Inspectors thought the behaviour of the pupils was very favourable. They recommended more consideration for entries by scholarship or bursary to increase the chances for girls with academic ability who could otherwise not afford the fees. Of great concern was the lack of any form of medical inspection or health regulation.[52] Yearly Kindergarten fees ranged from £14 3s 6d, and rose to Senior School fees of £25 4s 0d. Private music lessons ranged from £7 to £11 for violin, violoncello, solo-singing. The school received a grant of £1,650 from the Bristol City Council.[53]

In 1937 the Senior English mistress, Miss Andrews, produced Shakespeare's *The Tempest*. Drama productions were an extension of the study of English Literature, and enjoyed by those who took the leading roles, or made props and costumes or those who joined the appreciative audience. The School was involved with the Barton Hill University Settlement and the Sixth Form visited the underprivileged children, giving toys and presents and also holding a Christmas party in the Assembly Hall in 1936 and 1937.

In 1938 Miss Taylor forwarded proposals to the Council for temporary war arrangements but it was left to Bristol City Council in June 1939 to pay for the provision of air-raid shelters for all city schools. On 3 September 1939 the Prime Minister broadcast his devastating speech, 'as a consequence this country is at war with Germany'. In October 1939 the shelters were completed at Redland High School. Help was given by the School to the refugees from the Basque country as a result of the Spanish Civil War. At first the war made few changes at the school premises, the cellars, nicknamed 'the dungeons' had been made available and fitted out with seating to act as shelters. At the end of 1939 the country experienced a severe winter and as the heating system was not in use many girls complained of the cold conditions. Games were now optional as the sports field at Druid Stoke was commandeered for Army training. There was no Prize Giving and no magazine. Activities were confined to knitting socks with wool provided by the Admiralty.[54] The Second World War brought knowledge of the rest of the world and Redland girls were no longer sheltered from the problems of other countries.

In January 1940 Miss Taylor died from an illness from which she had suffered in the last years of her role as Headmistress. She had been described as 'not a tall dominating figure' but 'having a commanding presence'.[55] Madame Farquhar was appointed Acting-Headmistress until a replacement could be found. In May 1940 Miss A.F.H. Berwick was appointed as Headmistress.

NOTES

1 Avery, G., 1991.*The Best Type of Girl, A History of Girls' Independent Schools.* London: Andre Deutsch, p.273.
2 Bungay, J., ed., 1982. *Redland High School, 1882-1982.* Council of Redland High School, p.98.
3 Kean, H., 1990. *Deeds not Words.* London: Pluto Press, p.97.
4 Internet.
5 Redland High School, 1995. *Old Girls' Newsletter.* Archive (nyc).
6 Redland High School, 1917-1933. *Council Minutes, No. 3.* Redland High School Archive, BB 140. p.203.
7 ibid. p.205.
8 ibid. p.206.
9 Bungay, J., ed., 1982. *Redland High School, 1882-1982.* Council of Redland High School, p.91.
10 Shaw, M.G. 1932. *Redland High School.* Bristol: Arrowsmith, p.79.
11 Redland High School, 1917-1933. *Council Minutes, No. 3.* Redland High School Archive. BB 140. p.208.
12 Redland High School, 1913-1958. *Shareholders AGM.* p.63.
13 Shaw, M.G. 1932. *Redland High School.* Bristol: Arrowsmith, p.79.
14 Redland High School, 1917-1933. *Council Minutes, No. 3.* Redland High School Archive. BB 140. p.218.
15 ibid. p.218.
16 ibid. p.229.
17 Avery, G., 1991. *The Best Type of Girl, a History of Girls' Independent Schools.* London: Andre Deutsch, p.245.
18 ibid. p.258.
19 Redland High School,1917-1933. *Council Minutes, No. 3.* Redland High School Archive. BB140. p.234.
20 Shaw, M.G., 1932. *Redland High School.* Bristol: Arrowsmith, p.79.
21 Redland High School, 1995. *Old Girls' Guild, Newsletter* (nyc).
22 Redland High School, 1917-1933. *Council Minutes, No. 3.* Redland High School Archive. BB 140. p.254.
23 ibid. p.255.
24 ibid. p.262.
25 National Froebel Union, 1929. *Letter to Redland High School* (nyc).
26 Redland High School, 1917-1933. *Council Minutes, No. 3.* Redland High School Archive. BB140.
27 ibid.
28 Shaw, M.G., 1932. *Redland High School.* Bristol: Arrowsmith, p.82.
29 ibid. p.85.
30 Bungay, J., ed., 1982. *Redland High School 1882-1982.* Council of Redland High School. p.90.
31 Redland High School, 1917-1933. *Council Minutes, No. 3.* Redland High School Archive. BB140.
32 ibid.
33 ibid. p.330.

34 Redland High School, 1917-1933. *Council Minutes, No. 3.* Redland High School Archive. BB140.

35 Redland High School, 1913-1958. *Shareholders' Minute Book.* Redland High School Archive. BB139. p.74.

36 Redland High School, 1917-1933. *Council Minutes, No. 3.* Redland High School Archive. BB140.

37 ibid. p.370.

38 National Froebel Union, 1932. *Letter to Redland High School* (nyc).

39 Bungay, J., ed. 1982. *Redland High School, 1882-1982.* Council of Redland High School.

40 Redland High School, 1917-1933. *Council Minutes.* Redland High School Archive, BB 140.

41 Bungay, J., ed. 1982. *Redland High School, 1882-1982.* Council of Redland High School. p.91.

42 ibid. p.01.

43 *Western Daily Press*, May, 1933. Redland High School Archive (nyc).

44 Board of Education, 1933. *Inspection Report.* Whitehall, London (nyc).

45 ibid. p.2.

46 ibid. p.3.

47 ibid. pp.3, 4.

48 ibid. pp.4, 5.

49 ibid. p.6.

50 ibid. pp. 6-9.

51 ibid. pp. 12-15.

52 ibid. p.16.

53 ibid. p.16.

54 Bungay, J., 1982. *Redland High School 1882-1982.* Council of Redland High School. p.102.

55 ibid. p.98.

6
1940-1944 THE SECOND WORLD WAR

The death of Miss Taylor in the early part of 1940 was a great loss after her long service to the school.

Miss Taylor took every opportunity of getting to know us individually.
Barbara Vickery, Head Girl.

The responsibilities of directing and taking part in the training of youth are very great, the worries of organising a school must be a continuous strain.
Dr Francis, Chairman of the Council.[1]

The period of the phoney war from September 1939-1940 was surreal, as if people were living on borrowed time in the knowledge that at any moment death and destruction could come on an unimagined scale.[2] Gas masks had been issued in 1938 by the Air Raid Precautions (ARP), the fledgling nationwide civil defence organisation funded by the Home Office. Grey, silver-coloured, barrage balloons wallowed in the sky above London and were later seen on the Downs in Bristol. A month after the Munich negotiations for peace the Anderson air-raid shelter, named after Sir John Anderson, Lord Privy Seal, came off the production line in February 1939.[3] Attack from the air seemed the most likely and was born out with the taking of Czechoslovakia and the bombardment of Poland and entry to that country by the German Army on 1 September 1939.

On Sunday 3 September 1939 war was commenced by Hitler, Germany's leader.

During the last two months of peace and the first week of the war nearly four million people were evacuated from London and the east coast.[4] Children, with or without their parents or parent, were sent to the West Country, Cornwall, Wales, the Midlands and to the far north of England.

Dear Sir, Madam, The Medway Town Council at the request of the Government are now preparing plans for the voluntary evacuation of schoolchildren in the event of a national emergency. The object of the Government is to make plans in time of peace, so that, if an emergency were to arise, all concerned would know the part they ought to play.[5]

No large scale evacuation was to take place from Bristol until 1941. The phoney war at the end of 1939 had caused some panic and some children were sent to stay with country relatives during the months of October and November and returned home for Xmas. Trains leaving Temple Meads were packed with the British Expeditionary Force on their way to Southampton for embarkation to France. As one Redland pupil recalled:

We arrived at Temple Meads Station at eight a.m. in the morning. The train to Exeter was already full of servicemen. My father found a space in the corridor, standing room only, and I sat on the large suitcase. I remember looking at the brass buttons on a soldier's greatcoat with the insignia of a cannon. At Taunton civilians were ordered off the train and told to take a bus to Exeter or to their destinations. The twelve o'clock bus was full and after waiting for each hourly bus until four o'clock and still no vacancies, my father ordered a taxi to my Aunt's house at Honiton and back to Taunton for himself. The taxi fare cost him £30!

MISS A.F.H. BERWICK
(Headmistress 1940-1944)

Miss Alick Berwick had been a House Mistress at St Margaret's School, Scarborough. She graduated with an MA (Cambridge) where she studied classics. Miss Berwick arrived before the severe blitz on Bristol and the prospect of Germany invading England. This was not an auspicious time to take over a headship.

It was her youthful, progressive, outlook and vigorous dedication which enabled Redland to continue to flourish during those difficult days and which set the scene for its continuing success and it was due to her foresight that the School so easily made the transition into the post- war years. W. Barnett. P. Richardson. E. Stuart Smith.[6]

Many changes happened to families. Fathers were enlisted for military service or to help on the

38. c.1943. Miss Alick Berwick (Headmistress 1940-44) and Staff and Miss Berwick's dog

home front as a home guard, ambulance driver, special constabulary, fire warden. Holidays to the seaside ceased and the school organised activities in the holidays, weeding the garden, producing plays and trying out skills in craftwork. Gas masks had been issued to everyone and children were trained to put them on and to carry them at all times. Mr C. Ord and Miss Fry, Councillors, died in 1940. Miss Hilda Wills, a generous benefactor, resigned after many years of service to the School and Mrs Falk took her place. There are no preserved records of Council Minutes or a Headmistress Report for this period although The Shareholders' Reports are held in the archives. These reports were presented at the Members' Annual General Meeting and gave a summary of each year's achievements.

The Shareholders' AGM was not held in 1940 and the forty-sixth AGM was held in December, 1941. Pupil numbers had dropped from 320 to 250. Only one girl had taken the Bristol University's Higher Certificate and another had taken the Oxford Higher Certificate. Eighteen girls had taken the Cambridge School Certificate and two girls had obtained their National Froebel Teacher's Certificate. These were the final students to be trained at the recognised course held at Redland High School.[7] Girls left early to join the services and many returned to their studies after the war. The war opened up opportunities for women and several Redland girls continued in senior positions in the War Ministry after the war ended.

In 1941 the Rev. K.L. Parry was appointed Chairman. Members of the Council included Lady Baron, Lady Cook, Mr Latimer Thomas and Mr Hugo Mallett.[8]

Others to join the Council were Professor Fletcher, Professor James, and Mr Victor Allen, solicitor.[9] Pupil numbers had risen to 335. Four girls had gained the Bristol University Higher Certificate and thirty-five girls, the Cambridge School Certificate. One pupil had entered the West of England Academy of Art.[10]

In 1942 school numbers had risen to 434 and two Prize Giving ceremonies were held, one for the Junior School and one for the Senior School. Five girls had gained the Bristol University Higher Certificate and twenty-five girls had gained the Cambridge School Certificate with one girl gaining seven Distinctions![11]

1943 brought more Council retirements and Professor Young was elected Vice-President.[12] In December 1944 numbers had increased to 460, the highest number of pupils the School had ever known. Two Prize Giving ceremonies were again held. Mr Sharpe, Head of the Clifton College Preparatory School, presented the Junior School prizes and Dr Beryl Corner presented the prizes for the Senior School. Five girls had gained the Bristol University Higher Certificate and twenty-five had gained the Cambridge School Certificate.[13] A compulsory pass was needed in English in order to gain the Cambridge School Certificate. In 1943 Mr Parry became Chairman of the Council. Many long-serving staff stayed until the end of the war, and included Miss St John and Madame Farquhar.

Arrangements were made to use the cellars as air-raid shelters and each pupil kept a small case of supplies, mainly chocolate and biscuits.[14] Towards the end of 1940 the air-raids on Bristol increased and the night of 24 November 1940 was one of much destruction of the city. *It's all gone,* said the milkman, from the top of the steps of a house in Redland Road, *Jerry's bombed it all!* Miss Berwick set up bunk beds in her study for both girls and her Staff on duty as fire-watchers.[15] Many houses in Redland suffered fire damage from incendiary bombs and others were completely destroyed. The Bishop's Palace near the School was destroyed and Colston's Girls' High School lost its library. Except for a small fire in the roof, put out by the caretaker and teachers, Redland High School's historic house suffered no damage. Iron railings were removed for the war effort from houses in the Redland area but fortunately the wrought-iron gates of

Redland Court were saved through the intervention of the School Council.[16]

Food-rationing was something the British came to take for granted and was well-organised by the Ministry of Food so as to avoid the wartime shortages associated with the First World War when there was unfair distribution and profiteering. There was a certain amount of bartering by townspeople with their country neighbours, and eggs and potatoes were exchanged for services rendered.[17] Ration books with coupons were still needed until 1949.

Wartime rations for a week consisted of:
Sugar, 8 ounces; jam, 4 ounces; fats (butter/lard), 8 ounces; cheese, 2 ounces; bacon, 4 ounces; tea, 2 ounces; milk, 2 pints; eggs, 1.[18]

Oranges, one only, were for children under five years. Bananas completely disappeared from the shelves and young children did not taste them until the late 1940s. For children the rationing of chocolate and sweets was a devastating blow and the fun of the cone-shaped, paper bag, for a penny's worth of mixed-sweets and the additional *Dandy*, or *Beano* comic, had gone for ever.

Clothing coupons made it difficult to buy uniforms and were used for essentials such as Clark's sandals, which were compulsory indoor-shoes, and even these were in short supply. The slogan 'Make Do and Mend' became familiar. A second-hand 'school uniform cupboard', as it was known, held in the ante-room by the Assembly Hall was set up by the parents and continued for many years. Worn badges on old blazers were re-embroidered and a local tailor made one wrap-around skirt from two old ones by discarding the worn back-panels and using the front ones for the new skirt. Parents were recommended to visit him. Blazers of substantial woollen-material could be turned and re-made. Second-hand, pre-war, tennis racquets were sold at the 'cupboard' and thinly-shaped hockey sticks from the thirties were welcome as none of these sports goods were available to buy in the shops. Tennis balls, made of rubber covered with a white wool fabric, were also in demand, even if the covers were moth-eaten or worn! Panama hats were unobtainable and winter hats were worn in the summer.

The School managed to provide dinners, although at one stage there was a complete shortage of potatoes. Prunes and custard were a luxury. All imported cans of peaches and soft fruit after stocks had been depleted were not replaced.[19] After the terrible bombing at the end of 1940 and in 1941 parents were given the option to evacuate their children. For some children it was a horrific experience and yet others found love and comfort from their adopted families and enjoyed their stay in the countryside.

We were certainly not aware of the tremendous pressures Miss Berwick was under as a result of the bombing of Bristol. After the daily routine of teaching Latin and Religious Education she would don her warden's uniform and carry out her A.R.P. duties during the nightly air-attacks and at weekends she cooked for the Red Cross.
W. Martin, P. Holman, E. Stuart Smith.[20]

In 1942 in the summer holiday arrangements were made for the Senior girls to go to a harvest camp to help pick potatoes and fruit. They were

39. 1942. Second World War. Potato Harvest Camp

accompanied by a number of members of Staff, some of whom had been in the school for many years teaching sport, science and music. [21] This led to the establishment of clubs held on Thursday afternoons, as no after-school activities could be offered because of the 'blackout'. The 'blackout' was a period of no street lights and at night all windows were covered with dark curtains. Some of the older houses in the Redland area had retained their wooden shutters and these were perfect for blocking out any light which might have been seen from the road outside.

In 1941 Miss Weekes and Miss Shaw retired. Miss Shaw was the School Secretary and Clerk to the Council. Also in 1941 the Chairman of the Council, Dr Francis, died. The Francis/Francis Prize for public service to the School was endowed by Mrs Francis who died in 1944.[22] In August 1941 Bristol experienced its first daylight raid on the Bristol Aeroplane Company at Filton in which Barbara Vickery, who had been School Captain, was killed. She was working there before going to university.[23] A Barbara Vickery Memorial Plaque was unveiled in the School Assembly Hall in 2009. The Barbara Vickery Fund Prize was awarded for several years after her death to a pupil to help her financially to stay on in the Sixth Form.

Despite the financial hardships caused by the war every class raised money for the Red Cross, the Four Nations Appeal, and the Aid-to-China fund. The making of garments and knitting of socks continued as girls took on the task of fire-watching in 1941. Miss Berwick was always followed by her little dog, a Bedlington terrier, who became part of the school and was much loved by the pupils.[24]

On December 7 1941 the Japanese attacked Pearl Harbour which brought war to the Pacific and brought reaction from the United States of America who were now committed to join in the European war as well as defending their territory. As a consequence large numbers of American G.I.s were stationed in and around Bristol ready for the D-Day landings in France. Many large houses were taken over by the military, but Redland Court was spared this fate. In 1942 the School celebrated its sixtieth anniversary with a special service at the Cathedral and an open day.[25] There had been discussion on whether Kindergarten-age children should attend or be kept at home. Parents brought it to the Council's notice that Education Department's schools had not adopted this policy and they wished their children to attend despite the danger of daylight raids. .

The content of the curriculum was little affected during the war, although there were no trips to Europe to practise language speaking. Cooking classes focussed on what to do with dried-egg and dried-milk products and 'make do and mend'.[26] In 1944 School Certificate results were still high and although fewer girls stayed on in the Sixth Form they too achieved success. However, they were to experience stiff competition at the University when mature-age students, whose studies had been interrupted by the war, entered further-education courses. Teachers' Colleges offered a one-year teacher's training course to ex-military males and females. There was a demand for primary teachers owing to the loss of teachers, mainly men, killed in the war, and the increasing birth-rate after the war.

An Inspection took place in 1944 although the report was not available until 1945. The financial position was disclosed in the Inspectors' report but without Council Minutes available no details exist. When school numbers were low, income was low and without skilled labour available during the war years and limited financial backing very little was accomplished in maintaining the fabric of the building or the provision of new buildings essential for increasing numbers. The rise in numbers indicated the School was not in any financial difficulty if income exceeded expenditure.

In 1944 Miss Berwick announced she was leaving to become Headmistress of St. Michael's School, Bognor Regis and later in life she became an H.M.I. She continued in this role for another three years after normal retiring age. Miss Berwick's successor was Miss Sylvia Peters who became Headmistress in January, 1945.

NOTES

1 Bungay, J., 1982. *Redland High School, 1892-1982.* Council of Redland High School. p.103.
2 Hennessy, P., 2006. *Never Again. Britain 1945-1951.* London: Penguin Books. p.10.
3 ibid. p.8.
4 ibid. p.12.
5 'The Evacuee', 2010. *The Newsletter of the Evacuees Reunion Association.* Issue 162. p.4.
6 Redland High School, 1984. *Old Girls' Guild Newsletter,* Archive. p.3. (nyc)
7 Redland High School, 1913-1958. *Shareholders Minute Book.* Redland High School Archive. BB 139. p. 98.
8 ibid. p. 99.
9 ibid. p.103.
10 ibid. p.101.
11 ibid. p.102.
12 ibid. p.105.
13 ibid. p.107.
14 Redland High School, 2003. *Old Girls' Guild Newsletter.* Archive. p. 34. (nyc)
15 ibid. p. 34.
16 Bungay, J., 1982. *Redland High School, 1882-1982.* Council of Redland High School. p.107.
17 Hennessy, P., 2006. *Never again. Britain 1945-1951.* London: Penguin Books. p. 51.
18 ibid. p.49.
19 Bungay, J., 1982. *Redland High School, 1892-1982.* Council of Redland High School. p.107.
20 Redland High School, 1984. *Old Girls' Newsletter.* Archive. p.4. (nyc)
21 Redland High School, 2004. *Old Girls' Guild Newsletter.* Archive. p.34. (nyc)
22 Bungay, J., 1982. *Redland High School, 1882-1982.* Council of Redland High School. pp 103,104.
23 ibid. p. 102.
24 ibid. p. 106.
25 ibid. p. 104.
26 ibid. p. 107.

7
1945-1968 BECOMING AN INDEPENDENT SCHOOL

The Luftwaffe bombing of Bristol had ceased although London was experiencing the V2, a rocket-launched bomb from sites in France.[1] The Labour Government under Clement Atlee (1945-51) implemented the provision of the 1944 Education Act, regarded by many as the most important piece of legislation to be passed between 1939 and 1945.[2]

Children were no longer to be educated to the highest level at a Primary School. All were to receive a 'Secondary Education' with the phasing out of this for only those who could afford it through fee-paying. Five groups of schools existed before and in the war years and were arranged in hierarchical order of: Public schools, direct grant grammar schools (those receiving a direct grant from central government for scholarships, as well as taking fee-paying pupils), grammar schools, trade schools, elementary schools, and the new, secondary modern schools. There were also the 'religious schools' which, although under State legislation, could operate independently.[3] The main objective of the 1944 Education Act was to raise the school-leaving age to fifteen years.

Few repairs had been made to Redland High School's buildings during the war years and the Council made changes to its membership through resignations and deaths. In 1944 the Rev. K.L. Parry became the Chairman and an Inspection of the School was carried out and the report circulated in March 1945 when the headmistress's position had changed. The outcomes of the report became the concern of

Miss Sylvia Peters, who was appointed in January 1945.

Council Minutes gave detailed accounts of the actual process of debate concerning Council decisions. Strong debate, as it turned out, enabled the 'right' decision in the case of the Gamble science buildings. Financial losses were backed up by Council members who gave generous amounts of money and these were mentioned in the Minutes. Council was concerned with the maintenance of the historic building, lack of buildings to meet the Inspectors' demands, finance, number of pupils relating to fees charged, pupil and staff dismissals.

Reports by Headmistresses gave details of the functioning of the School, who did 'what', 'to whom' and 'why' and included staff appointments, supported by evidence of 'why' they were suitable candidates and discussion of their qualifications and experience. New trends in education, new developments, School House activities, drama, sports, community involvement, were also included in the reports.

The Council Minutes and the Reports from the Headmistress, Miss Peters, have not been retained in the archives, except for the Council Minutes of 1966, along with the Shareholders' Minute Book, 1913-1958, and the minutes of the Staff meetings. Additional information has been obtained through the responses to a questionnaire given to Old Girls who experienced the changes which took place when Miss Peters was first appointed as Headmistress.

MISS SYLVIA PETERS
(Headmistress 1945-1968)

Miss Sylvia Peters MA (Cambridge) had studied English and Classics. She was younger than the Headmistresses in the other girls' schools in Bristol and brought new ideas and zest to the Redland High School which had been run on fairly conservative lines. Her previous teaching experience in the subject area of English and position of Second Mistress had been at Croydon High School, a school which opened in 1874 and by 1880 had 220 pupils.[4] An appointment to a school with an historical background and housed in a Grade II listed building would have attracted Miss Peters to the role of Headmistress.

The last inspection of the School had taken place in 1933 and in 1944 the Inspectors from the Ministry of Education noted the boarding-school, St Margaret's, had ceased to operate.[5] They also drew attention to the decline in the number of pupils, particularly in the Junior School, although by 1945 numbers were on the increase and had risen from 250 to 461. There were twenty-two staff members and three part-time, giving a ratio of one staff member to twenty-five pupils. The Inspectors commented on the limited facilities and lack of equipment at the Kindergarten level but were impressed by the mixture of older and young teachers for this level who appeared to work harmoniously. 150 children were Junior School pupils and included sixteen young boys. There were thirty-nine pupils in the Sixth Form.[6]

An analysis of the girls leaving the Fifth and Sixth Forms in 1944 showed six proceeding to university, two to a Teachers' Training College, two to a School of Art, three for the training of nurses, and others for training in Froebel Teaching, housecraft and physical education. In 1943 only forty-three pupils from the whole school were exempt from fees and sixteen were part-exempt. The established leaving exhibitions were awarded through the Gamble Bequest and the Shekleton Memorial Fund.[7]

The Inspectors' report, while giving praise, emphasized that more buildings were needed if the School was to progress. The main criticism was directed at the inadequate accommodation for the Lower Junior School and suggestions were made to consider the purchase of a nearby house, thus releasing rooms for the Middle and Upper Junior School. The Inspectors reported the need for a 'proper' gym complete with changing rooms and shower facilities. They noted that the main library needed upgrading and although there were 4,000 books, many were covered in an unattractive dark-green, oilskin, protective cover.[8]

With the increase in numbers there were two parallel forms for every year except for the School Certificate year, which eventually had two parallel Forms after 1944. All pupils studied Latin for two years and at the end of the first year in the Middle School sets were made for mathematics and French, although the forms were not graded for ability in other subjects. A suggestion was made that housecraft could be introduced as a subject area for some girls or organised as an alternative Form. Owing to the war and non-recruitment of new staff it was felt the subject areas of English, history and geography needed attention because of poor examination results. The Senior English Mistress had been in the school for nearly thirty years and was a Cambridge graduate. Whilst recognising her skills and longevity the Inspectors were concerned with the content of the English Literature course offered and suggested a new, younger, member of staff would be able to bring 'modern' novels to the attention of the girls. Both the new geography and history teachers had only been in the school for a matter of weeks but their enthusiasm for their subject areas was evident.[9]

More recent appointments for French and German were also in their infancy and results were yet to be judged and Italian had been introduced. The appointed Classics teacher for the Senior girls was very well-qualified but had not taught in a classroom.[10] In 1944/1945, Latin was a compulsory subject for the Cambridge Higher School Certificate and University entrance. The teaching of mathematics was in the hands of a very capable teacher and the Inspectors were pleased with the progress of girls in the Sixth Form who were taking pure and applied mathematics for university entrance. The teaching of science was also considered to be good and the School was fortunate to have excellent facilities.[11]

Miss K. Taylor was the newly-appointed art teacher and the main change was in the allowance of two periods for an art lesson. The Inspectors noted the cramped room conditions when Middle School pupils used the art room. Miss Taylor could not develop any craft work because of the lack of facilities needed for pottery or fabric-printing and design work was carried out on paper.

Miss Taylor trained in Fine Art at the Royal College of Art and completed an art teachers' training course set up by Marion Richardson, an 'avante garde' supporter of the Child Art Movement. Miss Taylor had experienced the new form of pattern-making related to handwriting and it was proposed to introduce the Marion Richardson-style of handwriting which eliminated the loops in copperplate script.[12] A school rule stated that only girls in IVA and above were allowed to have self-filling pens, called fountain pens, and allowed to keep bottles of ink in their desks.[13] For the rest of the pupils ink wells, small china cups, were filled by the caretaker and replaced in the desks slots. In 1946 one girl had acquired a 'biro' from America, in a heavy, metallic-case, with purple 'ink' and she was forbidden to use it. Within four years everyone had a 'biro', a generic term used for the original invention. By 1955 art teachers were asked to teach italic handwriting

40. 1946. Miss Sylvia Peters (Headmistress 1945-1968) and Staff

41. 1949. The chemistry laboratory in the Gamble Science building

42. 1949. Middle School pupils in the Art Room

due to the reputed poor handwriting skills created by the 'biro'.

In a non-denominational school, Scripture was taught by the headmistress to the Senior pupils, a tradition introduced by Miss Cocks. Class teachers taught Scripture to their own pupils. Lessons took the form of discussions on alternative religions along with the study of passages from the Bible.[14]

Cookery, under the heading of housecraft, was not a subject area and was confined to a Thursday afternoon hobby-group developed from the holiday courses offered during the war years. The Inspectors suggested that housecraft could not be offered in the curriculum unless new facilities were made available. Music also was now in the hands of a newly-appointed senior music teacher and classes were held for each form and lasted for one period of forty minutes. A small orchestra had been commenced, supported by three members of the Staff. Four pupils received lessons from a visiting violin teacher and fifty-four girls were learning to play the piano under five members of the music staff. The Junior School had two music lessons a week taken by a Staff member who also taught recorder playing. It was felt the School had a promising music department to encourage girls to take music both in the School Certificate and the Higher Certificate Examinations, although this was restricted to girls who were taught an instrument by a member of the School Staff.[15] In 1944 the first orchestral Summer School for school pupils was held at Sherborne, Dorset and Hannah Weinberger, the Jewish refugee adopted by Miss Gill, was accepted as a cello player.

Gymnastic lessons in the hall were now more physical with exercises on vaulting horse and box set at different heights. Sports were well-catered for using the nearby fields belonging to Colston's Girls' High School. The need for a gymnasium with changing facilities was reported as being essential and with improved

43. 1949. Gymnastics class in the Assembly Hall

facilities the Inspectors advised the area of 'dance' could be added to physical education.[16] They concluded the School had carried on well though the difficult war-period although the increase in numbers showed the School had outgrown its premises and a separate accommodation venue was needed for the Junior School pupils. They were also concerned that academic standards were not being reached and new staff needed to be recruited if the School was to regain the distinguished level reached in the pre-war years.[17]

After receiving the results of the 1944 inspection Miss Peters set about recruiting teachers where she felt a need for improvement in teaching standards and would ultimately lead to excellent results in the external examinations. Miss Charlton, appointed as the Senior English teacher, was a teacher 'who made a difference'. Questionnaire recipients reported, 'if one was fortunate to have been taught by her' ... 'learnt more in one term than in the previous two years'.

Another new member of the Staff was appointed to teach mathematics. Miss Russell was an excellent teacher and the rules of homework being given in 'on time' were strictly followed. Homework books were delivered to a cupboard along the main corridor.

Miss Russell was remembered, along with Miss Gill, for taking mathematics into the world of Christmas decorations as three-dimensional mathematical models were painted and decorated to hang on the Christmas tree displayed in the Assembly Hall.

In 1949 Miss Slater was appointed to teach foreign languages, French and German, and stayed as a long-serving member of the Staff, becoming the Head of the Modern Languages Department. Miss Slater taught girls who became mothers and in her life-time taught their daughters. She died in 2010. Two French-born teachers, Madame King and Madame Williams, also taught French and Madame Williams was responsible in 1948 for acquiring pen-friends from Paris, through a link with the Lycee de St Cloud, Paris, set up by Miss Slater. The twinning of Bordeaux and Bristol led to many school holiday exchanges which took place after 1949. In 1948 exchanges had also been set up with Munster and Marburg in Germany and two German girls stayed in England and attended the Redland High School completing their studies in written English. Later, other German girls exchanged visits with English pen-friends. In 1949 there was a confrontation between the French and German girls in the courtyard. Occupation of France by Germany had affected many French lives and the French girls were not as forgiving as those less affected. One Jewish girl's father had been interned in a camp in the Bois de Vincennes and contracted tuberculosis and had died in 1954.

Under the War-Widows Scheme fees were paid by the military if a girl's father had held a Senior position. In these sole-parent families mothers worked or received a pension and could only afford second-hand uniforms although this was acceptable as rationing was still in operation and clothing coupons were needed for new clothes. After the war new uniforms and demands for specialised apparel were set in place and replies to the questionnaire brought responses of 'had to be purchased from expensive shops', 'bought one item at a time'. These items included hockey sticks with shortened curved ends, tennis rackets of new design, canvas hockey-boots, a 'must have' item bought at the new store of Daniel Neal, a London-based school uniform company, despite mothers knowing the old-fashioned, black-leather hockey shoes kept the feet dry. Another 'must have' was a leather brief-case which replaced the pre-war satchel. The 'must haves' were accepted as birthday presents. Younger mothers gave their daughters 'modern' freedom, allowing them to use lipstick and to wear nylon stockings, a luxury item from America. This was an era when teenage fashions had not yet reached England and could only be seen, with envy, in American and Canadian teenage magazines sent by pen-friends.

The main change to the summer uniform was from a dark-green cotton dress to one of green and white gingham material which varied from small checks to large ones. Dresses were often home-made and not regulation style. Miss Peters inaugurated a standard gingham material and dress style, with white collar and cuffs. Due to a number of 'larger' girls and when the Daniel Neal store became involved in supplying uniforms the material was changed to smaller-size green and white gingham and the front of the frock gathered from a yoke.

The winter uniform of a dark-green, round-necked, pinafore dress remained for the Junior and Middle School and Seniors wore the wrap-around games skirt. Long-sleeved white blouses, dark-green pullovers and a dark-green tie were worn by all the girls until the mid-1950s when prefects had a yellow, white and green diagonally-striped tie. Stockings or brown knee-socks were worn with brown lace-up school shoes. White ankle-socks were permitted in summer. Clarks' sandals were worn indoors, of which there were two styles, and the changing of outdoor-shoes to indoor-shoes was compulsory.

Hat bands were horizontally-striped colours of green, white and yellow worn on black, velour, winter hats and in summer, replaced on light-colour straw hats, known as 'panama'. The velour hat was phased out and replaced by a hat made of a green-coloured soft material and also a coat of green, tweed-material. The coat was an alternative to the raincoat which was also changed from navy blue to green. The School's blazer had not been altered since its pre-war introduction.

In Bristol there had always been an adequate number of Direct Grant Grammar Schools which received a grant from the Government in return for offering a number of places to local children in schools which also charged fees.[18] Redland High School had entered into this arrangement in the past because it needed Government money to survive. As a result of the 1944 Education Act and the forthcoming anticipated rise in population the Ministry of Education was pressing for some schools to become Government-owned with all places required for local allocation.[19] As is often the case, a situation is reported on, that is, pupil numbers were declining, and, 'How was Redland High School to survive?' When implementation time comes the situation has changed and a take-over by the Government is no longer seen as an option.

In February 1945 Miss Peters was present at a parents' meeting where they were addressed by the Deputy Director of Education for Bristol and Professor Basil Fletcher, Professor of Education at the University of Bristol. The main agenda was whether or not the School should continue with the Direct Grant scheme and risk being taken over completely by the Local Education Authority, becoming a Government-owned school, or to go down the alternative route of becoming fully independent.[20]

An archival document which survives appears to contradict the agenda for going down the alternative route. In June 1945 a letter was sent to the Ministry of Education for the continuation of Redland High School as a Direct Grant School.[21] Later in the month an Extraordinary Meeting of the shareholders was called because it was realised that to go down the path of a Government-owned school there would be more scholarship places and fewer fee-paying pupils and this would affect the right of shareholders to nominate pupils.[22] The Council's rationale behind relinquishing the Direct Grant may have been because a mortgage on the School's buildings was only £4,000 with a yearly interest of £180 and with a rise in numbers since 1942 income had exceeded expenditure.[23] There appeared to be little to recommend a 'take over' by the Local Education Authority. Many wealthy Councillors gave generously to the school and their bequests enabled the school to have additional facilities which they may not have chosen to give if the School had become a Government School.

At an Extraordinary Meeting held on 13 March 1946 the Council decided to apply to the Ministry of Education for the School to become a Recognised Independent School with a tapering grant for seven years to ensure no girl who had been admitted to the Direct Grant School should suffer if they had difficulty with affording the fees.[24] In restricting the entry of the eleven-plus scholarship winners from Government schools, the top 10% of children, Miss Peters recognised she might lose some children who would credit the School in the future. A bursary fund was launched to assist parents of able girls who might not be able to afford the school fees.[25] A parents' meeting was held in February 1946 and after listening to Professor Fletcher's argument for Redland High School to become an Independent School, 97% of parents voted for independence, although Miss Peters stressed she had not taken an appointment for an Independent School.[26] Scholarship girls had proven in the past their worth to the School as shown by their high achievements in the external examinations.

It was rumoured the eleven-plus scholarship would be phased out for entry in September 1945 but this was revoked and a parent, whose child was awarded a bursary with fees paid supposedly terminating in Fifth Year, turned it down in favour of the 11 plus, Government Scholarship with fees paid through to the Sixth Form. The child was reminded by Miss Peters of the inconvenience of the rejection and questionnaire responses from pupils included comments 'terrified of her', 'hated her', 'was in awe of her', although it was also reported 'in some instances she listened and offered advice'. Despite having a few unhappy memories, Old Girls who answered the questionnaire maintained Redland High School had offered them an excellent education.

The School had carried on well through the difficult war years and the effects of rationing of food and limited resource materials. In 1950 at a Staff meeting, Miss Peters reminded the Staff about wasting paper, switching off lights and gas, and the need to economise.[27] Miss Peters was instrumental in following the demands made by the Inspectors for Junior School accommodation. Number 1 Grove Park was purchased in 1947 from the Kemp family for £8,907.[28] The Kemp family of boys had attended Redland High School in the 1880s and 1890s and a family daughter also attended, leaving in 1926.

44. 1949. 1st Eleven Hockey team. Captain, Ann Cox, also Head Girl

The school kitchen was reorganised with ex-military equipment supplied by the Ministry of Health and was able to provide hot dinners at a cost of eight pence each for 400 children per day, although some children preferred to take a packed lunch and others living nearby had lunch at home. Half-penny, and later, penny buns, were on sale at morning break. Losses of money and purses were sometimes reported and instructions given, 'Keep your purse on your PERSON!' This led to the fashion of wearing an 'over the shoulder' small leather purse or having a zippered, skirt pocket.

In 1948/9 the balustrade of the terrace and steps were repaired with hand-cut stone at a cost of £3,000, also the roof and chimney stack which had been hit by lightning, and attention was paid to the main staircase after it was discovered wood beetles were destroying the timber.[29] The School was fortunate to have the services of another architect, Mr Ralph Brentnall, who had commenced his training with Sir George Oatley and later in 1950/51 he became the official School architect for the School. Both his wife and daughter attended Redland High School.

The next building project undertaken in 1949 was the enlargement of the domestic science room and the change over from a classroom, room 19, to a craft room linked to the art room. A parallel class with domestic subjects as the main objective had been suggested by the Inspectors for those girls not pursuing an academic career. The craft room became the hub for theatre costumes and props with storage for dyes and printing inks.

In the questionnaire the ranking for art was not very high and was due to the limited facilities and what was thought by some to have been 'poor teaching'. Unfortunately some girls chose to misbehave and there was deliberate upturning of patty pans containing the powdered paint.[30] For those girls with 'home grown' talent there was encouragement to continue with the subject area of art in the Sixth

Form which was greatly enhanced when the study of the 'History of Art' became part of the examination in the newly introduced Advanced Level.

Miss Taylor left Redland High School in 1954 to become an HMI for the teaching of art in schools. Her place was taken by Miss Stannard who had trained at Bath Academy of Art, Corsham. Competition for entry to Bath Academy of Art was highly competitive with only thirty places awarded each year from the whole of England. Three girls from Redland High School, during Miss Peter's time, the first in 1952, were awarded places. There is a record of a visit to the School by Mr Clifford Ellis, the Academy's Principal.

The newly introduced 'O' levels and 'A' levels of the General and Advanced Certificates of Education were welcomed as they introduced a higher standard of achievement. By 1962 in every subject at O level the percentage of passes was up to the same average as the Direct Grant Schools although Redland was now not one of these and only admitted a range of pupils who could afford the fees of an independent school.[31] The School was small in comparison with Government High Schools and pupil numbers were only 427 girls over the age of eleven years. In 1959 the Direct Grant List was re-opened and Redland High School was re-admitted which meant a large number of girls were applying for entrance to the Middle School and if accepted would complete their studies in 1966-1967.

In 1950 the school buildings were rewired, central heating installed, two new tennis courts were constructed on the wartime site of the static water tank and a Middle School library was established. A stream which flowed underneath the historic building which had supplied water to the well was finally diverted enabling use of the cellars for classrooms, cloakrooms and storage.[32] These works were carried out under the direction of Mr Ralph Brentnall who could now discuss future plans for the promised

gymnasium and the building of a second-storey over the Gamble science building. Mr George Oatley had designed a flat roof for this purpose and his design, a modern 'art deco' style, had caused debate amongst the Councillors. A conventional building with a pitched roof would have been costly to enlarge.

Although alterations were carried out in the main building two wooden buildings were still in use for music and a Form Room. Replies to the questionnaire indicated pupils were unhappy with these conditions and felt cold in winter and hot in summer. In 1952 the central heating system which had been causing further problems was finally overhauled at a cost of £3,200. The Sixth Form was moved constantly, occupying the room overlooking the Dutch garden vacated when accommodation was found for the Kindergarten and also the use of room numbers 5 and 6, or 1 and 2, and even the cellar, called rooms 20 and 21. At one stage the physics laboratory was a classroom in name only with possessions housed in metal cabinets some of which had locks and others not and as a consequence text-books and schoolwork went missing, causing distress.

A new floor in the Assembly Hall was laid in 1952/3 and Miss Peters was concerned that stiletto heels would damage the wooden, parquetry flooring and she banned the walking on the floor with heeled shoes. For assembly the Staff sat on chairs on the stage behind Miss Peters. Extra platforms were used for theatre productions. Miss Peters wished to have a Staff play every year. At a Staff Meeting the art teacher, Miss Taylor, expressed her concern at the time taken to make sets and costumes and said she would prefer it bi-yearly.[33]

In 1951 Miss Charlton and Miss Milton, who taught mathematics, published a book on the historic aspects of the area and the building of the Georgian mansion. One of the outcomes of this publication was a written account by every girl in IIIB and an appreciation of the Georgian building. In response to the question 'How did attendance at a school housed in an historic building affect you?' replies included 'sustained an interest in old buildings', 'I was lucky to be there, special feeling', 'loved everything antique', 'moved quietly around the corridors'.

Miss Peters's overall plan was to have everything in place for the School's seventieth birthday in 1952. A black-and-white film was made (available on video). The Bishop of Colchester preached at the Thanksgiving Service in the Cathedral and a supper was held on the terrace. The Old Girls gave the School the eighteenth-century Hepplewhite and Chippendale chairs for the front hall and a lectern bible was given by the girls, restored in 2010. A chandelier, silver salver, silver rose bowl and an eighteenth-century hall clock were presented by the Staff.[34] The clock was stolen in the 1990s. The entrance hall became a 'genteel' place to rest and to take in the atmosphere of

45. 1952. 70th Anniversary. Entrance Hall. Hepplewhite and Chippendale chairs donated by the Old Girls' Association. Chandelier and clock donated by the Staff

eighteenth-century living although for some girls it meant an anxious wait to see Miss Peters when the electrically-operated buttons changed from 'WAIT' to 'WAIT 5 MINUTES' or 'ENTER'.

Miss Peters was instrumental, at the cost of £850, in involving the School and Miss Hill in the new Nuffield Science which was of an exploratory nature for physics and chemistry learning, as part of the 'new approach to science' through the Nuffield Foundation. Redland High School also contributed to 'new' methodologies for the teaching of languages using the latest technology of audio-visual interaction with a French school.[35] In 1955 a second-storey was added to the Gamble science wing for a geography laboratory and a music room at a cost of £20,500. The building was officially opened by Sir Oliver Franks in 1956.[36] In 1956 the School was inspected by representatives from the Ministry of Education and the report issued in 1957.[37]

An ex-pupil described the involvement with drama, as, 'the school bristled with dramatic activity'. As well as the high-quality productions by the Staff, *A Quiet Weekend*, *Alice in Wonderland*, *Julius Caesar*, with Miss Peters playing that role, the School took on ambitious productions requiring girls to take men's roles in the chosen plays, for example, King Richard and Bolingbroke, in Shakespeare's *Richard II*, and The Chorus in *Antigone*, Hector, in *A Tiger at the Gates*, or Sir Thomas More, in *A Man for all Seasons*. The first two productions took place in the Assembly Hall which offered limited floor space. The later productions benefitted from having a marvellous stage and changing facilities in the new gymnasium. In addition, House dramatics offered parts to girls who would otherwise not have had the opportunity to participate.

Other pupils were involved in costume and stage sets often re-using 'flats' from previous productions. For the production of *Antigone*, a pair of bronze doors were required and were painted on the 'flats' laid out in different areas of the school buildings. When the 'flats' were hung on the stage on the evening of the performance the two doors did not match as the highlights were upside down on one of the panels. One of the Sixth Form girls involved in their production stayed after school to paint over and repaint the highlights and only just managed to finish before the audience arrived. For the Shakespeare production the design of the front panel of a female costume was taken from an illustration in a book on miniatures which had been used for a Sixth Form research topic in the alternative English course. Miss Taylor, the art teacher involved the Sixth Form girls in costume production and many new textile techniques were introduced, for example, painting the edges of the design with paraffin oil in order for the dyes to take up the pattern on the silk material. Stencilling, block-printing with lino cuts, and hand-painting were used for surface designs as silk-screening techniques were unknown in the school's art department at that time.

Music performance was also encouraged and there were concerts for parents, solo performances, choir, and orchestra at assemblies and Prize Givings. Although small and relatively in-experienced, members of the orchestra were encouraged to play their instruments with Staff members of a more professional standard giving simple renditions of Mozart. Later developments included wind instruments with one pupil returning as an Old Girl to teach the clarinet. House music concerts involved solo piano performances from girls who learnt a musical instrument out of school hours with private tuition and a tremendous amount of talent was shown. The School's music talents were used for drama productions. Miss Knowleden, a Senior member of the music staff was well known for her choir performances on special occasions and remained on the Staff for many years. She also taught singing and on one occasion when teaching pupils an Elizabethan song, 'Flora gave me fairest flowers, these I laid on Phyllis's bowers' she told the class that she had learnt this song when she was at school and her class had laughed because a girl in their class was called Phyllis BOWERS. As music teaching became more professional, playing in the School's orchestra led to playing in the Secondary Schools' Orchestra and acceptance in the National Youth Orchestra.

Enrolment of boys had ceased and numbers in 1956 were five hundred and sixty-six, with sixty-one pupils in the Sixth Form. Sixth Form numbers were down from the eighty of the two previous years and this was attributed to an increase in the term fees to twenty-nine guineas (£30 9s 0d) in the Senior School and twenty-six guineas (£27 6s 0d) in the Junior School. Bursaries were offered at half-fee reductions. Eighteen girls had entered University and thirty-two had entered Teachers' Colleges. There had been a high number of girls leaving at the age of sixteen to enter the nursing profession, secretarial and clerical training. Other areas of training included Art Schools and Domestic Science Colleges.[38] One girl had been accepted as an engineering student but for most the ultimate goal was to become a teacher, a nurse, or a secretary or to enter the academic field to become a scientist, a doctor, a linguist, or

46. Left: 1959 Junior School winter uniform
47. Right: 1966 Senior School summer uniform

perhaps a lawyer, in areas previously reserved for men. Miss Peters decided that entry to the Sixth Form was expressed as, 'has the ability to profit'.[39]

The Inspectors noted the purchase of a house for the Junior School and were impressed with the development of the Gamble science wing to include a second-storey providing toilet facilities, two classrooms, geography room, and a music room. The release of the room shared for geography and biology was now to be used for biology only. The music room was a gift from Miss K. G. Robinson in memory of her sister, Miss F. Robinson, a previous Councillor. Despite these improvements the Inspectors were still critical of the lack of a gymnasium and the use of the Assembly Hall for meetings, gymnastics, and even a dining-room. Staff facilities were noted as being cramped and cloakrooms were seen as over-crowded without adequate hand-basins The facilities for art and craft were still seen as inadequate.[40]

The curriculum included the usual Grammar School subjects with a choice in the second year between Latin, German, or domestic science which continued into the following years where sets were decided for mathematics and French and division of the sciences. In the Fourth and Fifth years a special form was made for the home science group to follow a different curriculum and a new approach in selection of either history or geography. An unusual feature of the Inspectors' Report is the inclusion of Miss Peter's point of view concerning the education of 'her' girls.[41]

They gave the work of the school unusually high praise, singling out those girls who did individual work based on experimentation and exploration of original sources ... related work in different fields of study ... we wanted our girls to face a world which would be different from the one we knew.[42]
Miss S. Peters, Headmistress.

In July 1960 plans were drawn up for the building of a new gymnasium complete with showers and changing-rooms. This facility had been requested by the Inspectors as being necessary for the development of the School. One Inspector had commented on the removal of skirts and tunics to reveal green knickers worn for gymnastics. A square-necked, white short-sleeved blouse was also changed into in front of the Form Class. With the new gym facilities any embarrassing situations could be eliminated, although as it turned out girls were reluctant to use communal showers and changing facilities. Included in the new building project were new staff rooms, cloakroom and office.

The brochure for the Appeal, with an attractive architectural drawing of the proposed building and photographs of the interior of the eighteenth-century building was ready in April 1961 and the Appeal set at £75,000. Some people fought against these 'improvements' but although seemingly a large parcel of land in the residential suburb, the Council were restricted in 'how' and 'where' they could build as extensions to the fabric of the old building were not permitted. The only way was to build sideways and upwards, and to keep a watch on nearby houses which might come up for sale.

Generous gifts of funds were made by Councillors, as in the past, the Dulverton Trust, the Old Girls, industry, parents and by Alderman Harry Crook, his wife being an Old Girl. The Parents' Association worked very hard on organising fund-raising events. The new buildings were opened by Lord Franks in June, 1964. Miss Peters had gathered a number of notable people from Bristol and other universities, the Arts Council, and historic families with past links to the school, the Franks, the Falks, and the Robinsons to help develop her ambitious plans for the Redland High School. Miss Peters was ably assisted by a succession of Chairmen, the Rev. K. Parry, Mrs George Falk and Mr Wynne Wilson.

48. 1964. Interior and exterior of the new gymnasium and sports hall

In October 1964 representatives from the School and Miss Peters joined in the march in protest against the Local Authority's proposal to abolish Grammar Schools and were interviewed on television.[43] In the local weekend newspaper Miss Peters was interviewed about the role of the Headmistress at Redland High School. She questioned the interviewer by saying the question should be, 'Not what I think the aim of general education IS, but what I think it OUGHT TO BE'.

I can say it is our business to help children to develop into sensitive, thoughtful, well-balanced people with a desire to find out, to discover things. I don't think we are educating them to pass exams but to give them the tools to go on learning all their lives.[44]
Miss Sylvia Peters, Headmistress.

In 1966 the Council bought 10 Woodstock Road for £2,500, the house the School had wanted to buy many years ago. This was planned to be used as a Sixth Form Centre and a craft facility and conversion was estimated to cost £8,750.[45] Finances were again tight and expenditure exceeded income by £3,972.[46] New buildings reached a total of £40,600 and repairs, £3,751. After the Colston's Girls' High School became an Independent School, Redland was paying two-fifths of the rent for the shared sports field at a cost of £1,250 and was not allowed to have a Redland High School sign at the entrance even though a visiting school hockey team had been unsure about the venue and had complained.[47]

By the time the Direct Grant recipients had reached the Sixth Form the Ordinary level results were outstanding and showed 100% passes in mathematics, general science, Greek and Latin and over 90% passes in English, English Literature, French, Nuffield Physics. There were successes at Advanced level and entries to Oxford and Cambridge and eighteen entrances to other universities.[48] Miss Peters saw these results as a result of the acceptance and opportunity given to Direct Grant recipients and their tuition by dedicated and highly-qualified Staff members.

Miss Peters met all girls when they came to her to buy their hat badges and in an earlier period every girl was handed her school report personally, as she passed through the front door to commence her holidays. If the queue slowed down it was because a girl was either receiving an accolade or a dressing down! Discipline and punishments were part of everyday life. Strict rules of lady-like behaviour at all times were obeyed.

I let them see the things we mind about in this School. Hard work. Awareness of what is going on around them, awareness of service to the community from which they are getting so much. We felt it was the business of a girls' school to encourage the development of sensitive, eager, thoughtful and adaptable people who would be good wives and mothers and who would also have some training for work in the wider community. We tried to educate by asking challenging and stimulating questions and by encouraging the girls to develop into the kind of people who would go on asking questions and who would be prepared to go to some trouble to find the answers in a rapidly changing world.[49]
Miss Sylvia Peters, Headmistress.

Similar goals had presented in the 1880s by Miss Cocks and who addressed the 'spirit of motherhood' and at the same time embraced 'educated girls'. Margaret Scott (née Russell), became a successful writer and broadcaster in Australia and in her semi-autobiographical novel *Changing Countries* wrote: *Miss Peters corralled the girls she wanted, separating the sheep from the goats.* Margaret Scott died in 2004. Academic achievement was high on the list of Miss Peters's priorities. Miss Peters's ambition to have a successful school after the difficult period of the Second World War, was achieved through her determination to provide the 'very best' of everything, commencing with new staff, new buildings and new educational thought.

In 1966 the uniform was changed and the green and white gingham-material dresses were replaced by a choice of 'dirndl' skirts, skirts gathered at the waist, in strong colours of turquoise, red, or russet brown, worn with a white open-necked blouse. Ties and hats were no longer part of the uniform although the green blazer and daisy emblem remained.

Miss Peters retired in 1968 after twenty-three years of service to the School and her place was taken by Miss Storm Hume. Many tributes were paid to Miss Peters after her death in 1982, the year when Redland High School celebrated its one-hundredth Anniversary.

Miss Peters was a woman of high expectations, the girls knew that only their best was acceptable. She knew every girl's name although many did not realise it until they left.
Old Girl's tribute to Miss Peters.

The word 'nice' should only be used for rice pudding.
Miss S. Peters, Headmistress.

NOTES

1   Bungay, J., 1982. *Redland High School, 1882-1982.* Council of Redland High School. p.117.
2   Chitty, C., 2004. *Education Policy in Britain.* Basingstoke: Macmillan. p.18.
3   ibid. pp.20-21.
4   Avery, G., 1991. *The Best Type of Girl. A History of Girls' Independent Schools.* London: Andre Deutsch. p.61.
5   Ministry of Education, 1944. *Report by H.M. Inspectors of Redland High School for Girls, Bristol.* Redland High School Archive. p.2 (nyc).
6   ibid. p.3.
7   ibid. p.2.
8   ibid. p.2.
9   ibid. p.6.
10 ibid. p.8.
11 ibid. p.8.
12 ibid. p.9.
13 Redland High School, 1950. *Minutes of Staff Meetings.* Redland High School Archive (nyc).
14 Ministry of Education, 1944. *Report by H.M. Inspectors of Redland High School for Girls, Bristol.* Redland High School Archive. p.4 (nyc).
15 ibid. p.10.
16 ibid. p.11.
17 ibid. p.20.
18 Bungay, J., 1982. *Redland High School, 1882-1982.* Council of Redland High School. p.117.
19 ibid. p.117.
20 ibid. p.117.
21 Redland High School, 1913-1958. *Shareholders Minute Book.* Redland High School Archive. BB 139. p.109.
22 ibid. p.109.
23 Ministry of Education, 1956. *Report by H.M. Inspectors of Redland High School for Girls, Bristol.* p.2 (nyc).
24 Redland High School, 1913-1958. *Shareholders Minute Book.* Redland High School Archive. BB 139. p.112.
25 Bungay, J., 1982. *Redland High School, 1982-1982.* Council of Redland High School. p.118.
26 ibid. p.117.
27 Redland High School, 1950. *Minutes of Staff Meetings.* Redland High School Archive (nyc).

28 Redland High School, 1913-1958. *Shareholders Minute Book.* Redland High School Archive. BB 139. p.120.
29 Bungay, J., 1982. *Redland High School, 1882-1982.* Council of Redland High School, p.118.
30 Redland High School, 2004. *Redland High School Old Girls' Guild Magazine.* Redland High School Archive. pp. 23-25 (nyc).
31 Redland High School, 1913-1958. *Shareholders Minute Book.* Redland High School Archive BB139.
32 Bungay, J., 1982. *Redland High School, 1882-1982.* Council of Redland High School, p.118.
33 Redland High School, 1950. *Minutes of Staff Meetings.* Redland High School Archive (nyc).
34 Bungay, J., 1982. *Redland High School, 1882-1982.* Council of Redland High School, p122.
35 ibid. p.121.
36 ibid. p.119.
37 Ministry of Education, 1956. *Report by H.M. Inspectors of Redland High School for Girls, Bristol* Archive (nyc).
38 ibid.
39 Redland High School, 1950. *Minutes of Staff Meetings.* Redland High School Archive (nyc).
40 Ministry of Education, 1956. *Report by H.M. Inspectors of Redland High School for Girls, Bristol* Archive (nyc).
41 ibid.
42 ibid.
43 *Western Daily Press,* October, 1964.
44 Redland High School, 2003 *Redland High School Old Girls' Guild, Newsletter.* p.40 (taken from Bristol Weekend, 1964) Redland High School Archive (nyc).
45 Redland High School, 1950. *Minutes of Staff Meetings.* Redland High School Archive (nyc).
46 Ministry of Education, 1956. *Report by H.M. Inspectors of Redland High School for Girls, Bristol.* Archive (nyc).
46 Redland High School, 1950. *Minutes of Staff Meetings.* Redland High School Archive (nyc).
47 Redland High School, 1913-1958. *Shareholders Minute Book.* Redland High School Archive. BB139.
48 Redland High School, 2003. *Redland High School Old Girls' Guild, Newsletter.* p.40 (taken from Bristol Weekend, 1964) Redland High School Archive. SN24.
49 Redland High School, 1982. *Day's Eye.* Redland High School Archive (nyc).

8

1969-1985 LABOUR TO CONSERVATIVE MRS THATCHER, PRIME MINISTER. CHANGES IN EDUCATION POLICIES

The reputation of the School had never been higher under the guidance of Miss Peters who strove for academic excellence and made pupils aware of the responsibilities of citizenship.

In 1960 the School had been able to borrow money, albeit only £20,000, through the Charities Commission, set up in 1960. Previous purchases and conveyances, titles to land, including Redland Court, land (playing fields) at Druid Stoke, 1 Grove Park and 10 Woodstock Road provided security for borrowing. In 1970 the Direct Grant system came under increasing attack from a Labour Government. Redland High School was left with two alternatives, to close the School or to become fully independent as it had done in the past. Following the Dennison Report the School could only become independent if the annual fees were set at £210 for the Junior School and up to £220 for the Senior School, a rise of over fifty to sixty pounds.

In 1972 annual fees were subjected to an increase, £162 for the Senior School and £161 for the Junior School, not quite as high as the initial estimates necessary for sustainability.

Mr Croxton Smith, Clerk to the Council, entered into negotiation with the Charities Commission for borrowing money, because *We are not likely to be offered a place in the Maintained School System…because there are already more places in schools than there are pupils to fill them.* Another foreseen problem was the losing of Charity status which would enable the Government to inherit any property the School owned. In 1974 an Independent

Schools Joint Committee had been set up to safeguard Independent Schools' land ownership and development.

Further to this was the introduction of the Sex Discrimination Bill and whether or not single-sex schools would be allowed to operate. Along with this was the employment of both male and female teachers under the rule of 'discrimination'. Securing the interests of the School to remain single-sex was under constant review. One of the Council's main concerns was that the loss of the Direct Grant should not prevent children of promise from attending the School and in 1976 an appeal was made for bursaries.[1]

In 1975 Margaret Thatcher was elected as Leader of the Conservative Party. Previously, in 1970 she had become Secretary of State for Education and Science and was remembered for 'no more free milk' for school-children. During her leadership and from 1979 onwards until 2000, thirty Education Acts were passed and a new emphasis was placed on choice, competition and parental control of schools.

Even the very concept of a 'national system, locally administered' was being called into question in an attempt to break with the past.[2]

As has been shown in the previous chapters the School was always in a position of wanting to make improvements which cost money. Some of the demands to add additional facilities were made by the Inspectors indicating the School should be offering specialist subjects. In November 1979 the Council applied to the Charities Commission for extension of their

9. Water-colour painting of Redland Court by Fanny Sarah Hodges (née Martin), 1808-c.1875.
Purchased by Redland High School, 2010, from family estate.
The Martin family are related to the Innys family. Martha Innys married John Cossins.
Photograph courtesy of RHS Development Office, 2010

10. Redland High School, Assembly Hall, built in 1894 by the Cowlin Building Company.
Carved wood panel, with motto, donated by the girls in 1905 to celebrate the School's 21st Anniversary.
Photograph courtesy of RHS Development Office, 2006

11. Dutch garden. Established in the Elizabethan period and part of a previous
Manor House before the building of Redland Court.
Photograph courtesy of RHS Development Office, 2008

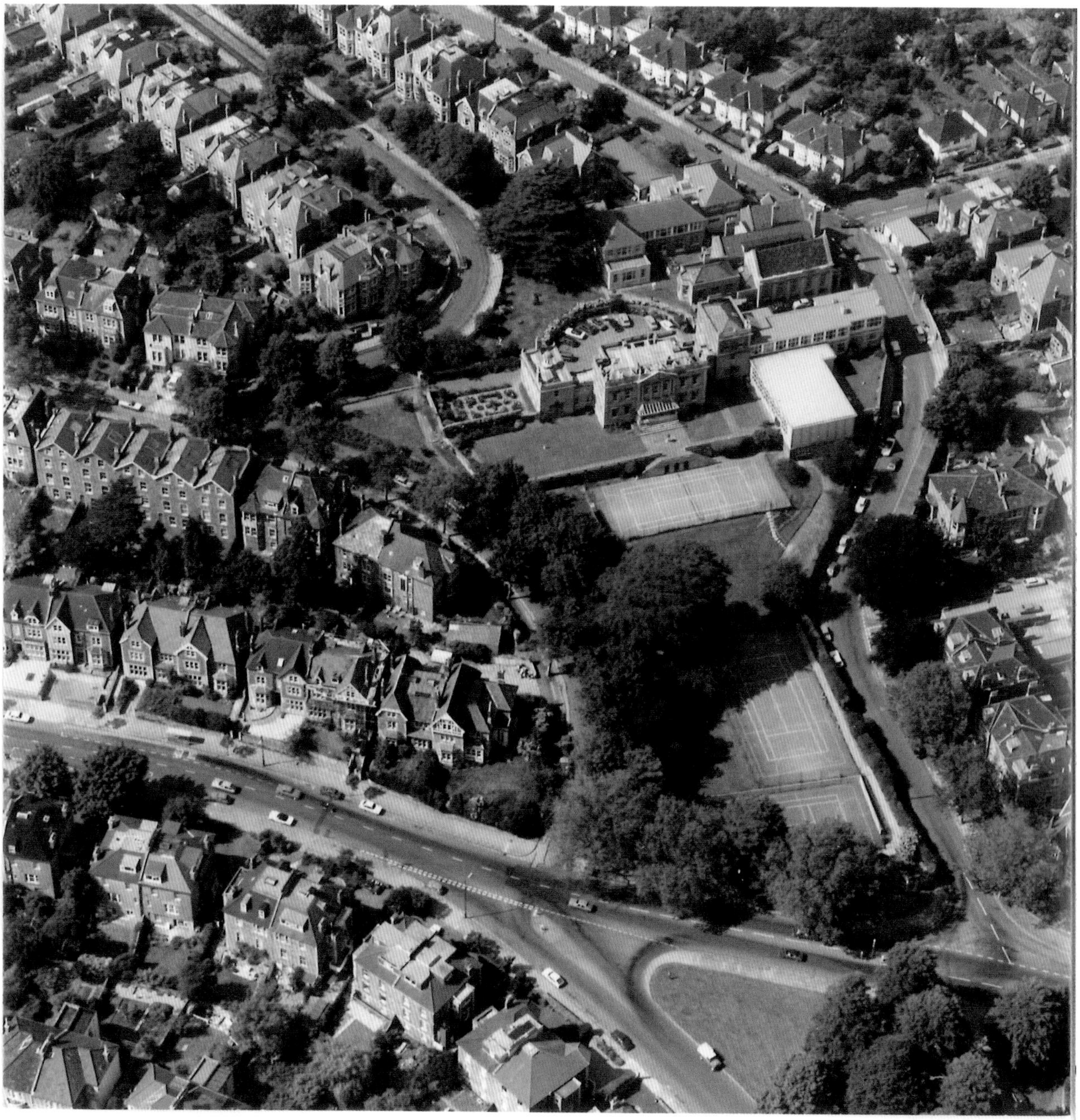

12. Aerial view of the district of Redland, showing Redland High School with new flat-roofed gymnasium and buildings. c.1986.
Photograph courtesy of the RHS Archival Collection

13. Redland High Junior School. Situated at Redland Grove/Redland Road.
Photograph courtesy of RHS Development Office, 2009

14. Side entrance. Hand-wrought, iron gate. Designed and constructed by Nathaniel Arthur, c.1740.
Photograph courtesy of RHS School Development Office, 2008

15. East wing, interior staircase, Redland Court.
Photograph courtesy of RHS School Development Office, 2008

16. Entrance hall, Redland Court. Furniture given by the Old Girls for
the School's 70th Anniversary in 1952.
Photographer Heather Kent, 2008

£35,000 loan to £90,000. The reason given was that the School was moving from the Direct Grant to full Independence and was in need of capital allowance. Later this was amended to £100,000 following the increase in teachers' salaries under the Burnham Award and repayments guaranteed with an increase in fees, the number of fee paying pupils and the intended Centenary Appeal to be launched in 1982. The loan was granted with the provision it be paid back within 12 years. Once again in the history of the School finances were traded and bought often on a precarious footing. However, investments in property – Redland Court in 1884, land at Parry's Lane in 1904, 1 Grove Park and 10 Woodstock Road – were to prove their worth when the value increased and land which belonged to the School could be sold.[3]

MISS STORM HUME
(Headmistress 1969-1985)

Miss Storm Hume, MA (Cambridge) was appointed from the Newcastle-on-Tyne Girls' Public Day School Trust School and she brought 'modern' changes. The past decade had seen opportunities afforded to Redland High School pupils and now the 'Roaring Sixties' heralded 'out with the old, in with the new' in a break with traditions. The Parents' Association formed in 1941 was discontinued and became the Friends of Redland High School with a broader membership and two parents were invited to join the Council.[4] The Sixth Form and Staff ceased to elect prefects in the belief that all Sixth Formers sharing the same privileges should share the same responsibilities. However, the responsibilities were left to a few. The 'all involved' policy was later changed to 'one girl elected as Head Girl, with seven Committee Members'.

In 1970 Houses ceased to be part of the School as extra curricular activities were replaced by clubs and the Duke of Edinburgh's Award Scheme. In 1973 there was agitation to restore the House system and a trial period commenced with new Houses under the names of two colours, Red and Yellow, which were seen as an avenue to unite girls of different ages. Four Houses were assigned the names of Innys, Cossins, Baker and Vaughan in memory of the owners of Redland Court.[5] After a year's trial the usefulness of Houses was discussed and the plan dropped. The music pupils reported they did not have enough time to prepare for inter-house music performances.

In 1971 Miss Edith Bancroft, one of the first pupils, died at the age of 101 years just a year before the School's ninetieth Anniversary in 1972. The Anniversary was the first notable event during Miss Hume's time as Headmistress. Miss Hume, the Staff and the girls dressed for the celebration in period costume of the 1880s. The photographs of this event are reminiscent of the early archival examples, such was the effort by everyone to 'get it right'. Boaters seem to have been easy to obtain and white sheets were easily converted to long tennis-dresses. Miss Hume dressed as a headmistress of the 1880s and cut the iced, birthday-cake decorated with a daisy-design. The Old Girls also celebrated the occasion with a birthday-cake and a toast was proposed by Mrs Joanne Spencer (née Franks), an Old Girl herself, reminding those present of the School motto *So hateth she derkness,* as darkness bred fear, and fear bred violence.[6]

In 1972 it was reported in the Council Minutes that the two portraits of Mr and Mrs John Cossins were cleaned once again. Smoking was not banned for the Staff and many were heavy smokers and may have been the cause of the build-up of surface staining. The cleaning was not well done.

1973 saw the last of the School Prize Giving, a decision which came through the Council electing not to give prizes for academic achievement with a new style for the Cathedral Commemoration Service.[7] In 1974 after finishing O levels pupils were encouraged to take up voluntary work with children or other members of the community, thus giving them an insight as to the direction their lives might take in the fields of nursing, teaching and social work.[8]

In 1975 a statement was issued by the Council:

> The Council at their meeting on June 5, 1975, decided to continue to run Redland High School as a Direct Grant School so long as their status is open to us and thereafter as an Independent School.
>
> The removal of the Direct Grant status by Westminster and the inability of the Avon Authority to offer any sort of integration or collaboration within their programme have left us with only the two alternatives.
>
> a. to close the School.
>
> b. to become fully Independent.
>
> The Council considered to close the School would be a breach of trust with the founders, our predecessors, the Headmistress and Staff...and parents who have shown confidence in the School.[9]

An appeal for money for Bursaries was launched in 1976. £56,000 was raised by this appeal and an annual sum of £20,000 was given by John James, philanthropist, (£200,000 over ten years). Eighty-three bursaries were awarded to the Senior School over a period of four years.[10]

A Special Committee was set up in 1977 to look at the idea of amalgamation with another school, which the Committee rejected, and to consider the issues of:

a. that Redland should continue as a single-sex school.

b. that Redland should become co-educational.[11]

Committees, with representatives at all levels, debated the proposals over a period of ten months and the conclusion reached was that Redland should keep a close watch on educational developments in Bristol and changes in other schools. There was even debate on the historical aspects of the Junior School having been co-educational until the 1940s implying this had worked in the past. The Council was fortunate in having the Rev. Rupert Davies as Chairman as a positive decision-maker.

In 1976 the School produced Benjamin Britten's opera *Noye's Fludde* which involved 200 participants, including musicians, and was part of the School's contribution to the fund-raising appeal which had begun through a School Fête with other organised sales and a Beetle Drive which raised £14.[12]

In 1977 Professor Andrew Robertson died. As an engineer and a Councillor he had given much time and expertise to the restoration of the historic building and on new buildings making sure that 'good' decisions would enhance the School's profile.[13]

In 1979 a new home economics unit had been erected and equipped and the room used previously was converted into a classroom. As has been seen previously there was still juggling for room-space. With a change of Government in November 1980 to the Conservatives the Education Regulations (Assisted Places) came into operation. Discussion at Council level took place concerning the debate over cuts in Government spending at a time of recession, all too familiar in 2011. It was decided to accept the Government's offer and in 1981 twenty-four girls were either entering with a Bursary, a John James Scholarship or an Assisted Place.[14] The art department moved into their new premises and the 'old' art rooms reused for the Sixth Form. The ceramic area became a pleasant Sixth Form study and the basement turned into a new cloakroom. Even the old Sixth Form cloakroom was turned in a laboratory for small Sixth Form, teaching groups.

The School continued to have long-standing members of Staff. Miss Mawle had been Head of history for thirty-two years. Old Girls were returning as Staff members. Miss Audrey Shepherd returned to teach mathematics and she noted the change in the number of girls taking applied mathematics compared to when she was a pupil at the School. Mrs Burkett also retired after eighteen years in the Junior School. Miss Russell, who taught mathematics, retired in 1977. Other long-standing Staff who retired were Miss Hill, Miss Fleure and Miss Hampton. Miss Knowleden had left in 1975. Miss Stannard, the art teacher, left in 1980 after twenty-eight years as Head of the art department.

The School had been involved since 1971 in the Duke of Edinburgh's award. By 1979 one hundred and seventy girls had gained Bronze Awards and fifty-eight girls had gained Silver Awards. Thirty-one girls had completed the Gold Award and had visited the Lake District and in 1979 a group visited the Isle of Skye.[15]

In 1979 a list of entrances to universities, colleges of education and training shows a continuation of Redland High School's successes in the academic field with girls gaining entry to Oxford to study physics and Cambridge to study natural sciences.

The continuation of girls studying science and forging careers in medicine was being upheld. New areas of further study were broadened with placements at agricultural college and in town and country planning. There was a 90% pass rate for Ordinary level results. Seventeen girls, an incredible number, studied physics.[16] In 1980 there was a 91% pass rate for the Advanced level and an 85% pass rate for Ordinary level. Numbers of girls studying the sciences was high with twenty-six girls studying chemistry. An additional subject at Ordinary level was Swahili/Afrikaans with two students.

Visits to Bordeaux continued with 1,200 children travelling from Avon schools and the exchange scheme celebrated its twenty-fifth anniversary. The link with Marburg was a school-exchange. The visits gave English children the opportunity to be involved with the culture of another country and to practise language skills. Exchanges were ongoing with the schools in Bordeaux and Marburg and involved thirty or so girls going to Bordeaux and over twenty girls going to Marburg. Lifelong friendships were formed and even marriages!

In 1980/81 the eight-lesson day was introduced in order for clubs to operate in the lunch-time. The School was for ever grateful for the benefits of the John James legacy and in return the School looked after the interests of elderly people and young children through visits and entertainment.

Under Miss Hume's guidance it was decided to allow girls in the Sixth Form to attend in day clothes although the wearing of a school uniform was compulsory up to, and including, the Fifth Form. The wearing of hats and ties had been phased out. In 1978 summer frocks of yellow and green check material with dark-green collar, or alternative frocks of a dark-green or a very pale-green material, had replaced the coloured skirts and white blouse. School visits included Wimbledon, the Tate Gallery and an art camp at a school study-centre near Lyme Regis organised by the art master, Mr John Icke appointed after Miss Stannard's retirement. Some of the drawings of Lyme Regis were reproduced in the magazine, Day's Eye.[17]

1982 was the year for the celebration of the School's one hundredth Anniversary and a Centenary Appeal was launched. School numbers had risen to 600 with thirty-four full-time teaching members of Staff. Inadequate facilities existed for the Junior School and library facilities for Senior girls and two temporary buildings had orders on them for removal. Of upmost importance was the need for a music centre as music, along with theatre arts and drama, provided girls with opportunities for their future development. In 1979 four new pianos had been purchased and the Senior orchestra practised with Cotham Grammar School and some girls were members of the County of Avon Schools' Orchestra, with performances in the Colston Hall. The Secondary Schools' Orchestra had toured Norway and Germany in the 1970s. The County of Avon Schools' Orchestra, of which Redland High School was a part, toured the Gulf States in 1981 and again in 1984. In drama productions the girls learnt to take a male role with a convincing performance as a sixteenth-century Spanish cavalier in the production of *The Royal Hunt of the Sun*.

The School had excelled itself in the sporting area being the finalists in the English Schools' Netball competition from 1974-1978.

The School had acquired 98 Redland Road next to the Junior School building, 1 Grove Park and plans were in place to link the two together, releasing space in the Senior School. Of utmost importance was the need for a computer centre and an extended library to house and show video-tapes. The amount needed for the alterations was £110,000 for Phase 1. Phase 2 would require a further £70,000 and would involve creating a 'Centenary Library' within the building area of the existing library or to develop a second-storey building within the framework of the 1904 building. Phase 3 was the planning for a music and art centre within the main complex, or in an adjacent house. The estimate of this cost was £70,000. Subscriptions to the appeal were asked for under a deed of covenant, so that tax could be recoverable.[18]

Redland High School had set its fees, as it had done in the past, to cover its costs although in the past Councillors, as shareholders, had personally paid the overdrafts. Although recognising the property was now a valuable asset borrowing money was not an option with

49. c.1980. School hockey team

50. c.1980. School netball team

51. c.1980. Group display on the playing fields

52. 1980. Art lesson in the 'old' Art Room

launched into a cloudless, blue sky. On the 12 May 1982 there was a re-enactment of the day when Redland High School moved into Redland Court. The girls and the Staff dressed in period costume and lessons were conducted in an 'old-fashioned' Victorian-style. The Centenary Appeal Fund continued to benefit from money raised and donations destined for the purchase and conversion of 98 Redland Road for the use by the Junior School.

In 1983 the School welcomed Princess Michael of Kent who, with great charm, officially opened the new extension to the Junior School. Also in 1983 Miss Hume was able to take sabbatical leave to tour Asia, Australia and New Zealand and the United States of America. In 1984 the range of entry to universities for further study included fashion, art history, computer science, economics, accounting and finance, along with psychology, classics, and the traditional subject areas.

Career counselling had also become part of school life and a department was set up in the

high interest repayments. For the celebration of the Centenary the Old Girls' Guild gave the School the gift of a grand-piano for the hall. Framed prints of Redland Court, once the home of Sir Richard Vaughan, were offered as a fundraiser and are still available. The Centenary celebrations began in September 1981 when a hundred balloons, green, yellow and white were

53. 1983. Princess Michael of Kent's visit to open the new extension for the Junior School

1980s. In the past it was the headmistress, as in the case of Miss Peters, who advised on career paths, leaving some girls to take alternative routes using their own initiative.

Miss Hume retired in 1985 after seventeen years as Headmistress. In her last year she was proud of the achievements of Redland girls with entrances to Cambridge and Oxford to study Classics and to Oxford to study Medicine. The development of Classics owes much to Mrs Carol Lear, Acting-Headmistress and later to become Headmistress. Music and drama performances were highly professional. The School had produced Thorton Wilder's *Skin of our Teeth*. Redland High School was a school of which to be proud.

I am sure I speak for everyone when I note her high standards and expectations, her scholarship, her kindness and sympathy, her generosity, her magnificent stamina and her sense of humour. Susan Hampton, ex-member of Staff.[19]

In 1985 the two great Cedars of Lebanon were finally felled owing to fungal and beetle infestation, although the largest tree had been 'inoculated' in the 1950s for prevention of disease. The area was cleared for new muchneeded netball/tennis courts. The old Cedar tree had been a place to lose tennis balls, a place to sit with friends, shady in summer and picture postcard in winter when covered with snow. The tree was a subject for drawing and in 1951 a painting of it was exhibited in the National Childrens' Art Exhibition in London and Bristol City Art Gallery. Upkeep of the historic building was constant and dry-rot was discovered in the old art room and part of the old stables and needed urgent attention.

A school is a strange phenomenon, it is always changing, yet its essence remains the same. Miss Storm Hume, Headmistress, December, 1985.[20]

Mr James Dean, Chairman of the School Council, said the School owed much to Miss Hume's persuasion, energy and diplomacy when action needed to be taken over new building projects and raising money. In 1986 Miss Eunice Hobbs was appointed as Headmistress.

NOTES

1   Bungay, J., 1982. *Redland High School, 1882-1982*. Council for Redland High School. p.148.
2   Chitty, C., 2004. *Education Policy in Britain*. Basingstoke: Palgrave Macmillan p.46.
3   Redland High School, 1975-1979. *Letters and correspondence*. Redland High School Archive (nyc).
4   Bungay, J., 1982. *Redland High School, 1882-1982*. Council for Redland High School, p.235.
5   Redland High School, 1975-76. *Redland High School Magazine*. Redland High School Archive. p.3 (nyc).
6   Redland High School, 1970. *Old Girls' Guild Magazine*. Redland High School Archive. p.4 (nyc).
7   Redland High School, 1973-74. *Redland High School Magazine*. Redland High School Archive. p.3 (nyc).
8   Redland High School, 1975-76. *Redland High School Magazine*. Redland High School Archive. p.3 (nyc).
9   Bungay, J., 1982. *Redland High School, 1882-1982*. Council for Redland High School. p.149.
10 ibid. p.140.
11 ibid. p.150.
12 Redland High School, 1971. *Day's Eye*. Redland High School Archive (nyc).
13 Redland High School, 1977. *Redland High School Magazine*. Redland High School Archive. p.3 (nyc).
14 Bungay, J., 1982. *Redland High School, 1882-1892*. Council for Redland High School. p.150.
15 Redland High School, 1975-76. *Redland High School Magazine*. Redland High School Archive. p.6 (nyc).
16 Redland High School, 1979/80 *Information about the School*. Redland High School Archive (nyc).
17 Redland High School, 1984. *Day's Eye*. Redland High School Archive. pp.5, 8 (nyc).
18 Redland High School, 1982. *Redland High School Centenary Development Plan*. Redland High School Archive (nyc).
19 Redland High School, 1985/6. *Redland High School Magazine*. Redland High School Archive. p.3 (nyc).
20 ibid. p.7.

9
1986-1989 THE AGE OF THE MICROCHIP

The Eighties were forecast to be the age of the microchip and the loss in the job market due to this technology was considerable with redundancies in secretarial positions. Changes were also taking place in the academic field with rising unemployment. Having a degree was no longer a guarantee of future employment and Redland High School set up a Careers Counselling Service enlisting parent help.

MISS EUNICE HOBBS
(Headmistress 1986-1989)

Following Miss Hume's retirement Miss Eunice Hobbs an Honours graduate from Southampton University was appointed from the Godolphin and Latymer School in London where she had been Head of the Geography Department.[1] She was interested, as Miss Edghill had been, in the architectural heritage of Redland Court although she realised the limitations imposed by the building's architectural status. Anxious to have a more efficient secretarial department she set up an office in a former classroom next to her study. Mrs Carol Lear, as Deputy Headmistress, was given an office in the Strong Room and the contents of the Strong Room were given a home in the cellars.[2] In hindsight the cellars were not the ideal place for storing records and as a consequence they have suffered damage from damp, dirt and neglect. The restoration process is ongoing and they have revealed valuable information on the history of Redland High School.

Next on Miss Hobbs's list of upgrading was the setting up of a Middle School Library and the appointment of a part-time librarian who rapidly transformed the Senior School Library with a new stock of books and attractive furnishings. Considerable money was spent on these changes. In December 1986 the home economics and needlework rooms and a new classroom were officially opened by Mrs Caroline Waldegrave. A school tour to Greece was arranged and a 'History of Art' tour to Paris along with the Bristol/Bordeaux yearly exchanges.

54. c.1986. First computers installed

Miss Hobbs's contribution to the School's development included scholarships to girls with outstanding achievement in sport, music and the arts and she was responsible for introducing the Young Enterprise Scheme and a weekly lecture for the Sixth Form on a wide variety of topics.[2] Redland High School was the winner of the South West Region and attended the National Achievers Conference at the University of Warwick. The School continued to support charities for the homeless and the aged. A large floral mural was added to the Redland railway station. A production in 1989 of *The Boyfriend* involved all members of the School.[3] High level results were achieved in 1989 with a 92% pass rate in Advanced Level and a 91% pass rate for the new GCSE. Three girls had been offered places at Oxford University. The Duke of Edinburgh's awards continued to attract girls to take Mountain Leadership Certificates.

Miss Hobbs was Headmistress for just over three years and the position was advertised nationally which resulted in the appointment of Mrs Carol Lear who had been Deputy Headmistress at Redland for a number of years.

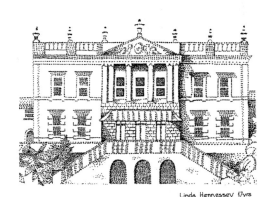

55. 1988. Redland Court. Computer drawings by Leah Occleshaw and Linda Hennessey

NOTES

1   Redland High School, 1989. *Day's Eye*. Redland High School Archive. p.3 (nyc).
2   Redland High School, 1986. *Day's Eye*, Redland High School Archive. p.3 (nyc).
3   Redland High School, 1989. *Redland High School Old Girls' Guild, Newsletter*. Redland High School Archive. p.4 (nyc).

10
1882-2006 EDUCATING YOUNG CHILDREN
HISTORICAL DEVELOPMENT, JUNIOR SCHOOL

A Junior School by definition refers to children under the age of eleven years and their entry via Kindergarten at an earlier age. In 1882 the younger children were all in the 'Kindergarten' and divisions into Kindergarten, Junior School, Middle School and Senior School did not occur until numbers had increased.

In Part 2, Chapter 2, 'The Founding of the Redland Girls' High School', mention was made of the methodology to be used for educating young children, Froebelian-based, including elements recognised by the Froebel Educational Institute.

Principles
1 Recognition of each child's capacity and potential.
2 Holistic view of the child's development.
3 Importance of play.
4 Recognition of the child, as part of the family, community, natural world.

Pedagogy
1 Professional teachers, appropriately trained.
2 Child capabilities, imaginative, creative, symbolic, linguistic, mathematical, musical, aesthetic, scientific, physical, social, moral, cultural and spiritual.
3 Activities which have sense and purpose for the child.
4 Autonomy and self confidence.

Environment
1 Safe, promoting creativity, enquiry, sensory awareness.
2 Opportunities for creative play.[1]

Fredrich Froebel, 1782-1852, a German educator, was inspired by his love of drawing as he had originally studied architecture and he understood the world was filled with objects which had shape and form, colour and texture, size and number. This led him to design 'play' equipment where learning could take place which he called his 'gifts'. These 'gifts' were 'concrete' objects, soft coloured balls, a solid wooden sphere, cube and cylinder, a wooden cube formed by eight smaller cubes, a two-inch cube which divided into eight rectangles.[2]

During the 1915 inspection the concept of 'integrated knowledge involving the senses' was not understood by one of the School Inspectors.

56. 1915. Kindergarten and Junior classroom overlooking the Dutch garden. Staff members assisted by trainees enrolled in the Froebel Student Training Award

57. 1915. Junior School pupils, boys and girls, in the courtyard.
(Elizabeth Cocks Library and Assembly Hall in the distance)

Unfamiliar with Froebel training he criticised the throwing of balls, which when dropped moved away and he suggested the use of beanbags![3] The soft, coloured balls were one of Froebel's 'gifts' to be used in conjunction with understanding 'objects in space'.

Miss Baker, a Froebel-trained teacher, commenced teaching at Redland High School in 1883. Boys and girls, with an average age of four years, attended the Kindergarten as it was then called. Miss Baker was assisted by pupil-teachers, girls who wished to become teachers. After Miss Baker's death in 1900 her place was taken by Miss Ida Deakin, also Froebel-trained, who stayed in the position for twenty years and was the Class teacher of IIA. In 1908 Miss Deakin established the Froebel Kindergarten Student Training programme for the Higher Certificate of the National Froebel Union and her student-teachers observed and taught the Kindergarten pupils.[4] After moving into Redland Court in 1885 the twenty–five Kindergarten pupils were housed in the gardener's cottage and pulled down later in 1894 for the building of the Assembly Hall. In 1886 there were enough pupils to form a Junior School replacing the name 'Kindergarten' which was only used for the very young children. In 1898 Kindergarten term fees were: five shillings for children under six years, £1 10s 0d; over six years, £2 2s 0d; eight to eleven years, £3 3s 0d.[5]

In 1901 the Junior School moved into rooms at the boarding school premises which in 1910 the Inspectors reported as being unsatisfactory. After the 1910 report the Kindergarten and Transition forms were housed in the room overlooking the Dutch garden and the room divided by a partition. A Junior School Form was housed in an ex-Army hut from the First World War. Complaints were made by parents about the heating of the wooden building and reported their children were cold. One parent objected to the school fees charged for inadequate accommodation.[6] By 1915 the term fees had been increased by £2 for the Kindergarten and by £5 for the Junior pupils. Miss Mayers, another Froebel graduate, taught the Kindergarten children. In 1916 six boys attended the Junior School. In 1918 the fees per term for pupils under the age of eight years was raised to £3 and for pupils aged eight to eleven years the fee was raised to £4.[7]

In 1918 Miss Daltry, a National Froebel-trained teacher, was appointed. After Miss Deakin's retirement in 1920, Miss Byrne became the Headmistress of the Junior School. The training of Froebel Kindergarten teachers was transferred to the University of Bristol as it was considered that teachers already at the school did not have the necessary skills to assess the training.[8] There were six boys enrolled in the Kindergarten and Transition and four student-teachers were finishing their Froebel training. In 1923 the Kindergarten and Transition forms were moved back to the boarding house premises and the Junior School to the room near the Dutch garden. An Old Boy (yes, Redland has a few!) remembers his classroom in the early twenties was called Form I and housed in the room overlooking the Dutch garden.[9] In 1924 the boys, all eleven of them, had their photograph taken and a print of the photograph is held in the School archives.

The Junior School used the cellars of the building for their cloakrooms, shared by the boys and the girls. A roster was drawn up for toilet use by both sexes, which hopefully didn't cause any accidents to occur!

We sat in the front row of the hall while the 'big' girls sang their House songs.
Urijah Thomas sang 'work while it is CALLED today' and I thought they said, 'work while it is COLD today.
Dorothy Milton, 1923-1937

Dorothy Milton was an Old Girl and later a Staff member of the mathematics department.[10]

Miss Moxley, also Froebel trained, joined the Staff in the late 1930s and later became Head of the Junior School After the closure of the Boarding School the Junior School occupied the west wing by the Dutch garden, called Room 1, and Rooms 2, 5, 6, 7, and Room 9 on the next floor. Miss Moxley's artistic skills were well-known in the production of costumes and her interests were in nature study, poetry and drama. Another successful and well-loved teacher was Miss Hodges. She was appointed in 1942 as a class teacher for IIIB, the Senior Form of the Junior School. Her love of music was conveyed to her recorder class and Junior School singing. Miss Hodges stayed at the School for twenty-five years, retiring in 1967. Staying for periods of between fifteen and twenty years and beyond indicates the dedication of Staff to the School. Both Miss Moxley and Miss Hodges taught the joined-up, no loops, Marion Richardson-style of handwriting.[11] This was still in practice in 1963 after being introduced in 1947.

When girls from the Junior School entered the Middle School in IIIA they were joined by girls from Government Primary Schools many of whom were the eleven-plus scholarship holders at that time until the scholarship was discontinued in 1945. There was a notable difference in the Froebel teaching method and practices at Redland High Junior School which contrasted with the teaching of the three R's at the Government Schools. The Junior School pupils took a written examination to enter the Middle School and very few were denied the opportunity. They were not as adept at mathematics as the scholarship girls and although taking mathematics as a subject were not always placed in the A group. However, their writing and creative skills, art and drama, were highly developed and they showed confidence in play-reading, acting, directing and story-writing. There was a distinct gap between

58. 1932. Junior School, puppet theatre

59. 1932. Junior School on the terrace of Redland Court

School had rooms above the study. In 1955 Junior School fees were twenty-six guineas (£27 6s 0d) per term.[12] Girls from Redland High School were leaving to attend the London-based Froebel Training College in the 1950s and entry to this establishment was considered a higher achievement of acceptance than for a 'normal' teacher-training college as this was a specialist area and trained teachers were likely to find teaching positions in private schools.

Miss Peters kept in contact with the Junior School and visited the School on Wednesday mornings to take Assembly. The Junior School pupils walked up the hill for lunch to the main school. When pupils reached the year IIB and IIA they moved into classrooms in the main building and entered the Middle School, Class IIIB, with intakes from Government Schools. In the 1970s the Junior School playground was fitted out with a climbing frame, fibreglass slide and a trampoline. Without records it is difficult to follow the progress of the Junior School up to 1970. Further development did not occur until the opportunity came to purchase 98 Redland Road, a house next door to the Junior School building at 1 Grove Park.

In 1982 work commenced on the house which had been purchased for £110,000 and would release Junior School pupils from the main school premises and in turn would give more accommodation to the Senior School. The Junior School had taken part in the 1982 Centenary celebrations with a Victorian musical evening. The curriculum was extended through camps and an interest in nature stimulated by setting up a Junior School programme as part of the Avon School's Conservation Project. In 1983 Her Royal Highness, Princess Michael of Kent, officially opened the new addition to the Junior School. For the purchase of 98 Redland Road, parents had donated £58,000, Old Girls, £18,000, Staff and Council, £11,000. Other money had come from charitable trusts, industry and fundraising. There was still a further £28,000 needed

the two groups and new friendships were only made if a Scholarship girl was seen as 'creative'.

1945 saw the last intake of boys with only one Junior pupil that year and the decision was made by Miss Peters for Redland High School to become a single-sex school in both the Junior and the Senior Schools. In 1952 four boys were still attending the Kindergarten but when the final move was made to the Junior House the facilities at 1 Grove Park were not set up for mixed-classes. Until the move the Kindergarten was held in the room next to Miss Peters's study and the Junior

60. 1982. Junior School pupils

to complete Stage 1 and plans were being laid for Stage II, the enlarged Senior School library.[13]

In 1985 Mrs Marilyn Lane replaced Mrs Kay as Head of the Junior School. Mrs Lane had held the position of Head of the Junior School at Badminton School. One of her initiatives was to introduce Junior School pupils to study Science, previously not a Junior School subject. She also gave Junior School pupils the chance to study modern languages and information technology. In 1986 the Junior School visited the Hippodrome to see *Peter Pan* and the Colston Hall for the Proms. Visits to the School were made by the Police during Police Week and representatives from the Help the Aged. For the older pupils visits were made to Winchester, London and Skerne Lodge.[14] A report for the Council was prepared by Mrs Lane, Head of the Junior School, and presented in November, 1985. There were currently 187 pupils. A marketing drive was needed to promote entry at Reception level and a video was prepared. An open-evening was held for parents and friends. Staff attended a course on School Development Plans and Mrs Lane was asked to formulate a School Improvement Plan.[15]

In 1996 after the visit by HMI Inspectors, Mrs Marilyn Lane prepared a report for the Council after the established move to the new building. Standards were reported as 'generally good' and the Inspectors praised the introduction of

'Senior' subjects. They were impressed with bringing in parents to engage with the children on topics such as 'buildings'. The Inspectors noted the 'freedom' to be 'creative' both in art and English (creative writing). More computers were needed in order for the children to become familiar with the new technology. The Inspectors spoke of the children as 'very nice children' and praised the pastoral care.[16] Activities beyond the classroom included visits to workshops at Willsbridge Mill, the Big Pit in South Wales and the Old Vic and the Redgrave Theatre.

After raising money for new facilities and books the library was moved to vacated office space and planning was helped by the school library services. Plans were in place to commence work on a School Development Plan, mainly curriculum based, with information from the Bursar concerning future buildings and resources. Salaries for Junior School Staff in 1995 ranged from £20,145 to £29,500 per annum.

In 2003 Mrs Lane retired after serving nineteen years and had gained respect from successive Chairs of Governors, beginning with Mr James Dean, Dr Beryl Corner and Mr Peter Breach. Two Governors, Mrs Nicky Kennedy and Mr John Pool had a particular interest in the progress of the Junior School.

Mrs Lane's position as Junior School Head Teacher was filled by Mrs Judith Ashill who had been appointed as a Junior School teacher in 1995 and later in her role as a Senior Teacher in the Junior School was a member of the School's Senior Management Team. Family lifestyles had changed considerably over the years and in many two-parent families both parents worked. In 2003 a summer holiday club, named previously Redland Rascals by Mrs Marilyn Lane, was set up for children aged three to eleven to alleviate the situation. Play equipment was updated and purchased by the Friends of Redland High School and included rope and log bridges and stepping stones which had appeal for children.[17]

MR JONATHAN EYLES
(Head-teacher Junior School 2006-)

In 2006 Mr Jonathan Eyles, BEd (Hons), MEd (Hons) (Bath Spa University), was appointed as Head-teacher of Redland High Junior School. The appointment of a male Head-teacher was a first for Redland High School and ironically having a male in this position was bitterly opposed by the first Headmistress, Miss Cocks, who at that time in 1882 was fighting for a girls' school to be run by a woman. Male staff have been employed at Redland over a number of years and even in those early days in the 1880s 'drill' was taken by an ex-sergeant major and art by an art master from the Bristol School of Art. Over the recent years male staff were employed to teach mathematics, art, science, drama and music. In 2006 the Junior School was inspected by the Independent Association of Preparatory Schools (IAPS) who found pastoral care and guidance was a particular strength of the School. The Inspectors recognized the high-quality of teaching from dedicated staff and strong partnerships between the School and parents.

The Inspectors also recorded that our pupils show respect for the value and feelings of others, pay attention in discussions and respond seriously to opinions different from their own.
Dr Ruth Weeks, Headmistress 2002-2006.

The curriculum was enhanced by drama and music and 2006 saw the production of *The Flower of the Holy Night* and children participated in National Book Day and enjoyed dressing-up as favourite book characters. In 2008 an extension was built in Grove Park providing classrooms for Years 5 and 6 and freeing up space for increased 2009 enrolments. This was officially opened in 2009 by the children's author, Amanda Mitchison, through the character Professor Georgie Blink. The Redland and Cotham Amenity Society awarded the building a gold star, given for high quality new developments and contribution to appearance in the area.

As well as giving us enough room for further Year 5 and 6 classes, we will be able to enhance the educational experience of all the girls through creating a multi-purpose Activity Hall... to accommodate our extensive programme of clubs and activities.
Mr J. Eyles Head-teacher, Redland High Junior School.[19]

The philosophy of the Junior School, according to Mr Jonathan Eyles, was to ensure that each girl should reach her potential and foster her own self-esteem. The Junior School decided to have a hymn which they could call their own and 'Shine, Jesus, Shine' was chosen to be sung at Commemoration Services and on special occasions. Other developments were the award of a silver flag for the Junior School as an Eco School with the installation of a water-butt, hand-dryers and a children's scooter-rack.

In an interview in October 2010, Mr Jonathan Eyles stressed that the ethos and climate of the Junior School is essential to the child's level of independent thinking particularly with regard to the inter-related curriculum development and learning. The children were working on objects, the eye, the sea, and how these relate to the real world, blind people's needs, and the R.N.L.I, Royal Navy Lifeboat Institute.

Another initiative for developing 'gifted' children's talents in Thinking Skills for those with an above average I.Q., after identification, is the Pandora Club (after Pandora's Box). Problem solving and creative thinking can be developed when children are confronted with an unusual situation. Edward de Bono's work with children in the 1980s, 'Children Solve Problems', has provided the background for continuation of the notion of developing the creative brain-power of children. The Synectics group of inventors claimed the 'flip top can' was invented as a solution for a design for a 'better' can opener. The philosophy behind Froebel's 'gifts', and ways to develop these continues with those concerned with today's education of young children.

It is not about 'to learn', but 'HOW to learn and the transference of skill.'
Mr J. Eyles, Head-teacher, Redland High Junior School. 2010.

NOTES

1   Wikipedia, n.d. Froebel Educational Institute. 'Elements of a Froebelian Education for Children from Birth to Seven years'. *In:Wikipedia: the free encyclopedia* (on line). St. Petersburg, Florida: Wikimedia Foundation. Available from http://w.w.w.froebel.org.uk/elements.html. (Accessed 2 March 2010)

2. Manning, J., 2005. 'Rediscovering Froebel: A Call to Re-examine his Life and Gifts'. *Early Childhood Education Journal*, 32(6), pp.371-376.

3   Board of Education. 1915. *Inspection Report.* London: Whitehall. Redland High School Archive. p.17 (nyc).

4   Shaw, M.G. 1932. *Redland.* Bristol: Arrowsmith. p.54.

5   Redland High School. 1893-1898. *Council Minute Book.* Redland High School Archive, BB043.

6   Redland High School. 1917-1933. *Council Minute Book. No. 3,* Redland High School Archive, BB140.

7   ibid.

8   Shaw, M.G. 1932. *Redland.* Bristol: Arrowsmith. p.67.

9   Bungay, J., 1982. *Redland High School 1882-1982.* Council of Redland High School. p.82.

10 ibid. p.93.

11 ibid. p.153.

12 Redland High School. 1917-1958. *Shareholders Minute Book, AGM.* Redland High School Archive. BB139.

13 Redland High School. 1983. *Progress Report. Centenary Appeal.* Redland High School Archive (nyc).

14 Redland High School. 1986. *Day's Eye.* Redland High School Archive. p.54 (nyc).

15 Redland High School. 1995. *Junior School Headmistress, report to Council.* Redland High School Archive (nyc).

16 Redland High School. 1996. *Report after HMI visit.* Redland High School Archive (nyc).

17 Redland High School. 2005. *Newsletter.* Redland High School Archive (nyc).

18 Redland High School. 2006. Spring. *Newsletter.* Redland High School Archive (nyc).

19 Redland High School. 2008. *Newsletter.* Redland High School Archive (nyc).

11

1989-2002 ACCOUNTABILITY. NEW LABOUR, 1997

In the 1970s there was a powerful shift from 'partnership' to 'accountability' as a result of the economic crisis of 1971-1973 and education moved towards the needs of the consumer, the pupils, parents, and industrialists. Schools and teachers were to be more accountable to the public and were to be involved in presenting the 'core curriculum' of 'basic knowledge'. How was this to be achieved? Curriculum models for discussion included 'integrated-curriculum', 'compulsory-curriculum', 'a common-curriculum' and settling for 'a national-curriculum'.[1]

The professional common-curriculum approach was clearly outlined in the three HMI Red Books between 1977 and 1983. The essentials of a good common-curriculum according to the Schools Council were to give importance to personal development, aesthetic experience, experience of the material world and of society and 'transcendentalism', that is, ideals and inspiration.[2]

In Red Book One, 1977, eight areas were identified:

- the aesthetic and creative
- the ethical
- the linguistic
- the mathematical
- the physical
- the scientific
- the social and political
- the spiritual[3]

This was set out for Secondary schools and later in 1985 encompassed the curriculum for five-year olds to sixteen-year olds. Red Book Three, published in 1983 placed special emphasis on 'pupil entitlement'. Schools were to offer all levels of attainment, not just academic.

In 1983 the Charity Commission allowed Redland High School to borrow £95,000 from the Bristol and West Building Society on security against 98 Redland Road and 1 Grove Park with the proviso it was paid back within ten years. By 1990 the School again wished to expand. The consultant planners received a fairly condemning letter from Bristol City Council Planning Department which criticised what had been done in the past which made Redland Court (the original building) not higher than a Grade II listing and further work might see it taken off the list. The only expansion they would consider were extensions to the rear garden of 10 Woodstock Road. They also pointed out that a pledge had been made not to exceed the Middle and Senior School numbers of 450 girls.

When the large Cedar had been removed, the Planning Department had requested a slow-growing, not overtly-spreading, replacement tree to be planted in its place and they had recommended that a standard-size oak tree should be planted. They noted this had not yet been done.[4]

Mrs Carol Lear had been Deputy-Head-mistress for a number of years and was familiar with the development of the School and was well-suited to the position of Headmistress. A 1988 Sixth Form advisory publication was produced to attract pupils to stay on and take advantage of the special facilities provided at the Sixth Form House and the opportunity of individual study. It was also open to girls from other schools following along the lines of the new Sixth Form Colleges. Government assisted places, bursaries, and scholarships for those talented in a particular field, academic, sport, art, music, were offered at half-fees. The publication outlined the content and mode of study of each subject area.[5]

MRS CAROL LEAR
(Headmistress 1989-2002)

Mrs Carol Lear, MA Classics (London), DipEd (Bristol) was born in Bristol and was educated at Colston's Girls' School. Her first teaching post was at Cheltenham Ladies' College and later she returned to Bristol to teach at Red Maids' School. Here she taught the Cambridge Latin course and later when she came to Redland High School she persuaded the School Council to adopt this new and exciting course.

Mrs Lear's aims for the School were to bring about a broader and more balanced curriculum and to enable the girls to reach their potential. Through instilling confidence in them it was expected that Redland High School pupils would take a fulfilling role in society. Enrichment was offered through the extended curriculum and girls were encouraged to question and not to accept without questioning. Design technology was to be introduced into the curriculum and involved practical experiences in crafts, cookery, fashion design involving needlework, and home economics. New subject areas to be implemented were, Spanish, history of art, psychology, drama, information technology, economics and politics, all of which needed well-qualified staff.

In reviewing her first complete year as Head-mistress, 1990-1991, Mrs Carol Lear wrote:

Education can never be static for it is a process of continual growth and change but in the last five years or so, the rate of change has been unprece-dented with the removal of the O.L. and G.S.E. Examinations and the introduction of the new G.C.S.E. Examinations followed by the require-ments of the National Curriculum.[6]

More courses needed more space and more buildings. Two further rooms were created under the gymnasium, with approval from the Bristol City Council Planning Department, and the release of the workshop inside the School gates became the Centre for Information Technology accommodating twenty-eight computers necessary for this new subject. Later, this area, perhaps not the most attractive of extensions, became the Centre for Design Technology. The main building was also in need of continual maintenance, which included the painting of window-frames and doors, although in later years it was found necessary to replace the wooden window-frames of the Assembly Hall with low-maintenance plastic ones of similar design.

The girls continued to achieve a high standard in music and one girl was accepted as a cellist for the National Youth Orchestra, a position not awarded to a Redland High School pupil since 1946. Hannah Weinberger was also a cellist. Redland had always been well-represented in sports and the arts. The art department had grown in strength and an exhibition in Bristol Cathedral drew public acclaim.

Tours and excursions were widely extended and went as far afield as China and some girls worked in villages in Nepal for two weeks. Israel, Greece, Italy were also visited along with the annual exchanges with Bordeaux and Marburg. More places to visit and knowledge about Bristol, 'City of the Sea', the SS *Great Britain* and the Maritime Heritage Centre helped with written projects. The girls also visited the battlefields of the First World War. These were far more interesting than trips offered in the 1950s to visit Fry's chocolate factory where the smell of chocolate was overpowering, or Wills Tobacco Factory where the uncomfortable odour of the drying leaves might have prevented girls from taking up the socially-accepted habit of smoking, or a visit to the *Evening Post* where the clattering of the printing machines and smells of oil and toxic lead-based ink in the production room made the handling of newspapers lethal with the threat of lead poisoning. Softened in water, newspapers of that time made a very good cleaning rag for windows because of the lead content and the shine it left on the glass. Health and Safety regulations were non-existent.

The delightful Georgian House and the Red Lodge provided historic interest for those students interested in history and art and visits to the Bristol Old Vic provided an insight into Drama and Theatre production. At the end of the Sixth Form in 1952 a visit to hear Kenneth Clark (later Sir Kenneth) at the Bristol University give a lecture on the subject of Dutch landscape painters was never forgotten by one pupil. Kenneth Clark explained how the landscape was without high ground and the artists reversed the imagery by painting huge cows lying in the foreground to accommodate the loss of hills and mountains.

Inspiring girls to broaden their learning has opened up a whole new set of subjects to be studied at university level. In 1995 in the Head-mistress' Report to Council girls were obtaining places to read archaeology, anthropology, politics, philosophy and economics as well as classics, mathematics and medicine. Awards were won in creative writing, technology, food preparation, fashion and textiles, all outcomes from the expanded curriculum offered in the 1980s.[7] In conjunction with this a careers advice/ counselling service was set up. Nothing like this had been available in the 1950s and 1960s when advice was given only by the Head-

61. 1992. Entry for the Young Enterprise Scheme

mistress who pre-determined what a pupil 'could', or, 'could not do'.

The Young Enterprise Scheme founded in 1988, conceived with modest products of Christmas paper and stationery, continued to impress and in 1995 the girls produced a talking book of nursery rhymes read by celebrities along with a printed version. Jeans had also been recycled into oven gloves and other products. The Young Enterprise company 'Lyrics' went on to win the local rounds and was placed third in the national finals out of 3,000 companies. 'Tickled Pink' was the next Young Enterprise Scheme and featured jokes and anecdotes from famous people.

In 1990 at A Level, the highest mark ever recorded at Redland High School was 99.8% for the subject area of history of art and results in French were in the top 5% in the UK. 94% of the G.C.S.E. in 1991 resulted in Grade A-C and 91% of the A.L. resulted in a Pass. The Duke of Edinburgh Award Scheme continued to attract girls to acquire new skills and develop self-reliance. Involvement in this scheme could be added to a C.V. when applying for entrance to university and even for employment.[8]

In 1992 the Council purchased two houses in Woodstock Road. These houses faced the Sixth Form House purchased earlier. The Bristol City Planners were unlikely to approve any further building on the Redland Court site and having buildings available so close to the school was indeed fortuitous and the purchase was made possible through the generosity of the Harry Crook Trust. The buildings allowed for a caretaker's flat and new premises for the Sixth Form which had outgrown the existing accommodation and the buildings would also house the Bursar's office. In turn the music school moved into the caretaker's flat above the design technology room.[9]

The previous Sixth Form location, now empty, was converted and developed into an art centre by 1997. In turn the conversion of the former art studio into a modern library was estimated in 1995 to cost £370,000. Phase 1, costing £185,000 was anticipated to be operational by the summer term of 1996 and was to contain not only books but all the technological equipment needed for resource-based learning. Phase 2 at a cost of £185,000 would involve the creation of a new entrance to the proposed art centre with classroom above and re-landscaping of the courtyard.[10] An attractive colour-printed brochure was produced to attract funding.[11] The existing library for fewer pupils contained less books than today's requirements and was now inadequate. The new library would enable more books to be displayed and the setting up of an electronic cataloguing system.

Not long after the Woodstock Road purchases the opportunity came to buy 4 Redland Court

62. 1995. New double-storey library and computer facilities

Road, which had been an architect's office and presented no problems for its continued use as school premises. Computers had been installed and were used by the Junior School. The rooms were also used for music lessons. Money for these purchases came from the sale of the land at Druid Stoke which had been bought and donated by Mr Tait. He had predicted in 1903 that even if the School did not use it for playing-fields the land could be sold. And sold it was, raising enough to be able to spend a large amount of money on the new facilities with the balance used to keep the School financially sound. It is fortunate that the land was never sold earlier during the many financial crises the School had experienced for this 'nest-egg' was increasing in value, year by year and by 1992 was a highly-prized piece of land giving access to a new housing development.

In 1992 the Assembly Hall was used for an episode of the television programme 'House of Eliot' with pupils used as 'extras'. The results of the public examinations were very good, 96% of the GSCE results were grades A-C and the average number of subjects taken was nine. The Advanced level results were 88% pass rate and 48% of these passes were grades A/B. Mrs Lear expressed an opinion that the whole question of league tables was fraught with problems but they were here to stay.[11]

If a school is wholly judged on its results there is much that is left out about other individual successes. The success of the art department owed much to the staff who developed the talents of the pupils and was much talked about in art circles. Creativeness was also shown in developing products for the Young Enterprise Award and in 1992 the group 'Focus' made attractive notice boards with wooden frames. Another pupil won a prestigious fashion award and became the National Winner of the Lloyds Bank Fashion Challenge Competition. The award had been won previously by a Redland High School girl. In the competition for the world energy project a Redland girl was runner up in the national competition with 8,000 entries.[12]

Over the years new areas of sporting prowess had emerged in which the School took part and competed in cross country running and fencing. Fencing would have appealed to the Edwardian girls as part of their defence mechanism of being 'as good as the boys' in their efforts to free themselves from the institutionalised domestic ideology.

In 1995 Mrs Lear attended the Girls' School Association to discuss the new UCAS entry procedure for higher education.

Schools are very complex institutions and our responsibilities are very great.
Mrs Carol Lear, Headmistress.

Also in 1995 Mrs Lear presented a report to the Council. New staff were welcomed and included one Staff member mentioned as gaining her Certificate of Competence to drive the new mini-bus. Several girls had applied to Oxbridge and were hoping to read archaeology and anthropology, English, P.P.E. (politics, philosophy and economics), mathematics and medicine. Another girl had her letter, previously entered in the competition for 'Letters of Peace', printed in an attractive book. A pupil had won a cooking competition and was presented with cookware

63. 1994. School production of *The Wizard of Oz*

for herself and the School. A pupil in fashion and textiles was successful as a national winner for a sportswear outfit. The School benefited when Roger Black, the athlete, spent a day at the School giving advice on fitness and diet and took a sports-studies class, as well as reading a nursery-rhyme for the publication by the Enterprise Group.[13]

Music students continued to perform at a high level and were accepted into the National Youth Orchestra and the National Chamber Orchestra. Mrs Lear commended the School on these achievements adding that the School is not a large school and yet performance is exceptional. Marketing of the School had been improved by offering prospective parents the

64. 1991. Redland High School pupil at the Schools' Promenade Concert in the Albert Hall, presented by the Avon Schools' Orchestra

chance to view the School play as part of the School's Open Days.

It was considered very important for the Staff to attend courses concerning the teaching of girls with mild learning difficulties and courses on the counselling of girls with eating disorders. There was never any real counselling on health issues in the 1950s and 1960s and there were overweight and underweight girls in the School. It was left to Miss Jennings, the gymnastics' teacher, to meet the girls before School commenced and to help girls with posture problems. Girls who were on this programme wore a red-ribbon posture badge.

More space was needed for science and computing and these were next on the agenda together with drama which needed an area free from furniture.[14]

The School was very fortunate in being awarded the John James Bequest, endowment money from a wealthy Bristol entrepreneur. £30,000 per year had been given to support bursaries enabling girls with potential and limited means to enter the School. Money from the Harry Crook foundation had enabled the

65. 1995. New organ for the Assembly Hall. Note the portrait of Miss Hume (Headmistress 1969-1985)

purchase of the Sixth Form house. A contribution from the Old Girls had enabled the School to purchase an organ to be used for assemblies and by music pupils. Under the chairmanship of Mr Peter Breach, the Governors of the School spent money wisely and carefully, in developing the facilities of the School and drew on its members' expertise for advice.

In 1997 due to the results in the League tables and fees charged Redland High School was placed fifty-fifth in the 'value for money' in the national table, and the A level results placed the School in Division 1 in the league tables.

Every Head regards the League Tables with a degree of mistrust because there is so much else which needs to be said about a school but what they do tell us is that standards of teaching and learning are very high.
Mrs Carol Lear, Headmistress.[15]

Music students performed in concerts and the Chamber Choir visited Thailand. Miss Knee retired and her place was taken by Mr Nigel Davies. School drama productions continued to impress and in all cases the Staff gave their expertise and help with sets and costumes. Once again the Governors played an important part and provided the School with a new and spacious library and resources centre with new computers and also a refurbished science laboratory.[16] All the latest technology was provided and bought through the generous donation from the Wolfson Trust.

The winter uniform had not changed from the days of the dark-green wrap-around skirt and was still worn for most of the year. There was discussion on a change of style but this did not take place until several years later. However, there were special sports clothes for team games, hockey, netball and tennis.

In 1998 Redland High School achieved an outstanding double success by winning all the major awards in Bristol's Senior and Junior speaking competitions for local schools. In this year the School lost the Head of geography, Mr Chris Charlwood, who moved to the Bruton School for Girls. He had organised successful field trips and residential visits. A hundred years had passed since Miss Cocks had decided that her school should have an all-female Staff, with the exception of the teaching of music, violin, cello, choir and orchestra.

A school clothes cupboard was also still operating in much the same way as it did during the Second World War because in those days clothing coupons were kept for Sunday 'best' outfits and second-hand clothes did not require coupons. There was a demand for summer dresses as these were often not worn out as girls outgrew them or had not used them for any length of time. Sales were channelled into the Fund Raising Account.[17]

In 1998 Redland High School's award winning 'Young Enterprise Company' was invited to join a partnership with schools on the Continent. Redland was matched with a school on the Belgian-Dutch border. The group 'Stucco', made and sold cards, cupids, suns and moons. *Salad Days*, the famous musical, was produced with girls from Redland and boys from QEH and Cotham, and had its origins in a production in Bristol in the 1960s.

The A level results were again excellent with 72% of grades of A's and B's.

Long-serving Staff retired, notably Mrs Claypoole who taught Physical Education and advised on careers after thirty-four years at the School. Mrs Perry (science) and Mrs Schofield (Sixth Form) retired after nineteen years service to the School. Lady Macara who had been Deputy Head since 1989 and taught biology also left after many years of service. Changes had been made and the assisted places scheme phased out although Redland continued to attract very good students.[18]

The Headmistress was also President of the Old Girls' Guild and supported them in all they did and still do for the School. In 1999 membership was well over eight hundred and with advanced technology and the internet contact has been made with four times that number. In 2000 a Redland High School website was set up.

A school must move forward, adapting and changing but the underlying values remain the same.
Mrs Carol Lear, Headmistress.

In order to promote the School through publications, advertisements and events, a marketing office was set up. Publications had advanced into glossy magazines, beginning in 1998 with recording events through text with black and white photographs and moving into colour after the millennium. The newsletter of the Old Girls Guild was incorporated into these publications and the yearly school magazine, the *Day's Eye* is a way of keeping in touch with the past, the present and future events.

In 1999 a large party of Redland girls visited China accompanied by six Staff members and parents. Also in that year the School produced *An Inspector Calls* with sets made by A level art students and lighting by the A level physics students. Finally the new ICT suite was finished in the underground space behind the art centre. Every part of the school grounds has now been filled and architectural purists feel that the Georgian estate is only a shadow of its former glory. Educationists may ask the question concerning learning, 'Does the setting matter?' For Redland it does matter. The Georgian house is the central hub around which everything else revolves and is that part of the School fondly remembered by Old Girls.

A School Inspection was carried out in 1999 and the results were available on the internet and an oral report was presented to the Staff and Governors. The Inspectors were impressed with the confidence and enthusiasm of the girls. An

66. 2002. Mrs Carol Lear's retirement.
(Headmistress 1989-2002)

67. 2002. Cake made by Mary Walters (Old Girl), for the
120th Anniversary of the Redland High School

ICT suite was opened by Mr Ian Beer, former Headmaster of Harrow, who, while singing the praises of the computer, said the human brain was the best computer! In 2000 the Young Enterprise company calling themselves GAIA, produced a wallet containing advice on protection from the sun and a solar card allowing the monitoring of the sun's UV rays.

In 2002 Redland High School celebrated its one hundred and twentieth anniversary, and after thirteen years as Headmistress Mrs Carol Lear retired. She always maintained that Redland High School girls would continue to do well if they had acquired good habits of self motivation and learning, whilst receiving excellent tuition from highly experienced and dedicated Staff, especially if they had chosen wisely from a programme of subjects tailored to their needs.

The 120th anniversary was remembered by the cutting of a cake in front of all the girls assembled on the terrace. It was the year when Tanya Beckett, an Old Girl, opened the Wolfson Laboratory. The Wolfson Trust gave £50,000 towards the building and the School contributed the balance.

Redland is a beautiful place, the Staff are committed to teaching and encouraging the girls and to making opportunities available to them. I have been privileged to be part of the community as a teacher and as the Headmistress.
Mrs Carol Lear, Headmistress.

Mrs Carol Lear has continued her interest in Redland High School and in 2007 was appointed President of the School Council.

NOTES

1 Chitty, C., 2004. *Education Policy in Britain.* Basingstoke: Palgrave Macmillan. pp.189, 119.
2 ibid. p.120.
3 ibid. p.121.
4 Bristol City Council Planning Department. 1983. *Letter to Redland High School.* Redland High School Archive (nyc).
5 Redland High School 1988. *Sixth Form Prospectus.* Redland High School Archive (nyc).
6 Redland High School. 1991. *Old Girls' Newsletter.* Redland High School Archive (nyc).
7 Redland High School. 1995. *Headmistress Report to Council.* Redland High School Archive (nyc).
8 Redland High School. 1990. *Old Girls' Newsletter.* Redland High School Archive (nyc).
9 Redland High School. 1992. *Old Girls' Newsletter.* Redland High School Archive (nyc).
10 Redland High School. 1995. *FAX message to Bursar from Mr Peter Breach.* Redland High School Archive (nyc).
11 Redland High School. 1992. *Old Girls' Newsletter.* Redland High School Archive (nyc).
12 Redland High School. 1995. *Toward Tomorrow.* Redland High School Archive (nyc).
13 Redland High School. 1992. *Old Girls' Newsletter.* Redland High School Archive (nyc).
14 Redland High School. 1995 *Headmistress Report to Council.* Redland High School Archive (nyc).
15 ibid.
16 Redland High School. 1997. *Old Girls' Newsletter.* Redland High School Archive (nyc).
17 ibid.
18 Redland High School. 1998. *Redland High School, Spring Newsletter.* Redland High School Archive (nyc).
19 Redland High School. 1998. *Old Girls' Newsletter.* Redland High School Archive (nyc).
20 Redland High School. 2002. *Old Girls' Newsletter.* Redland High School Archive (nyc).

12

2002-2006 EXTENDING OPPORTUNITIES, RAISING STANDARDS

Underpinning New Labour's education policies was the notion of measuring performance, whether it was for an individual or for an institution as a 'whole'.

In the 2002 Green Paper, *14-19: Extending Opportunities, Raising Standards,* the Government was fully committed to the idea of the *14-19* as a single phase which enabled pupils to develop at a pace best suited to their needs and abilities ensuring 'economic prosperity and social justice for all in the new century'.[1]

Coinciding with the publication in March 2003 of a Secondary Heads Association policy statement on school accountability, the General Secretary of the SHA pointed out that Head Teachers were now accountable for twenty-one different bodies. These included parents, governing bodies, local education authorities, central government, the QCA, Ofsted, the LSC, partnerships (varied), child protection, health and safety, racial equality, Disability Rights Commission and Equal Opportunities Commission.[2]

This 'over-accountability' was seen by the SHA as a 'disincentive to creativity' and the obsession with examination results and studying subjects where higher grades were easier to obtain was leading to a shortage of graduates for science, mathematics and modern foreign languages. 'Intelligent accountability' was a framework to ensure schools worked efficiently and towards the common goal of giving the best to their pupils. The Redland High School has always given of its best.

DR RUTH WEEKS
(Headmistress 2002-2006)

Dr Ruth Weeks, BSc (Hons), PhD (Birmingham) had held the position of Deputy Headmistress at the Haberdashers' Girls' School in Monmouth. Appointed in 2002 to Redland High School she was young, vibrant, and quickly established a rapport with the girls, particularly with the Sixth Form whom she would invite into her study for coffee and biscuits. Here was a style of friendliness but firmness.

In Dr Weeks' first report she noted there was a 100% pass rate at A Level and all Sixth Formers who applied for university courses were accepted. These results were the outcomes of 'good' teaching, dedicated Staff, many of whom had been in charge of departments for a number of years. Dr Weeks had been appointed to a school with a very good track record. Success was achieved in the contest for the Bristol One-Act Drama Festival and once again the art department's exhibition had been outstanding. Individual performances in singing were rewarded with two girls selected for the National Youth Training Choir.[3]

Dr Weeks was responsible for re-establishing the House system, long forgotten and which had been part of the school's policy of the integration of different age groups and a driving force behind the notion of 'competitiveness'.

Many Old Girls sanctioned this as they felt part of School life and part of its heritage had disappeared when the House System was

68. 2003. Dr Ruth Weeks (Headmistress 2002-2006)
with Sixth Form pupils

abandoned. The new House names, Chestnut, Maple, Rowan and Willow followed the House System adopted in the Junior School who chose river names. English was to be taught in House groups. It has been seen that the re-establishment of the traditional House system continued the tradition of bringing girls together and brought out hidden talents.

100% pass rate at A2 level was achieved in 2003. Dr Weeks reported that, *These results are a great credit to pupils and staff alike.*

Year 11 also surpassed their predecessors when they set a new record with a 99.5% pass rate for GCSEs. One girl was awarded one of the top five marks in the country in the history of art, A2 level. Mr John Icke, Head of the Art Department, commented, *Obtained full marks for four of the six modules involved. A terrific achievement.* The study of the history of art comes alive when girls are able to visit actual works of art. In 2003, girls, parents and staff took a trip to Italy to study Renaissance art.

Other students visited Cambridge University's Open Day to explore opportunities beyond their experiences at Redland which provided them with a sound basis for further study. New areas of learning, government and politics studies, was enhanced by a visit to the Houses of Parliament and to the Greater London Authority (GLA)

which worked with Ken Livingstone to deliver strategic policies for London. Comments by the girls included, 'we were shown where it (politics) takes place, creating a great base on which to build future knowledge.'[4] The Sylvia J. Frost Memorial Prize for Grade 7 Piano was won by a Redland pupil for the highest score of those taking the Grade 6 and 7 piano examinations in the Bristol area. Music and drama are to be combined as a grade examination by the London College of Music.

In 2003 a new school uniform was introduced with decisions made by the girls who chose a tartan (Redland's own) for a kilt-like skirt, based on the previous navy-blue skirt, and worn with a blazer style mid-green coat and pale-green embroidered initials, RHS, on the pocket. A V-necked, navy, pullover with an aqua trim to match the colour in the skirt material, white shirt, black stockings or three-quarter length dark-green socks and black shoes completed the uniform. The wearing of a uniform was not compulsory for Sixth Form girls.

In 2003 Mrs Joan Bungay (Kay), an Old Girl, parent, and former member of Staff, died. She was responsible for producing a book to celebrate the School's one-hundredth anniversary which contained many personal accounts by Old Girls of their days at Redland High School. Dr Weeks worked closely with the Old Girls' Guild and was receptive to some of their comments about past traditions. She was impressed by the career achievements of Old Girls and invited them to talk to the Sixth Form. A distinguished Old Girl, Elizabeth Hoodless, was made a Dame (D.B.E.) for her responsibilities concerning the Community Service Volunteers after forty years of service to that organization, travelling abroad to promote the concept. She was invited in 2004 in her role as the Chairman of the London Branch of the Old Girls' Guild, to present the prizes at the School's Prize Giving held at Bristol Cathedral. An Old Girl spoke with girls taking art at A level and helped to promote future paths

69. New design of emblem

70. 2005. Mrs Carol Lear (Headmistress 1989-2002)
and Chairman of the Governors admiring the new
uniform, tartan skirt (the School's own) and light-weight
blazer-style coat

open to them through her own experiences and study into 'The Psychology of Children's Drawings'. She also showed the girls her art file, paintings and drawings produced under the direction of Miss Taylor in the 1950s, and these were 'very modern' when compared to the work produced in art lessons at other schools.

Another Old Girl was voted Britain's most admired Charity Chief Executive of the organization 'Guide Dogs for the Blind' and said she owed her success to the development of her drama skills, writing scripts and appearing on stage while she was a pupil at Redland. Confidence in the ability to succeed has always been part of the ethos of the Redland High School.

In 2004 the Young Enterprise team, NOX, won the first round of the competition held in Bristol. Other successes were in indoor cricket, Redland becoming the under-fifteen years, indoor, Gloucestershire champions. Girls visited the Somerdale Chocolate factory, though not as in the past just to sample the products but to note the health and safety regulations. How times have changed! However, they sampled some products and came away with a variety bag of goodies, after all, they are still children!

Debates on issues have always been part of Redland's education for girls and learning to gain confidence to speak out in public. Sixth Form physics' pupils took up a challenge to build a working crane which would use an electromagnet to pick up paperclips and transfer them to a dropping zone. Their teacher, Mr Sloan, said he was keen to see girls consider a career in engineering as there were many university scholarships only open to women for which they could apply.[5]

In 2005 the School took over the lease of the Bristol Rovers ground at Golden Hill. Earlier reports indicate this had once been offered to Colston's School after the lease of the nearby fields owned by the Bristol City Council and used by Colston's School were earmarked for a new Government school. The grounds included an all-weather pitch as well as five grass pitches. The Friends of Redland High School purchased a mini-bus for the School's use to visit the playing fields or to take small groups of girls on outings. In 2005 the astro-turf was re-carpeted and was officially opened by Isabel Palmer,

Captain of the Clifton Ladies Hockey Club and holder of the Captaincy of England's Ladies Hockey Team.

In 2005 for the fourth consecutive year Redland students achieved a 100% pass rate at A2 level. One student was in the top five, nationally, for French. The girls were also successful at GCSE with a 100% achieving 6 GCSE's at grades A*-C and an overall pass rate of 99%. Awards were received in music (piano composition).

The entry for the Young Enterprise Competition was entered as Young Enterprise Trading Initiative, YETI, commencing with a Christmas product trade-fair stand and using the profits to develop a fitness pack to become the Runner-Up Company of the Year.[6]

Another change was the combining of Prize Day with the Commemoration Service held at Bristol Cathedral although this posed problems for accommodating the girls, parents and visitors. Some Old Girls thought the two occasions should be held separately.

At the Girls' Schools' Association Meeting for Headmistresses a speaker from America announced that research had shown that girls were able to multi-task better than boys but were not as good in risk-taking as boys. Dr Weeks suggested that Redland High School girls should address this issue and be given some risk-taking tasks.

It was now suggested that a subscription paid each term would ensure life-long membership of the Old Girls' Guild and the money raised could be offered for bursaries. A new database of Old Girls was set up by the Development Officer in order to make contact with Old Girls and to record some of their stories. The Old Girls' newsletter is now incorporated into the magazine *Day's Eye* and the seasonal newsletter. The good work of producing an Old Girls' newsletter has been invaluable for information concerning the progress of Redland High School and has provided information, facts and dates. In 2005, Miss Fleure, who taught geography,

died. She had been in poor health for a number of years. Old Girls will remember her wonderful shared experiences, visits to a coal mine and the fossils she collected, or a visit to Egypt and photographs of the Sphinx.

Jamie Oliver's much televised series on healthy eating was being applied to the school's provision of dinners and a private company now has charge of these.

In 2006 thirty Redland girls went on a ski trip to America. Progress of House activities recorded that the Senior House debating competition was a great success with plans to extend to Junior House members. A pancake race proved popular and each house raised money for the future South West Children's Hospice and each House had a chosen charity. Fun was had with a Christmas dinner with each House providing the entertainment. Overall it was agreed that the House system provided an avenue for more girls to participate in activities.

In 2006 the house in Redland Court Road became the School's new music centre and involved moving eight pianos, three clavinovas, piles of music scores, music stands, keyboards, classroom instruments and hundreds of CDs and LPs, enabling Music tuition to be in one central place. The School received the gift of a Broadwood grand piano from the relatives of Miss Knowleden, Head of Music from 1944 until 1975. Miss Knowleden died in 2006.[7]

Modesty of bearing, rare in someone of such exceptional qualities, made Dr Weeks eligible for consideration by other schools. She resigned in 2006 after four years' service having been offered another position nearer to her permanent home. An inspector commented that 'Dr Weeks is leaving an excellent legacy to her successor'. Many Staff changes were made at the end of 2006 including the appointment of a male Head-teacher for the Junior School, Mr Jonathan Eyles, and a new Headmistress for the Senior School, Mrs Caroline Bateson.

NOTES

1   Chitty, C., 2004. *Education Policy in Britain.* Basingstoke: Palgrave Macmillan. pp.145-146.

2   ibid. p.204.

3   Redland High School. 2002. *Day's Eye.* Redland High School Archive (nyc).

3   Redland High School. 2003. *Newsletter, Autumn.* Redland High School Archive (nyc).

4   Redland High School. 2004. *Newsletter.* Redland High School Archive (nyc).

5   Redland High School. 2005. *Day's Eye.* Redland High School Archive (nyc).

6   Redland High School. 2006. *Day's Eye.* Redland High School Archive (nyc).

7   ibid.

13

2006-2011 DEVOLVED POWER AND INTELLIGENT ACCOUNTABILITY, COALITION GOVERNMENT (2010)

The historical development of Redland High School has shown that 'fear of the educated woman', that is, women no longer staying in their 'womanly' prescribed role, women invading men's guarded territories, along with difficulties and criticisms of combining productive paid work with family life is no longer appropriate in the twentieth-century.[1] Miss Peters saw girls' attendance at Redland High School as being 'privileged' for those who could afford it and both 'privileged' and 'rewarding' for those with talent who entered though scholarships and bursaries. Miss Peters never wished Redland High School to become an Independent School. As a consequence of losing the Direct Grant she strove for the setting up of bursaries for able and talented girls in order for the School to achieve academic success.

1997 saw a return to a Labour Government which brought educational changes.

Over the years girls had been seen to be 'improving' in their results due to the increase in the number of girls taking science, mathematics and technology (IT) and the boys appeared to be 'failing'.[2] When computers were first introduced into Australian schools in the mid-1980s for children selected on a 'gifted' children's programme the boys were very possessive over their use. In a sharing situation, with equal numbers of boys and girls with one computer between two, the girls were reluctant to commence. As one girl commented, 'They (the boys) can be the computer operators and we (the girls) can be the computer typists'. The gender roles were clearly defined, 'girls as typists', 'boys as engineers, with an understanding of technology and all things masculine'. Fortunately the roles have now changed, although a co-educational school's Prospectus in 2010 shows a boy at the computer and a girl sitting alongside him holding a pencil!

In 2002 the dangers of 'over accountability' were emphasized by Dr O'Neill, the Principal of Newnham College, Cambridge in her Reith Lecture. She saw performance indicators, although defended as a means of regulating and enhancing the performance of public sector institutions, were actually chosen for ease of measurement and control rather than because they measured quality of performance accurately.[3] In 2003 David Milliband, Schools' Minister, talked of the Government's plan of 'the combination of devolved power and intelligent accountability, a framework to ensure that schools work effectively and efficiently towards the common good and development of their pupils.[4]

In the 'catch up' period since the late 1990s girls were now outperforming boys. There was an increase in the number of girls taking those subjects considered mainly for boys and there was an increase in girls' performance scores. Boys' underachievement was receiving publicity and there was some concern for boys to be taught separately, in special boys' streams, within co-educational schools. In some historic single-sex schools for boys the authorities had been forced into becoming co-educational in order to maintain their place in the top level of Independent Schools with girls' examination scores helping to boost League Table results. In 2010 the Headmaster of Harrow School, Mr B. Lenon, maintained the less popular boys' schools were forced to take girls and they were doing so in order to survive. He supported the argument that teenage boys and girls learn in different ways, boys overestimate their ability, girls underestimate their ability and as a consequence, WORKED HARDER! The statement, 'Girls have to work harder' was used by Miss Cocks, Redland High School's first Headmistress. Mr Lenon took into account the recent developments in identifying, through brain imaging, the differences in the chromosomes present in the female brain and those in the male brain. Girls use both sides of the brain for language development and the difference is greater at the age of fifteen years.[5]

In 2010 the highest achievements in examination results came from the established boarding schools. These schools are available to those who can afford to pay the extremely high fees although there are some scholarships available. The results would indicate that the pupils are free from any distractions, are highly competitive, and have highly educated parents. Under the banner of Parent Power schools have been placed in a position where acknowledgement of examination results has led to a demand in teachers' performance. The Teachers' Union have strongly supported and defended their members. Opposition to League Tables is no longer confined to the teacher unions, as in 2001, the Welsh Assembly decided to ditch them and since that time many Primary Schools in England have supported this decision. Other established Independent Schools have the option of not handing over their League Tables for public scrutiny.

The A* at A level is now the goal to aim for although some educationists are worried about the dropping of other A level subjects in order to concentrate on a particular subject to gain entrance to one of the top universities. Mr Anthony Seldon, Headmaster at Wellington College, comments that the grade inflation is already happening. The only question is 'How long will it be before the Coalition Government has to create the A**?' His guess is 2020.[6]

How will the single-sex school, boys or girls, fare in the future? What is a Redland Girl? How does she differ from a girl who attends a co-educational school? Answers to these questions will require further research.

What is the future for 'free' schools set up by parents, teachers, and other groups? They will need to show evidence of demand and location of a suitable site according to the Coalition Government's requirements following on from the Government's education policy of finding 'the best school for each child'. The opposition to 'free' schools is based on 'without profit they will not succeed'. Proponents of 'free' schools say they will offer the best as they are being set up by teachers in areas where there is a need for a 'better' school. Christine Blower, the General Secretary of the National Union of Teachers, NUT, reports, 'Adopting such a business model to own a school will amount to the sweeping dismantling of our education system. "Free" schools will have to follow the National Curriculum'.

The Government plans to publish the annual amount of money every school receives for each pupil and they believe that a single national-funding formula which sidelines local authorities makes sense because of the growing number of academies financed by Whitehall. Academies have been set up through endowments and business investors. Any shortfall cannot be made up by the increase of fee paying pupils when the physical buildings limit the number of pupils who can be accommodated.

In Bristol several historic schools which commenced as single-sex, for girls, or for boys, made the decision to become 'co-educational'. In the hard economic times their reasons may have been financial, demographics of catchment areas, and as has been suggested, to gain a prestigious place in the League Tables. Some endowed schools remain single–sex because of the nature of the endowment which stipulates it is for the education of 'boys only' or 'girls only'. Redland High School is a school founded on the tradition of 'education for girls'. Chris Woodhead, Chief Inspector of Schools, maintains that 'good schools' are those which have dynamic leaders, high quality teachers, good facilities, offer a wide range of extra curricula activities, and have dedicated and talented staff.

In November 2010 the Education Secretary, Michael Gove, unveiled some sweeping school reforms in the Coalition's Government White Paper. First on the agenda was the transformation of teacher-training, followed by the shake-up of League Tables in order to focus on children's performance in academic subjects. More power was to be given to Headteachers for the dismissal of teachers who were not performing, and finally, Headteachers would have the power to exclude disruptive children.[7]

Mr Gove also announced the introduction of a new award, the English Baccalaureate.

In addition the League Tables were to recognise the merits of schools which offered physics, chemistry and biology as separate subjects. He believed that the adoption of a school uniform also raised standards of behaviour along with prefects and house systems. There should be a smarter attitude towards schooling and fixing up the schools which are seen as failing to provide an adequate level of schooling and subsequently are failing children. These issues are being addressed by the setting up of academies and free schools. The Independent schools which have not failed in their duties should continue to uphold their traditions.

MRS CAROLINE BATESON
(Headmistress 2006-)

Mrs Caroline Bateson was appointed as Headmistress in September 2006. She had previously held the position of Deputy Head of Badminton School and had been Head of the History Department since her appointment at Badminton School in 1986.

Mrs Caroline Bateson is a strong advocate of single-sex education, believing that,

Girls undoubtedly flourish and gain confidence in a secure and nurturing environment, free of gender stereotyping.[8]

In 2006 and for the fifth year running, the girls achieved a 100% pass rate at A level. One girl had achieved one of the top five marks in the UK for her Psychology B paper from 5,900 candidates. The GSCE candidates were also extremely successful. Other successes included awards for textiles in the sustainable category and the technical textile category. The new music school at the house in Redland Court Road was proving to be an invaluable resource and was attracting entrants for the Music Scholarships offered. Workshops were offered in physics and engineering with tutors from the Royal Engineers, giving the girls the opportunity to be inventive and voicing their ideas without worrying about the gender difference. Exchanges with Marburg in 2006 celebrated fifty-five years of existence.

In 2007 Dr Beryl Corner, OBE, a distinguished Old Girl, died. At a time when women doctors were few in number she forged a career in paediatric medicine. In her early days as a young doctor she was asked to convert an empty swimming pool into a temporary ward to cater for the number of wounded soldiers rescued from the evacuation from Dunkirk. She also supervised the evacuation of child patients on the night of the bombing of the Bristol Royal

Infirmary and managed to find them accommodation at the Homeopathic Hospital. These children, one of whom later attended Redland High School, were at the Bristol Royal Infirmary because of the severity of their illness which could not be treated at the Children's Hospital. This patient's little sister saw the damage to the Bristol Royal Infirmary with exposed beds hanging over the edge of the wall, previously the ward, and marvelled that anyone could have escaped from this horrific scene. Dr Beryl Corner recalled this event in a talk to the Old Girls and added 'remember we were working in the dark, calling out to the children to tell us where they were. One little boy was hiding under the Matron's table'. Dr Corner was devoted to her 'old' school and she always reminded Old Girls that it was 'The Redland High School FOR

71. 2007. Celebratory cakes for the School's 125th Anniversary made by Mary Walters (Old Girl and past Chairman of the Old Girls' Guild)

GIRLS'. In her retirement years she served as the Chairman of the Governors and President of the Council.

2007 was the year for Redland High School to celebrate its one hundred and twenty-fifth anniversary. Three iced-cakes were made by Mary Walters, an Old Girl, featuring badges and the historic Redland Court. The cakes were shared with the whole school. A silver daisy brooch was presented to all girls leaving in Year 13 to show their allegiance and membership of the Old Girls' Guild. Three girls were offered places at Oxford and Cambridge. UCAS applications include not just academic excellence but a range of activities and contributions to society. The Young Enterprise competition is highly competitive. In 2007 there were more successes in the competition with entries by two teams, Skye and Eden. Skye were the runner-ups as 'Best Company Overall' and moved forward to the regional finals. A popular visitor was Jake Meyer the youngest man to climb the seven summits and was part of the campaign to build a climbing-wall in the gym. In conjunction with the one hundred and twenty-fifth anniversary the Friends of Redland High School organised a Victorian fair.[9]

In 2008 new events included taking netball teams overseas to Barcelona and promise of the same for hockey teams. The climbing-wall, at a cost of over £7,000, was officially opened by Jake Meyer, thanks to the financial help from the Friends of Redland High School. Mrs Bateson commented: *This is something different, not offered by other schools and is part of a fitness programme.*

The School's involvement in drama has produced many fine actresses over the years, some in the past appearing in British movies and television. A pupil, Lucy Briggs-Owen, landed a major part in *Troilus and Cressida*, playing the role of Cressida.

In 2008 Mrs Carol Lear, ex-Redland Headmistress, was appointed as the new President of the Council of Redland High School replacing the late Dr Beryl Corner. Mrs Carol Lear had been on the Staff of Redland High School for thirty-one years, thirteen of those as Head-mistress.[10]

In 1906 acquiring a telephone was heralded as a new innovation and the installation of the electric light in 1921 enabled huge changes to be made. By 2008 the School had excellent IT facilities with access to web-outlook enabling monitoring of appointments and absences. The girls could also use the shared areas of computers and work from home with computer connections to the School.

In 2008 Mrs Bateson explained there had been many changes and even uncertainties for Independent schools. Redland's strengths lay in its pastoral care and academic success in the provision of a single-sex school. Peer mentoring had been a success throughout the School and a publication 'Getting it Right' had helped new girls to settle in at Year 7. The School has always supported charities and the House system provides an avenue for focussing on a special event and a special charity, chosen by the House. Attendance at school plays and sports' days are also a source for fund-raising. The School was able to welcome distinguished visitors including Dr Adam Hart-Davis talking on the feasibility of 'life in space'. The School had also welcomed historians, linguists, scientists, actors, musicians, environmentalists and engineers to inspire the girls.[11]

In 2009 the girls at Redland High School achieved success in local and national competitions in a range of curriculum areas, and also in their examination results. Two sisters were successful in appearing on the 'X Factor' television talent show and made it to the final twelve acts out of a total of 180,000 entries. The School's provision for 'extra-curricular activities' had led to the development of talent across a wide spectrum. There is evidence of strong teamwork in producing science research, art

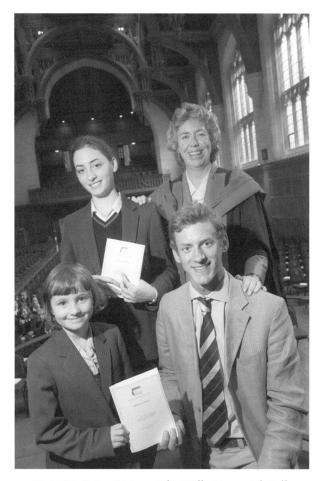

72. 2009. Prize Giving at the Wills Memorial Hall, University of Bristol. Mr Jake Meyer, guest presenter, with the Headmistress Mrs Caroline Bateson and prize-winning pupils

exhibitions, drama productions, musical performances, at all levels of development. A dedicated Staff has always been a major part of the development of Redland High School.[12]

In the Annual Report of the Council, 2009, the Council's main objective was to maintain the standing of Redland High School as a top-quality Independent Girls' Day School in Bristol. They saw the need for further financing of scholarships and bursaries. Fee increases were inevitable although the Council had tried to keep these as low as possible.

In Autumn, 2010, Redland High School students achieved the highest percentage of A* grades at A level in the whole of Bristol and every Year 13 pupil gained entry to the University of their choice. Three students took the Extended Project Qualification which counts as half an A and is highly regarded by universities as it is directly related to the subject candidates wish to study at university. The GCSE results were also the highest for five years.

The results prove that the teaching here is of the very highest quality and I congratulate my Staff as well as our students.
Mrs Bateson, Headmistress.[13]

The School contributes to, and occasionally edits, the Bristol Schools publication *Banter* produced by the *Evening Post* newspaper and is an excellent introduction to a career in journalism.

At the end of the summer term the art, PE/dance and technology departments combined to produce the show 'Redland's Got Talent' with fashion and dance routines. The show was enhanced by artworks, sculpture, ceramics, fine art, printed fabrics and appreciated by parents and guests. A welcome change which commenced in 2009 was the separate occasion for the Commemoration Service in the Cathedral and the Annual Prize Giving in the Great Hall of the University of Bristol.

Redland High School is very successful in providing 'added value' not just in academic standards. Extra-curricular activities such as the Duke of Edinburgh's Award, School plays, concerts and sporting activities, House events and the myriad of Clubs we offer at Junior and Senior level are all life enhancing experiences to build confidence.
Mrs Bateson, Headmistress.[14]

The Bursary Fund continues to support entries for those who have the ability to succeed. The Harry Crook Foundation generously supports girls in the school whose families suffer hardship or bereavement: it acts as a much needed 'life line' enabling the girls to continue their education at Redland High School. The Harry Crook Trustees also give an Annual Award to a pupil for an 'Enterprise and Innovation Project'. The John James Trust helps Bristol girls by awarding bursaries at Year 7 entry and also gives the 'Tools of the Trade Award' each year to a Sixth Form recipient. In 2010 the Pool Bursary Fund was established as a legacy from Mr and Mrs John Pool. John Pool had been Vice-Chairman of the Governors and his wife, Sadie, an Old Girl.

Redland High School has an Appeals Committee to encourage donations to the Bursary Fund and carries out events which contribute to the fund. The Development Office has information on ways in which contributions can be made.

An appreciation of Redland's history and connection with John Cossins's personal chapel on Redland Green is enhanced by the Junior School choir who perform there. Other history projects have helped in the appreciation of the building, Redland Court, around which the school is centred and it is hoped that the accessioning of the archives will enable these to be used for school projects with a greater understanding of the history of the School. Recently a letter was received from Miss Charlton, co-author of the book on the history of Redland Court, who is in her ninetieth year.

Entrance to the School at the 11-plus age group is through an examination and an interview in which the child is asked to bring an object they like or a hobby they enjoy and 'to talk about it'. In this way the potential of the child can be assessed, which may be creative, artistic, academic, or musical. Potential music students can sit for the music scholarships or entry. In addition the previous school records are taken into consideration.

Girls in Year 10 made a video on 'what does happiness mean for them?' Texting, shopping, playing in the rain and the snow, friends on the bus, TV food programmes and maths! Was that the male teacher?! A very healthy cross-section of the girls' enjoyment of life.

The skills acquired at Redland High, as it is now known, are skills acquired for life, as many Old Girls will testify. This book has set out the pattern of the development of Redland High for the first one hundred and thirty years. More details are now recorded electronically and published in the yearly School magazine, the *Day's Eye*, the daisy being the School's flower as in the poem by Chaucer, and in the publication of the newsletters enabling the continuing story to be told. Historians will need to have access to these, electronically, or saved as printed material housed in the archives.

Now have I than switch a condicioun
That, of all the floures in the mede,
Than love I most these floures white and rede,
Switche as men callen daysies in our town.

Of all the flowers in the meadow, I love most these flowers, white and red, such as men call daisies. *The Legend of Good Women*, Geoffrey Chaucer (1343-1400)

A Redland High education is a gift for life. A Redland High girl is part of a vibrant community of family loyalty and shared ethos.

SCHOOL SONG

1   When darkness shrouds and shadows reign,
   and light runs out like sand.
   We wear a smile with cheerful hearts,
   and take hope by the hand.

   For at Redland High we know that if
   We look doubt in the eye,
   Bright futures will await us all
   As girls of Redland High.

2   Both strength of mind and warmth of heart
   At Redland we pursue
   And Redland girls are not afraid
   To make their dreams come true.

   For at Redland High we know that if

3   So when our years at Redland end
   We have to leave, but yet
   Close friends we've made, good times we've had
   As girls of Redland High

   For at Redland High we know that if

NOTES

1 MacKinnon, A., and I. Elgqvist-Saltzman., and A. Prentice., 1998. *Education Into the 21st Century. Dangerous Terrain for Women*, London: Falmer Press. p.1.

2 Chitty, C., 2004. *Education Policy in Britain*. Basingstoke: Palgrave Macmillan. p.192.

3 ibid. p.205.

4 ibid. p.206.

5 Wikipedia, n.d. Lenon, B., Education, Co-ed or Single-Sex. *In Wikipedia: the free encyclopedia* (on line). Available from www.firstelevenmagazine.co.uk 2010.

6 Griffiths, S., 2010. 'The new A-level stars', *Sunday Times*, 14 November, p.v.

7 Wikipedia, n.d. Michael Gove unveils sweeping school reforms. *In:Wikipedia:the free encyclopedia* (on line). St Petersburg, Florida: Wikimedia Foundation. Available from: http://www.guardian.co.uk/education/2010/nov/24/michael-gove-sweeping-school-reforms/print

8 Redland High School. 2006. *Newsletter, Autumn*, Redland High School Archive (nyc).

9 Redland High School. 2007. *Newsletter, Spring*. Redland High School Archive (nyc).

10 Redland High School. 2008. *Newsletter, Spring*. Redland High School Archive (nyc).

11 Redland High School. 2008. *Day's Eye*. Redland High School Archive (nyc).

12 Redland High School. 2009. *Newsletter, Spring*. Redland High School Archive (nyc).

13 Redland High School. 2010. *Newsletter, Autumn*. Redland High School Archive (nyc).

14 Redland High School. 2010. *Day's Eye*. Redland High School Archive (nyc).

CONCLUSION

The story of Redland High School for Girls is interwoven with the development of the district of Redland. It has been shown how it suffered setbacks and was even in danger of being closed down by His Majesty's Inspectors. Shortage of land for further development, even though the School was situated on two acres, and the limitations placed on additions to a Grade II building added to the prospect of closure. A fortuitous purchase of a piece of land, a few miles away destined for a sports ground, although distance prevented its intended use, proved to be a 'nest-egg' which could be sold. Sold it was and the money raised has given Redland High the very best of facilities seen today.

In the past the Council of Redland High School was always trying to negotiate the sale of land belonging to the Bristol Corporation used as playing fields by Colston's School and shared with Redland High School. However, the land was always seen as a site for a Government High School when transport, private and public, became more available, serving not only Redland but surrounding districts where there was a shortage of Government Secondary Schools. In 2002 it was announced that Redland Green School, a modernist curved wonder of glass and bricks, costing over £36million would be built on the site of the playing fields. Redland Green School opened in 2006. By 2010 all year groups were on site and the school achieved Specialist Science Status, thus building on the strengths of those achieving in mathematics and science. There is a great deal of movement of children, people, and cars, in the narrow streets around two schools in close proximity to each other.

Thus the district of Redland is changing. Gone are the pre-war children's playing areas on Redland Green as children do not play outside on their own any more. Gone is the Bishop's Palace bombed out of existence. Gone are the wartime allotments and the finding of Roman coins and in their place a Bowling Club for older members of the community. Redland Chapel remains in pristine condition although other buildings of this period have been demolished and replaced with blocks of attractive and not so attractive flats. Fortunately, the district of Redland and Cotham is monitored by Redland and Cotham Amenities Society who keep a watchful eye on additions or changes which may spoil 'how things are'.

The first Redland High School Magazine was published in 1886. Today the School magazine is published yearly under the title *Day's Eye* (daisy) with interim newsletters, all of which tell the story of life at Redland High School. Academics studying 'the education of girls' have commented on the lack of written and published social histories of schools complaining that the present-day communication of events through magazines, videos, and computer technology may be lost if these are not stored in a retrievable format.

In 2010 an opportunity arose to make use of the School archives rescued from a damp cellar by the School's librarian, Mrs Catherine

Spalding, and a band of willing girls prepared to get their hands dirty! The mammoth task of cleaning and organising the archives was undertaken by a group of Old Girls and involvement led to the decision to publish a social history of Redland High School.

Without archival records how we would know about women's educational achievements at Cambridge University? How many of you know that women up until 1948 were not formally presented at this university for admission for degrees? It was not until 1998 that an apology was given to those with degrees taken before 1948 (Miss Hume was one of those students), giving them entitlement to full membership of Cambridge University.

In 2012 Redland High School celebrates its one-hundred and thirtieth Anniversary and the next twenty years will see many changes in 'the education of girls' before the one-hundred and fiftieth Anniversary is celebrated.

BIBLIOGRAPHY

Allen, M. and Ellis, S., 2010. *Nature Tales, Encounters with Britain's Wildlife*. London: Elliott and Thompson.

Avery, G., 1991. *The Best Type of Girl, A History of Girls' Independent Schools*. London: Andre Deutsch.

Bungay, J., 1982. *Redland High School, 1882-1982*. Council of Redland High School.

Charlton, J. and Milton, D.M., 1951. *Redland 791-1800*. Bristol: Arrowsmith.

Chitty, C., 2004. *Education Policy in Britain*. Basingstoke: Palgrave Macmillan.

Gibson, C., 1997. *The Bristol School Board 1871-1903*. Bristol: Bristol Branch of the Historical Association. University of Bristol.

Hennessy, P., 2006. *Never Again. Britain 1945-1951*. London: Penguin Books.

Hunt, F. ed., 1987. *Lessons for Life, the Schooling of Girls and Women, 1850-1950*. Oxford: Blackwell.

Ison, W., 1952. *The Georgian Buildings of Bristol*. London: Faber and Faber.

Kean, H., 1990. *Deeds not Words*. London: Pluto Press.

Kingsley, N., 1992. *The Country Houses of Gloucestershire, Vol.II. 1660-1830*. Chichester: Phillimore Press.

Kingsley, N., 2001. *The Country Houses of Gloucestershire, Vol.I. 1500-1660*. 2nd ed. Chichester: Phillimore Press.

Mackinnon, A., and I..Elgqvist-Saltzman., and A.Prentice., 1998., *Education into the 21st Century. Dangerous Terrain for Women*. London: Falmer: Press.

Morris, S. and Mowl, T., 2002. *Open Doors*. Bristol: Redcliffe Press.

Ollerenshaw, K., 1967. *The Girls' Schools*. London: Faber and Faber.

Perceval, F., 1998. *Chaucer's Legendary Good Woman*. Cambridge: Cambridge University Press.

Purvis, J., 1991. *A History of Women's Education in England*. Buckinghamshire: Open University Press.

Shaw, M.G., 1932. *Redland High School*. Bristol: Arrowsmith.

Sturge, E., 1928. *Reminiscences of my life*. Bristol: Arrowsmith.

Wilkins, H.J., 1924. *Redland Chapel and Redland*. Bristol: Arrowsmith.

ACKNOWLEDGEMENTS

This book has grown from my interest in the preservation of the Redland High School's archives. 2012 is an important year in the School's history, namely the 130th Anniversary of its commencement in the district of Redland in 1882. My thanks are given to Mrs Caroline Bateson, Headmistress and to Mrs Carol Lear, former Headmistress and Chairman of the Board of Governors of Redland High for their support, encouragement and reading of the text before publication.

Without the mammoth undertaking by Catherine Spalding, (former School Librarian) and the girls to remove the archives from their thirty years' storage in a cellar, to dust and clean them and bring them into the library, this story could never have been written. My thanks go to the Old Girls' Archive group, Jane Bruce (née Storrs, 1963), Philippa Crabbe (née Cheyne, 1962), Sue Phillips (née Dennies, 1963), Margaret Westgate (née Lobb, 1959), Shirley Whittaker (née Bosanquet, 1952) and other helpers who are responsible for further cleaning, sorting, cataloguing and accessioning the archival material which includes hundreds of photographs. Catherine Spalding's interest and scholarship provided the guidelines for the professionalism expected for the caring of the archives, enabling the history of the School to be written and referenced.

The archives, along with this book, will provide pupils, students and researchers into girls' education, with a wealth of starting points for further study. A book without pictures only tells half the story and my thanks are given to those whose photographs enhance the publication. Support has been given within the School for reproducing images and permission granted from Jane Butterworth (Public Relations), Linda Spencer-Small (School Development Office) and Heather Kent (School Receptionist) to use their photographs. Vickie Howard (B.I.I.P.), a professional photographer, was engaged to supply photographs of the environs and buildings and the front cover photograph is a detail from one of these. I would like to thank the members of the Old Girls' Guild who replied to a questionnaire concerning their time at Redland High School when Miss Peters was Headmistress and their feedback provided information where there was a lack of archival material.

Professional expertise on the development of the district of Redland was provided by Dr. Peter Malpass from the University of the West of England and I thank him for his permission to use excerpts from his unpublished manuscript. Nicholas Kingsley, Head of Archives, National Archives, Kew, has been more than generous in allowing use of the image of an early drawing of Redland Court and providing for publication a previously unseen architectural image of Redland Court. Correspondence with David Stockham, Divisional Commercial Director of the Cowlin Group informing him of that Company's building of the School Hall in 1895 resulted in the sharing of archival material and a donation towards the publication. A donation was also received from the School. Costs are to be covered by the sale of the book and any profit from sales will go towards the Bursary Fund.

I would like to thank Dr. John Sansom and his daughter Clara Hudson, of Redcliffe Press Ltd, for their expertise in the production of this book.

Jenny Allen-Williams

INDEX

LIST OF ILLUSTRATIONS

LIST OF COLOUR PLATES

COLOUR PLATES

1   Redland Court, built in 1735. Purchased by the Redland High School for Girls in 1884.
Photographer, Vickie Howard, b.i.i.p., 2010

2   Entrance gate. John Cossins's 'Coat of Arms' includes the 'Golden Lion of
Cossins'. The ram's horns signify fecundity, rebirth, renewal and rejuvenation.
The five goat horns represent the five planets, where the goat of lust is attacking the heavens.
Photographer, Vickie Howard, b.i.i.p., 2010

3   Map of the district of Redland, 1841. Shows Redland Court, Redland Chapel,
Turnpike gate on road (Redland Road). *Bristol Record Office as supplied by
Dr P. Malpass (School of the Built Environment, UWE)*

4   Lithographic print of a drawing by Storer, 1825, showing Redland Court as a residence
for Sir Richard Vaughan. (Colour has been added to the original black and white print)
Note the 'Halley's Comet' weathervane on the East wing. The Comet was sighted in 1761 and
the weathervane was installed by Martha Cossins in memory of her husband's death in 1759.
The East cupola and weathervane pulled down when accommodation built in c.1886 for
Miss Cocks, the first Headmistress. Now seen on the West Wing, or may be one of a pair
originally on the East and West wings. Also note the figure, with outstretched arm, in the alcove.
Two metal figures were removed to help the war effort in the First World War. The figures were
described by Miss Shekleton, the second Headmistress, as 'hideous'.

5   *Above:* Oil painting of John Cossins, first owner of Redland Court.
Below: Oil painting of Martha Cossins, wife of John Cossins.
Painted by John Vanderbank (1649-1739) *Photographer, Heather Kent, 2008*

6   West wing, interior staircase, Redland Court. *Photographer, Heather Kent, 2008*

7   Coloured pencil drawing. Redland Chapel, built for John Cossins in 1743.
Drawn by R. Farnsworth, c.1940s. Donated to Redland High School by
Jenny Allen-Williams in 2006. *Photograph courtesy of RHS School Development Office, 2010*

8   Weathervane, showing Halley's Comet, West cupola. *Photographer, Vickie Howard, b.i.i.p., 2010*

9 Water-colour painting of Redland Court by Fanny Sarah Hodges (nee Martin), 1808-c.1875. Purchased by Redland High School, 2010, from family estate. The Martin family are related to the Innys family. Martha Innys married John Cossins. *Photograph courtesy of RHS Development Office, 2010*

10 Redland High School, Assembly Hall, built in 1894 by the Cowlin Building Company. Carved wood panel, with motto, donated by the girls in 1905 to celebrate the School's 21st Anniversary. *Photograph courtesy of RHS Development Office, 2006*

11 Dutch garden. Established in the Elizabethan period and part of a previous Manor House before the building of Redland Court. *Photograph courtesy of RHS Development Office, 2008*

12 Aerial view of the district of Redland, showing Redland High School with new flat-roofed gymnasium and buildings. c.1986. *Photograph courtesy of the RHS Archival Collection*

13 Redland High Junior School. Situated at Redland Grove/Redland Road. *Photograph courtesy of RHS Development Office, 2009*

14 Side entrance. Hand-wrought, iron gate. Designed and constructed by Nathaniel Arthur, c.1740. *Photograph courtesy of RHS School Development Office, 2008*

15 East wing, interior staircase, Redland Court. *Photograph courtesy of RHS Development Office, 2008*

16 Entrance hall, Redland Court. Furniture given by the Old Girls for the School's 70th Anniversary in 1952. *Photographer, Heather Kent, 2008*